Organizing and Managing Your Research

A Practical Guide for Postgraduates

Renata Phelps, Kath Fisher and Allan Ellis

SAGE Publications

London • Los Angeles • New Delhi • Singapore

SAGE Publications Ltd
1 Oliver's Yard
55 City Road
London EC1Y 1SP

SAGE Publications Inc.
2455 Teller Road
Thousand Oaks, California 91320

SAGE Publications India Pvt Ltd
B 1/I 1 Mohan Cooperative Industrial Area
Mathura Road, Post Bag 7
New Delhi 110 044

SAGE Publications Asia-Pacific Pte Ltd
33 Pekin Street #02-01
Far East Square
Singapore 048763

British Library Cataloguing in Publication data

A catalogue record for this book is available from the British Library

ISBN 978 1 4129 2063 6
ISBN 978 1 4129 2064 3 (pbk)

Library of Congress Control Number 2006930619

Typeset by C&M Digitals (P) Ltd, Chennai, India
Printed on paper from sustainable resources
Printed in Great Britain by The Cromwell Press, Trowbridge, Wiltshire

Contents

Foreword		vi
Preface		viii
Acknowledgments		xii

1 Introduction — **1**
How do you become both an efficient *and* an
effective researcher? — 1
Why become an efficient and effective researcher? — 2
Who should use this book? — 3
What does the book do (and not do)? — 4

2 Establishing Technical Fundamentals — **10**
Learning about technology — 11
Hardware fundamentals — 13
Software fundamentals — 15
Networking fundamentals — 26
Increasing your technical efficiency — 30

3 Managing Yourself, Your Ideas and Your
Support Structures — **35**
Know thyself — 36
Managing your time — 37
Managing your ideas — 41
Managing your supervisor — 45
Setting up a peer support structure — 49

4 Organizing Your Work Environment — **56**
Organizing your physical environment — 56
Constructing a universal filing schema — 62
Electronic or hard copy? — 64

Managing your paper resources   67
Managing your electronic resources   69

5 **Planning and Overseeing Progress of Your Project**   **79**
Developing a research plan   80
Timelines and milestones   83
Project management software   87
Budgets, grants and resource management   91

6 **Communicating and Networking Electronically**   **104**
Using the Web for professional networking   105
Asynchronous communication   106
Synchronous communication   117
Translation resources   122
Establishing your own presence on the Web   123

7 **Effective Literature Searching**   **128**
The changing nature of information literacy   129
Fundamental searching strategies and skills   129
Tools for locating literature   135
Monitoring literature   146

8 **Strategic Web Searching**   **150**
Web-searching tools   151
Improving your search results   157
Managing important websites   159
Ready references on the Web   162
Evaluating Web-based information   162

9 **Managing and Organizing your Literature**   **166**
Bibliographic software   167
Strategic handling of your literature   173

10 **Designing Data Collection Systems**   **179**
Planning and managing data collection   180
Multimedia data collection   181
Computer-based data collection   190
Simulation software   194
Collecting data online   195
Data from the Internet: some examples   199

11 **Managing Data Analysis**   **207**
Qualitative data analysis   208
Quantitative data analysis   217

12 Improving Your Writing Efficiency   **238**
      Word processing skills for research writing   239
      Typographical considerations   251
      Improving writing efficiency   252
      Writing for screen   255

13 Presenting and Publishing Your Research   **258**
      Oral presentations   259
      Using presentation software   263
      Publishing your research   274

Bibliography   282
Index   286

Foreword

Over the past decade I have witnessed quite radical changes in the landscape of postgraduate and university research in my role as a research leader and administrator. Internationally, research training and research output at the institutional level have become major priorities, retention and completion rates of doctoral candidates are more critical than ever, and advances in information and communication technologies have changed the way that research is being done. It has become imperative to support research students, as well as their supervisors, to work in the most efficient and effective ways possible to produce excellent research.

For these reasons this is a book whose time has come. It is a research book like no other as it steps new researchers and students, as well as career researchers, through the skills they need to conduct their research efficiently. It will also be an invaluable resource for supervisors, who, if they are like me, don't have time to either keep up with the latest technological developments or pass these on to their students. Not only will this be important for experienced supervisors (who will no doubt pick up useful tips for managing their own research projects as well), but academics who are new to supervision will be able to help get their students off on the right foot in their postgraduate research with some confidence. Usually new supervisors and researchers have to pick up tips from their colleagues and learn from painful experience. Reading through this book, it is obvious that many of the tips provided here are a distillation of advice from many experienced researchers, including the authors, advice which is not usually found in a book but rather picked up through corridor conversations or chance meetings at conferences.

Managing and organizing skills are critical to successful research projects and being systematic and organized is an essential way to build research capability and output. However, these skills are usually not systematically or comprehensively addressed as part of research preparation and training programs, which tend to focus more on the methodological and writing aspects of candidature. I can see this book becoming an essential resource for students and supervisors alike, the book you'll go to when you get a question that relates to the day-to-day practicalities of doing research, whether it's how to organize your files, how to speak to the media or how to manage long documents on your word processor, questions I know I'm not particularly good at answering! Not only that, you can be confident you will be preparing your students for a research career in industry or academia by introducing them to cutting edge research practices that make the most of technological innovation.

Prof. Peter Baverstock
Pro Vice Chancellor (Research)
Southern Cross University
Australia

Preface

Why write a book on organizing and managing research? There are so many helpful resources available to students embarking on a research project, why add another to the pile?

The answer comes largely from our own (quite different) experiences as research students, as academic researchers and as supervisors. Each of us worked out how to manage our doctoral projects and subsequent research in our own ways, drawing on other researchers' tips and experiences, our own organizational habits, learning from plenty of bad decisions and wishing we'd known at the beginning what we knew at the end of the process. In supervising our own students, we find that all benefit from, and some definitely need, considerable guidance in the day-to-day managing of their information and research process. Yet this information didn't seem to be available to them in any systematic form. It is often assumed that students already know or will pick up organizational skills and management strategies. We came to the conclusion that a book focusing specifically on this undocumented part of the research process was long overdue.

We don't want to give the impression that we are all meticulously organized in our practices and respond calmly and impeccably at all times to the stresses that beset academic teachers and researchers. We know from experience that the gap between ideal practice and reality can be very wide. No matter how organized we want to (and know how to) be, the realities of day-to-day life and work conspire against all our good intentions. We also know that it is when we start to get too disorganized, when we have a huge build-up of e-mails and piles of paper cluttering the desk, that our productivity diminishes significantly and the stresses of juggling multiple commitments keep compounding. The collaborative process of writing this book while working around our other personal and professional demands, has challenged all our intentions of good organization and management! We have had to continually reflect on our practice and think about how we could or should have done things differently. This is exactly why the book is so important – to learn from others' experiences and mistakes.

Despite the challenges, we found that our varied experiences and preferred ways of working complemented each other very well. Renata's background as a librarian developed her skills in organization. Later, as a research assistant employed to help academics in a university department, she became familiar with the management issues that both beginning and experienced researchers confront on a daily basis. While teaching educational technology to pre-service teachers she worked full time on her PhD, which explored how computer users develop capability. This demanding workload required her to be incredibly efficient in both her work and research practices. She liked technology, but realized she couldn't always afford the best and the greatest and had to learn how to make do with what was available. Many of the useful organizational tips and tricks in this book come from the strategies that Renata developed during this time. Now as a supervisor of research students, she recognizes what students require in terms of organizational and management strategies. The idea for a book like this arose from these understandings and experiences.

Kath has a background in social science teaching, primarily in the fields of group processes, communication, economics, politics and sociology. She did her PhD part-time as a mature-aged distance student with two growing children and found that the only way she could manage was to set up peer support groups with other research students. Now, as a supervisor and mentor, Kath helps students develop collaborative networks to support their research. Kath's insight into the emotional needs of research students, combined with her facilitation skills and a good editorial hand, complement Renata's and Allan's organizational and technical skills.

Allan did his PhD in geochemistry in the era before advanced computer technology. His writing and management tools were a manual typewriter and a card index file for his references. His recollections of literature searching include wandering along library stacks looking for lost journals. Allan has been using computers since the days of punch cards and mainframes, developing an interest in the Web from its inception. He continues to have a pivotal role in organizing national and international Web conferences (http://ausweb.scu.edu.au and http://www.iw3c2.org). Allan specializes in the use of educational technology in adult education, and he supervised Renata's PhD. His technical knowledge and experience in PhD supervision have been essential in contributing to the book's substance and detail.

The book is much more than a cobbled-together accumulation of what we have learnt through bitter experience. We have had to do a lot of research ourselves and systematically explore and document what is available and how others use different technologies and strategies in their research. Our research included a survey of postgraduate students across Australian universities, asking them about their experiences and needs in relation to organizing and managing their research (Phelps et al. 2006). We also talked to a number of experienced researchers and supervisors nationally and internationally.

Of course, experienced researchers and supervisors have known about the importance of these skills and strategies for years. In fact, the inspiration for this book came from the following quote in Sternberg's 1981 classic, *How to Complete and Survive a Doctoral Dissertation*[1]:

> The key to completing a dissertation is not brilliance or even inspiration, but organization. Indeed, many a long-term [postgraduate research student] is overloaded with brilliant insights which keep him darting in various noncumulative directions; the definitive quality of brilliance is a short, illumination that quickly burns out. This is precisely not what the [postgraduate research student] needs. What he does need is a master plan in the form of some kind of filing system which keeps him on the right track(s), helps him evaluate his progress on various dissertation fronts, keeps him on keel, "flash-freezes" occasional "brilliant" insights so that they can be reconsidered within the framework of the total plan.

Our intention in this book is to assist you to appreciate the value that good organizational skills and strategies can offer as you go on the mysterious, creative, challenging and wondrous journey that research can be. We will be your tour guides, helping you map out your adventure, giving you some advice on what to pack, pointing out the attractions you might want to visit and suggesting some productive and efficient routes to take. Like any traveling experience, though, it will ultimately be up to you to make the most of the journey. Which brings us to a story that arose during our own journey of researching this book.

Brad is an early career academic researcher we know who is incredibly well organized and who also eagerly embraces technology. He is continually looking for new opportunities that technology might open up and exploring new hardware and software to support him to achieve his personal and professional goals, from qualitative data analysis software to pen scanners, digital music composition to palmtops. The following is a tale (with a moral), told to us by Brad, which may prompt reflection from you on your own research process.

> ...All the gadgets and software programs are, in effect, only as smart as the stuff that you put in. They can help you access your previous thoughts in a faster, more systematic and rigorous way, but only if you have put them in there in the first place. They cannot have the thoughts for you.
>
> An illustration of this comes with the singularly most useful technological innovation I found during my candidature, and one that I use still. I was in my literature review, and there were too many concepts, and the computer screen was too small for all my mind maps, because I wanted to see the whole mess all at once. I really wanted a huge whiteboard, but whiteboards can be over $800 for 2 × 3 metres, and I was wanting one 2 or 3 times this size. So, I went to the newsagent, bought 10 sheets of the stiffest white cardboard they had, and a whole bunch of good quality contact. I spent the night in front of the telly covering them. Then presto, I had a 6 × 3 metre whiteboard for under 25 bucks! I am still using the

same bits of cardboard 3 years later. The whiteboard markers just rub off, and it is completely portable. A white board this size has allowed me to see all the arguments and lines of logic in the whole thesis, book, article all at once. It's like Google Earth for academic argument! Once I get this picture, then it goes into NUD*IST and the other technological 'Tupperware' containers. With all the expensive toys I lust after, this has still been the thing that lets me be most productive, in terms of generating original material.

I can tell whether the technology I am using is any good or not because after a small start-up learning curve on its technical (how to drive) aspects, it then fades into the background, (or even better becomes invisible), and I am just left with me and my thoughts again … it's a Zen thing... If I find that I am being pulled out of me to re-engage with the technology all the time, then this is a good reason for me to ditch it, and I have had to do this on a couple of occasions.

Whether you are someone like Brad who is an "early adopter," keen to embrace change with enthusiasm and try out innovations as they become available; or whether you are more cautious, a "late adopter," who waits until technology is well established, we hope that this book will stimulate you to move closer to the edge of your comfort zone and be more curious and adventurous in your research travels. More importantly, we trust that as you travel down the road towards completion of your research degree or other research projects, the guidance we offer allows you to stride confidently towards your research goals.

Note

1 Sternberg 1981, p. 57.

Acknowledgments

We wish to acknowledge the support of the Grain Foods CRC for sponsoring the writing of this book and in particular Carol Morris, the Education Officer of the Grain Foods CRC. Peter Baverstock, Pro Vice-Chancellor of Research at Southern Cross University, has been an enthusiastic supporter of the book from the moment we floated the idea past him in 2004. Special thanks go to Carrie Maddison and Brooke Maddison for tireless and accurate research assistance, especially in helping develop the software tables. Many thanks must also go to John Revington for producing the cartoons.

We also have many people to thank for their ideas, tips, thoughts and experiences that contributed much to the substance of this book, as well as others who gave us extremely helpful feedback on the text in the process of writing. The following postgraduate students, researchers and academics deserve our heartfelt appreciation (listed in alphabetical order):

Alan Anderson	University of Otago, New Zealand
Ruth Anderson	Southern Cross University, Australia
Lynne Bertram	Southern Cross University, Australia
Annie Bolitho	University of Melbourne, Australia
Lyndon Brooks	Southern Cross University, Australia
Clare Brett	University of Toronto, Canada
Dale Burnett	University of Lethbridge, Canada
Sally Campbell	University of Technology Sydney, Australia
Clare Brett	University of Toronto, Canada
Lyn Carson	Sydney University Australia
David Coleman	University of New Brunswick, Canada
Lee Duncan	Deakin University, Australia
Katie Ellis	Queensland University of Technology, Australia
Phil Finnimore	Southern Cross University, Australia
Niel Fligstein	UC, Berkley, USA
Anne Graham	Southern Cross University, Australia
Rik Hall	St Thomas University, Canada

John Hammond	Southern Cross University, Australia
Carolyn Hendricks	Australian National University, Australia
Grete Jammison	Oslo University College, Norway
Mike Keppell	The Hong Kong Institute of Education, Hong Kong
Keith Lyons	Australian Institute of Sport, Australia
Judy Mousley	Deakin University, Australia
Meg O'Reilly	Southern Cross University, Australia
Karey Patterson	NTech Media, Australia
Rob Phillips	Murdoch University, Australia
Catherine Pocknee	Swinburne Institute of Technology, Australia
Aaron Roodman	SLAC, Stanford University, USA
Rafe Schindler	SLAC, Stanford University, USA
Kurt Seemann	CRC Desert Knowledge, Australia
Jason Sharman	University of Sydney, Australia
Brad Shipway	Southern Cross University, Australia
Des Stewart	Southern Cross University, Australia
Michelle Townsend	Centre for Children and Young People, Australia
Lyn Turney	Swinburne Institute of Technology, Australia
Brigid Veale	Southern Cross University, Australia
Mim Weber	Southern Cross University, Australia
Juliet Willets	University of Technology Sydney, Australia
Mieke Witsel	Southern Cross University, Australia

We are particularly grateful for the patient support and guidance we have received from our publishers, Sage Publications. In particular, Patrick Brindle recognised the value of a book such as this and was an enthusiastic champion of our proposal. Gita Raman was a tirelessly efficient and cheerful project manager in the final stages of production, and was well supported by Vanessa Harwood and Heidi Cormode.

Thanks also to Lynne de Weaver and Katie O'Rourke for help with publicity, and finally many, many thanks to the unfailing support from our families throughout the whole process of producing this book.

Chapter 1

Introduction

Doing research, whether it's gathering information on an archaeological dig, examining the behavior of bacteria through a microscope or exploring the role of song in indigenous cultures, is exciting and rewarding. Making a contribution to knowledge and satisfying our curious natures provide the impetus for many a research project. However, no matter what the field of inquiry, ask any experienced researcher what doing research day to day is really like, and they are likely to tell you that it is much less about flashes of insight and fine theoretical abstractions than it is about methodical, organized activity. Behind every piece of efficient and cost-effective research is a sound and efficient organizational system.

It is this behind-the-scenes aspect of research that is the subject matter of this book. No matter what stage of the research process you are in, whether you are just thinking about doing a postgraduate research degree or are well into your research career, this book will assist you to manage your research more efficiently and overall to become a more effective researcher. Through offering many practical tips and suggestions we aim to help you develop effective organizational systems that use not only common sense strategies that have stood the test of time, but also to introduce you to readily available computer technologies that have revolutionized the way that research can now be done. By developing skills and strategies that allow you to be more efficient in your day-to-day organizational practices, you will save time, increase the effectiveness of your research practice, improve the quality of your research output and, most important of all, keep you sane throughout the process.

How do you become both an efficient *and* an effective researcher?

In this book we emphasize the value of research being done both efficiently and effectively. Being efficient means making the most of your available resources, particularly time, while being effective involves achieving your research goals and producing quality outcomes. We all know researchers who might well be very organized and efficient but whose research outcomes fall below their potential. We can also all think of researchers who have produced wonderful, ground-breaking research, but it has taken double the time it could have due to their inefficient work practices.

To become *both* an efficient and effective manager of your daily research activities, you need good strategies, in particular:

- **time, project and process management skills and strategies;**
- **systems for organizing your hardcopy and electronic resources** and your physical workspace;
- **information literacy skills,** such as efficient and effective library database and Web searching, as well as strategies for continual monitoring and management of the huge quantity of information you are likely to access;
- **professional networking skills,** including the use of a range of communication technologies;
- **skills in collecting, managing and analyzing (often) large amounts of data**, whether quantitative or qualitative, and the ability to make a decision about what data analysis software to use;
- **efficient writing and word processing skills,** including those that support the creation and management of large documents such as theses and reports;
- **skills in presentation and publishing** of research and research in progress, including public speaking, presenting to the media and planning a publication strategy.

Why become an efficient and effective researcher?

Our response would be "Can you afford not to?" Developing these skills will allow you to:

- **save time** by creating systems that stop you from spending many hours in unproductive or tedious activity;
- **maintain your sanity** by, for example, being able to find things quickly when you need them or effectively managing information overload;
- **maintain a balance** between your research, other work commitments and personal life;
- **pursue a career in research,** by building skills essential in an environment characterized by continual tightening of research budgets;
- **develop effective work practices** beyond your period of research training, benefiting both your professional practice and personal life;
- **work smarter not harder.** Academic and industry environments are constrained by the need to meet deadlines and be cost efficient. The days of

extended research timeframes are (sadly for many) coming to an end as governments and industry are increasingly reluctant to fund research that takes too long to produce an outcome.

Who should use this book?

If you are a research student this book is an essential guide. Whether you are at honors, masters or doctoral level, and whatever your discipline (physical, biological, social sciences or humanities), you will find material relevant to your research process. This is certainly not a research design or methods text. In fact, it provides something completely different. It is a very practical resource that will enhance *all* aspects of your research activity. The book is also not a substitute for the guidance your supervisor can offer, but can be a valuable supplement to supervision as well as input from your peers. You might delve into sections of the book that are most applicable to your research. Alternatively, you may prefer to skim through several chapters to gain a general overview of the skills and strategies suggested, and then return to those most relevant as you travel along your research journey. This is certainly not a book that you are likely to read from cover to cover, nor one that you would engage with once and never pick up again.

If you are an early career researcher there are likely to be aspects of your research practice which you feel could be more efficient. While some systems, skills or strategies may be familiar to you, a skim through the various sections may reveal new ideas to enhance your practice.

If you are a supervisor (or advisor[1]) of postgraduate research students, you will see your role as a teacher and trainer of the next generation of researchers. Like most supervisors, the time available to work individually with your students will be limited and very valuable. You probably do not want to spend it introducing students to basic technical and organizational processes. Nor would you want to discover that they are simply not employing good strategies to manage their (and your) time, resources, and effort. For you, this book can provide a valuable point of referral for your research students.

If you are an experienced researcher you already know the benefits of good practice and the necessity of using efficient tools. You might find this book a useful resource if you want to hone your skills, improve your organizational strategies or be updated on innovative developments in research practice.

If you are teaching a course in research methods, you may find this a useful text as specialized methods texts usually don't cover organizational systems and strategies. The reflective questions and suggested activities provided at the end of each chapter offer a stimulus for your students to critically examine the impact of their personal work practices on the effectiveness of their research.

We do recognize that different research cultures give rise to significant differences in expectations and experiences of staff and students involved in research. The level of collaboration, explicit discussion, training, resource availability and emphasis placed on technical and organizational aspects of research will vary between countries, between research institutions, between faculties (not just disciplines) and between individual supervisors and students. In some contexts, technology is embraced, emphasized and readily available, creating a culture of support for using specific software. In other contexts few people may use or even be aware of such products resulting in research students having minimal exposure or opportunity to make an informed decision about their relevance. In these contexts this book could be particularly valuable.

What does the book do (and not do)?

The approach we take in this book is to:

- **provide very practical advice**, resources and tips;
- **build your** *capability* as a researcher, i.e. our philosophy is to focus on skills that allow you to adapt and build on knowledge, rather than just become competent in a particular area;
- **provide references** that encourage you to seek out further information;
- **outline the broad features of particular software** but then refer you to the software manufacturers' websites for the most up-to-date information, since such information changes rapidly as new versions are released;
- **assume that you are relatively familiar with general research processes** and management but may be less familiar with the use of technology to support these activities;
- **assume that you will be familiar with basic computer functions**, but like most people may not have considered the many ways that technology can enhance your research;
- **provide you with online, downloadable resources** via the book's website.

However, this book:

- **is NOT an introduction to research methods** or approaches to writing a proposal or a thesis[2];
- **is NOT a "how to" manual** and does not deal in-depth with particular software or statistical techniques;
- **DOES NOT cover technologies or techniques specific to particular disciplines,** but instead focuses on those common and relevant to all researchers;

- **DOES NOT recommend any specific software products**, providing instead short summaries and references to a wide range of programs.

How is this book organized?

The book is organized around broad aspects of researchers' everyday practice, whatever the discipline. While to some extent a research sequence is implied in the arrangement of chapters, you can read them in any order.

- **Chapter 1: Introduction** emphasizes the importance of being efficient in your everyday research practices. Without understanding the value of good technical and organizational systems, skills and strategies you are unlikely to be motivated to read on.
- **Chapter 2: Establishing Technical Fundamentals** defines and explains terms and concepts used throughout the book as well as outlining some basic skills, all within the framework of an exploratory learning philosophy.
- **Chapter 3: Managing Yourself, Your Ideas and Your Support Structures** suggests you take a critical look at your personal work practices and identify areas for improvement in aspects such as managing time, notes, ideas, your supervisor and your support systems.
- **Chapter 4: Organizing Your Work Environment** explores a range of suggestions for managing your physical and electronic research environments, particularly through using consistent file management strategies.
- **Chapter 5: Overseeing Progress of Your Project** addresses aspects of research such as establishing timelines and milestones, budgeting, applying for grants and managing other resources, including the use of project management software.
- **Chapter 6: Communicating and Networking Electronically** covers a range of synchronous and asynchronous communication technologies that can support your professional networking.
- **Chapter 7: Effective Literature Searching** covers a range of literature searching tools and emphasizes those strategies that are essential in making searches both effective and efficient.
- **Chapter 8: Strategic Web Searching** focuses on sophisticated and informed approaches to locating, managing and monitoring Web-based information.
- **Chapter 9: Managing and Organizing Your Literature** is the essential companion to Chapters 7 and 8 and considers the role of bibliographic software for filing, sorting and summarizing print and electronic literature.
- **Chapter 10: Designing Data Collection Systems** presents a range of issues, challenges and solutions encountered in collecting and managing both qualitative and quantitative research data in a range of multimedia formats.

- **Chapter 11: Managing Data Analysis** addresses the fundamental principles of both qualitative and quantitative data analysis, focusing specifically on issues you need to consider in choosing appropriate software.
- **Chapter 12: Improving Your Writing Efficiency** explores a wide range of foundational and more advanced aspects of word processing to support both individual and collaborative writing process, including online and nonlinear forms of writing.
- **Chapter 13: Presenting and Publishing Your Research** considers tools and strategies that allow you to communicate your findings to others in a variety of ways, in particular public speaking, poster presentations, using presentation software and planning a publication strategy.

Because the book is not designed to be read sequentially, you will find extensive cross referencing between chapters and chapter sections.

Distinctive features used in this book

Throughout the book we use a number of formatting devices to differentiate specific types of information and to guide you to the type of information you will find most useful.

Practical tips that we have drawn from our own experiences and from discussion with supervisors and other experienced researchers are highlighted as follows:

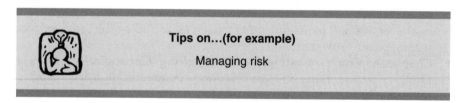

Tips on...(for example)

Managing risk

Feature examples of researchers and their practice, software or Web resources that are illustrative of the book's practical approach to research are identified as follows:

Feature Website: (for example) StatCrunch

http://www.statcrunch.com

Forms and templates that could be useful for you to use as they are, or to modify to suit your own needs, are found on the website associated with this book (see below).

See the **Organizing and Managing Your Research Website**

http://www.sagepub.co.uk/phelps

"Want to know more" feature provides where appropriate, a list of print or Web-based resources for you to explore in more detail.

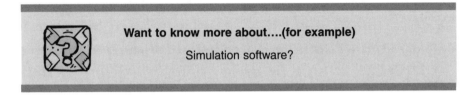

Want to know more about....(for example)

Simulation software?

Software tables, featuring a selection of relevant programs, appear at the end of relevant chapters. We certainly don't make any claims that these lists are comprehensive, or even that the specific examples that we discuss are necessarily the ones you might use. Rather, they provide a basis upon which you can begin your investigation of such research tools. Information provided includes:

- the **name** of the software;
- the **manufacturer** or developer of the software;
- the **platform** for which it was developed at the time of writing (i.e. Windows, Macintosh, Linux, Unix);
- a **website address** where you can find further information. If the link does not work, try a search using the name of the software;
- **licensing** details, principally, whether it is freeware, shareware or commercial ware (as explained in Chapter 2);
- **demo** on website, i.e. whether there was a demonstration version of the software available at the time of writing;
- **points of interest**. These are aspects that caught our attention. Note that mentioning a particular feature does not mean that other programs do not also have that feature.

Software availability and features (including licensing) change so rapidly that you are the best person to assess what is most suitable for your particular research. Consider these tables as a starting point and conduct your own searches for more recent or relevant applications (see Chapter 2 for further advice).

Each chapter concludes with an **"Over to you"** section, with some questions and tasks designed to challenge you to consider the relevance of the content to your own research field and to apply your learning to your project.

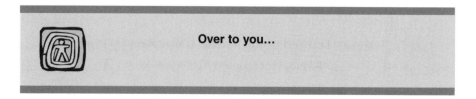

Over to you...

Using the book's website

This text is accompanied by a website which provides additional support if you want to follow up the issues and strategies outlined in the book. The website serves a number of functions:

- To provide **live links to the many web-based resources** that are mentioned in the book, allowing you to "point and click" to visit sites, rather than having to retype URIs. It also allows us to update links which might move or change over time.
- To provide **useful templates** referred to throughout the book, enabling you to download these directly rather than re-creating them yourself.
- To **supplement the resources mentioned in the book** with others that either have been identified since publication, or that we simply weren't able to incorporate here due to space limitations.
- To **give you the opportunity to provide feedback to us** and make further suggestions, which we can in turn share with others via the site.
- To **provide an opportunity for discussion** with other readers of the text and support the establishment of a community of researchers interested in issues related to organizing and managing research.

The Organizing and Managing Your Research Website will grow and develop in response to the interests and needs of users. We hope that you will join us in contributing to this enhancement to the book.

Now that you are ready to explore more of what this book has to offer, start by reflecting on these questions:

Over to you...

1. In what ways do you think this book could be useful for you and your research?
2. What stage of research are you at now? What sections of the book seem immediately relevant?
3. Take a moment to visit the book's website and consider how you might make use of and/or contribute to this environment.

Notes

1 Throughout this book we use the term "supervisor" to denote the advisory role taken by senior academics with postgraduate research students.
2 There is a wide range of such texts available to the beginner researcher, such as Rudestam and Newton 2001; Bryant 2004; O'Leary 2004; Oliver 2004; and Roberts 2004.

Chapter 2

Establishing Technical Fundamentals

What sort of computer user are you? Are you comfortable using computer hardware? Are you experienced in trialing new software? Do you take a problem-solving approach when things don't go to plan? Or are you uncertain about your computer technology skills and feel anxious about moving outside your comfort zone? We recognize that people come to research from diverse backgrounds, and some researchers return to the role after an extended career break. Sometimes new (and experienced!) researchers are reluctant to acknowledge their lack of understanding of computer basics and can struggle along inefficiently without seeking appropriate assistance. The topics we cover in this chapter are what we consider to be the computer fundamentals that might be expected of you as a researcher, but which many new researchers don't necessarily have. If you are a confident computer user, the earlier sections of this chapter will already be familiar to you. However some of the later sections may offer you something new and useful.

This chapter is not an A-Z on how to use computer technology and we *do* assume you are already making some basic use of computers. We offer here guidance on key fundamental concepts that provide a foundation for other sections of the book. We also provide you with skills and strategies that, from our experience, help all computer users (particularly novice ones) to become more confident in their computer learning. In this chapter we cover the following fundamental strategies:

- tips on how to learn about new technologies;
- the different types of computers available;
- guidance on downloading software and using spreadsheets, databases and graphics applications;
- basics on connecting to the Internet and accessing information from the Web;
- tips on how to use your computer more efficiently.

Learning about technology

Proficient computer users rarely develop and maintain their computer skills from using a manual or doing a formal training course. Most just "get in and have a go." To be an effective researcher you continually need to develop new strategies and skills as your needs and context change. When it comes to learning about technology it is quite likely that "you don't know what you don't know." Unless someone has shown you how to use a program, or you have seen it demonstrated or read a review, you are unlikely to be aware of how it could be useful for your research. This book is designed to serve exactly that function. It will raise your awareness of the range of technologies available to you and give you the confidence to have a go at using them yourself.

Our philosophy is that you will learn best through being an "exploratory learner," rather than relying on formal group or individual instruction. We have a lot of experience working with computer learners and we know that strategies that facilitate ongoing, independent computer learning can be taught and learnt. For many of the individuals we work with, gaining these insights and strategies is empowering and opens up a whole new world of independent computer learning.

Strategies for exploratory learning

Nothing major can go wrong when you explore the features of your computer or software, providing you use common sense and follow the suggested strategies below:

- **Develop good risk management practices,** including backing up, versioning and virus protection (see Chapter 4). If you're confident that you are not in danger of losing work, you can explore without fear.
- **Set goals and have the confidence to try new things.** View your learning about technology as an investment in your own professional development, not as a waste of time. Even if you try out a new piece of software and decide not to use it, you will have enhanced your general knowledge and technical skills and have increased confidence to explore other applications.
- **Look through the menus** within any program that you use. Even a program you use all the time is likely to have useful features you are not aware of. Exploring the menus and adding a new skill or two every so often can increase your skills and confidence significantly.

- **Try right clicking** on icons, on desktop items, on highlighted text, in fact on anything, to discover features you weren't previously aware of. This will display a menu with all sorts of options related to that item (on a Mac the equivalent is Control-click).

- **Experiment with "drag and dropping."** There is more to it than just moving files. This action is central to the functionality of many programs.

- **Learn to use the different types of Help.** While lots of people claim that "Help" isn't very helpful (and, we agree, sometimes it isn't), frequently it is unfamiliarity and inexperience with using Help that is the problem. Spending a little time exploring the various Help options is a sound investment in research time. The three most common Help formats are:

  - **Help Contents**, which is like the table of contents of a book, with chapters on each topic. Use this when you want to read a comprehensive guide on how to do a particular task.

  - **Help Index**, which is like the index of a book. Use it to look up very specific pieces of information. Sometimes you need to try a couple of terms before you find what you are after (just as in a book index).

  - **Help using natural language searching**, which lets you type in a question when you don't know exactly what to look up.

- **Explore the Preferences, Options and/or Tools section** of any program. This is where the default settings that control how the program behaves can often be adjusted. Later in this chapter we discuss some ways you can use these to customize programs.

   Want to know more about....

Computer terminology?

While we aim to keep computer jargon to a minimum and explain most terms in straightforward language throughout this book, if you encounter a term that is unfamiliar to you, try one of the following Web-based technology dictionaries:

- Webopedia   http://www.webopedia.com
- Computeruser.com   http://www.computeruser.com/resources/dictionary

- Whatis.com   http://whatis.techtarget.com
- FOLDOC   http://foldoc.org
- Computer Hope   http://www.computerhope.com/jargon.htm

Hardware fundamentals

In 1948, the journal *Popular Mechanics* predicted that "in the future computers will probably weigh less than 1.5 tons." Such a notion seems laughable to us today, given the diversity of professional and consumer level hardware that sit on our desktops, our laps, or in the palms of our hands. Advanced research is exploring the development of molecular level computers, several hundreds of thousands times smaller than silicon-based circuitry. Super fast, million dollar supercomputers measure their calculating speed in tera-flops (trillions of calculations per second). Some are purpose-built machines (such as IBM's Blue Gene) while others such as Virginia Tech's System-X consist of more than a thousand Apple Mac G5 servers, the same G5s that you can buy over the counter.

Researchers' computer hardware needs vary greatly, as do their budgets and the level of support provided by their institutions. No doubt you do already have access to some form of computer configuration. However, in our experience, many researchers find themselves reconsidering their hardware needs when beginning a new project or phase of their research career. For example, you may to date have used a desktop computer, but because of a new need to travel or collect data in the field, may be considering a laptop or palmtop. Our intention here is to list the main types of computers you are likely to encounter and some of the issues associated with each, focusing on general purpose rather than specialist computers.

Types of computers

Desktops take up the space of about the size of two A4 pages and with the need for a separate monitor, keyboard and mouse they certainly are not the sort of computer you want to be moving around on a regular basis. Desktops tend to have faster processor speeds and more storage space than average laptops and are generally cheaper. They are also more easily customized. For instance, you can replace or upgrade components, add extra hard drives, or increase Random Access Memory (RAM).

Workstations are computers that use the latest and most powerful processors. They are suited to handling large amounts of data or running specialist software and might be considered as "desktops on steroids."

Laptops, also called **powerbooks or notebooks**, weigh in at one to two kilos, have adequate processing power for most office jobs, but often have limited hard disk storage and only modestly sized screens. Their advantage over desktops is their portability. If needed, their capabilities can be boosted by attaching external hard disk drives and a large monitor. In your office, you can use a docking station, a piece of equipment that sits on your desk with all the peripherals (such as mouse, keyboard etc.) and cables already connected.

Palmtops (or their less sophisticated cousins, **Personal Digital Assistants** or PDAs) are small computers that can be held in one hand and operated by the other. Processing speed and storage are sacrificed for portability and size. If you need a computer to support your data collection in the field, or an electronic organizer which you can carry with you and synchronize with your main computer, these machines may be just what you need. Most now allow you to handwrite on the screen and the palmtop performs character recognition to convert to typewritten text. While it is generally very effective, it can take a little time to adjust to how some characters need to be formed. Palmtops and PDAs can also incorporate digital camera and video capabilities, wireless and Bluetooth (a short-range form of wireless) connectivity, inbuilt mobile phones and Global Positioning Systems (GPS).

Servers are computers (or related devices) that have been set up to provide a specific type of network functionality. They are usually permanently connected to the network they serve and run 24 hours a day, 7 days a week. One of the oldest types of servers is a file or FTP server. Its role is to control the secure storage and transfer of files between other computers on the network. Another common server is a mail server, one specifically set up to move and store e-mail. Other servers include chat, discussion list, proxy, Web etc. In fact, more than one server function can run on one machine at the same time, but in high traffic environments each function is often dedicated to a separate machine. Consumer laptops such as Mac Powerbooks have the Apache Web server application built into the operating system so you can run your own Web server whenever you are on a network.

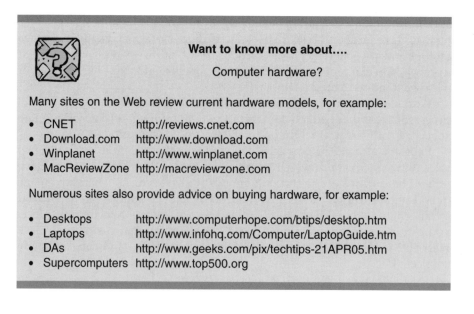

Want to know more about....

Computer hardware?

Many sites on the Web review current hardware models, for example:

- CNET   http://reviews.cnet.com
- Download.com   http://www.download.com
- Winplanet   http://www.winplanet.com
- MacReviewZone http://macreviewzone.com

Numerous sites also provide advice on buying hardware, for example:

- Desktops   http://www.computerhope.com/btips/desktop.htm
- Laptops   http://www.infohq.com/Computer/LaptopGuide.htm
- DAs   http://www.geeks.com/pix/techtips-21APR05.htm
- Supercomputers http://www.top500.org

Software fundamentals

Software is a generic term that refers to the programs that allow your computer hardware to do what you want it to do. Without software, your computer would only really be useful as a paper weight! There are two broad categories of software, operating systems and application and utility software.

Operating system software

Operating system software provides a user-friendly environment for you to interact with your computer's hardware. Common operating systems (or platforms) are:

- **Windows.** Examples include 2000, Millennium and XP.
- **Macintosh.** Examples include OS8, OS9, OSX (as in Roman numeral 10).
- **Linux** is a free, open-source operating system, meaning that its underlying source code is available to the public and anyone can freely use, modify, improve or redistribute it. Originally used by technologically oriented people (some might say "geeks"), Linux has become much more user-friendly and is now widely used, particularly by people wishing to avoid being locked into big proprietary software companies.
- **UNIX** is the oldest and most well-established operating system. It was developed by programmers for programmers and provides multiuser and multitasking capabilities.

Various software products allow you to run (or emulate) a Windows environment within a Macintosh or Linux operating system. As you might expect, the software runs a little slower than on a similarly powered Windows computer, but the big advantage is that you can instantly switch (or "toggle") between operating systems.

Want to know more about ...

Emulating a Windows operating system?

Macintosh

VirtualPC	http://www.apple.com/macosx/applications/virtualpc
	http://www.microsoft.com/windows/virtualpc
iEmulator	http://www.iemulator.com

Linux

CrossOver Office	http://www.codeweavers.com

Unix

Wine	http://www.winehq.com

Application and utility software

Application and utility software provides particular functionality to your computer. Applications are large, multifunctional programs while utilities are smaller with a defined function. While there are thousands of applications and utilities available, there are some fundamental types that are essential aids to research, most of which we consider in this book:

- word processing (Chapter 12);
- e-mail applications (Chapter 6);
- Web browsers (this chapter with further detail in Chapter 8);
- spreadsheets (this chapter with further examples throughout the book);
- databases (this chapter with further examples throughout the book);
- graphics applications (this chapter, with further references in Chapters 3 and 13);
- utilities such as note taking (Chapter 3) and virus protection and backup (Chapter 4).

Of course, throughout this book we also consider a range of additional specialist software relevant to research.

Applications often come bundled as a package, for example, Microsoft Office includes word processor, spreadsheet, e-mail, calendar, database, Web browser and presentation applications. There are other bundled (and individual) applications available, including some which are shareware, freeware or open source (free). For example, you might like to investigate and perhaps even try out OpenOffice (http://www.openoffice.org) – an open-source multiplatform and multilingual office suite, free to download, use, and distribute (see below regarding software licensing). Other examples include NeoOffice http://www.neooffice.org/ and Thinkfree Office http://www.thinkfree.com/common/main.tfo.

File formats and file names

When you save a document created in any one of these many applications, it will be saved in a particular file format. On many operating systems the format of the file is distinguishable by 1–4 letters (typically 3) that appear at the end of the file name, separated by a full stop (period). These are known as file extensions. For example, Word files have a .doc extension; Rich Text Format is .rtf; and photos are generally in .jpg or .jpeg format (short for Joint Photographic Experts Group, and pronounced jay-peg). Some file extensions are proprietary to particular application software (for example .xls for Microsoft Excel; .nsf for Lotus Notes databases; and .dsf for Micrografx Designer). Other file extensions are more generally used, for example .wav are waveform audio files; and .png are Portable Network Graphics files. *It is important not to delete the file extension from the end of your file name or your computer may have difficulty identifying which program opens it.* A comprehensive listing of file extensions is provided on Wikipedia (http://www.webopedia.com).

Many programs allow you to open files in one format and save them to another (using the "Save As" function). This is highly valuable if you need to move files between different applications or share files with others (e.g. moving data from a spreadsheet to a quantitative data analysis program, or converting a project logo to a format that can be used on a website).

Software licensing

Throughout this book we refer you to many software products that you may find beneficial to your research. Knowing that researchers generally have very limited budgets, we have attempted to balance our coverage of commercial products with those that are free. It is, however, important to understand the meaning of several software licensing terms, so that you can make the most efficient budgetary decisions.

- **Freeware** is computer software that is made available free of charge, but with some licensing restrictions, e.g. that the software cannot be copied, modified or redistributed. This is different from *free software* that can be used, copied, modified and redistributed but may or may not be free of charge. In both cases, support may be limited or not provided at all. "Adware," a variation on freeware, doesn't require you to hand over any money, but you do pay a price in being exposed to advertisements embedded in the display. "Donationware" (sometimes referred to as "beggarware" or "nagware") is distributed for free with the authors asking users to make a donation to themselves or to a charity. More malicious are "baitware" products that are very limited or defective freeware intended to attract users to commercial products. **"Open source" freeware** (or public domain software) are applications where the source code for the program is available to the public. Anyone who knows how to write programs can change or modify it, although there are usually restrictions, such as not being able to market the original or change source code, or a requirement to include an acknowledgement statement with all modified code.
- **Shareware** is software that is fully functional and that you can download and try out to see whether you like it. If you do, you pay a fee to continue using it. Much shareware expires (usually in 14 or 30 days) and no longer works fully (or at all). Users are generally encouraged to copy and "share" unregistered versions of the software, with the aim that others will also pay the fee to gain full use of the program.
- **Commercial or proprietary software** is controlled by a single person or company (with copyright protection) and only they can change or distribute it and, of course, you pay for it. Many commercial programs are, however, provided as **demonstration versions** on the software website. In these instances (and there are many cited in the software tables throughout the book) you can install and use the program, generally for a set number of days (e.g. 14 or 30). Some demonstration versions provide full functionality while others are restricted (e.g. you may not be able to save files).

Selecting and downloading application software

General points to be aware of when selecting software to support your research are listed below. Note that we provide specific tips in relation to particular types of applications where applicable throughout the book.

- **Operating System compatibility.** Check that the software you are considering is compatible with your operating system, including the version of the system (e.g. some software may be compatible with Windows XP but not Windows 2000).
- **Hardware requirements.** The software should state the minimum memory, hard drive space, processor speed etc. it requires to run the software.
- **The user interface,** or how "user-friendly" it is, will be influenced by the familiarity of the menus and icons, its on-screen displays, the range of shortcuts provided and so on.
- **Support.** Your choice of software should be informed by the availability of support resources such as books, online help and tutorials, online user groups and perhaps the availability of people in your institution who are familiar with the program.
- **Export and import features.** The ability to move data between different programs will be important if you ever choose to change software or if you want your files to be accessed by other researchers.
- **Palmtop compatibility** may be a great bonus if you want to move data between your palmtop and desktop or laptop.
- **Cost and licensing.** Many programs are quite expensive if purchased as a single license. It is worth checking whether your institution or any other researchers already have a multiuser license or would be prepared to contribute to one.

 Want to know more about...

Selecting and downloading software?

Many sites provide reviews of software, as well as direct download access to demonstration or full versions of software, for example:

- TuCows   http://www.tucows.com
- CNET download.com http://www.download.com
- Versiontracker.com http://www.versiontracker.com

For Palmtops

- Handango   http://www.handango.com
- PocketGear.com   http://www.pocketgear.com

In the following sections we give detailed attention to four general purpose applications that are fundamental across the spectrum of research activity: spreadsheets, databases, graphics applications and programs that create and/or view PDF documents.

Spreadsheets

In our experience many researchers, particularly those from the social sciences and humanities, have had very limited exposure to spreadsheet programs. Yet they are one of the most versatile and useful applications a researcher can use.

Spreadsheets are specifically designed for entering, editing, manipulating and printing structured, tabular information, and were originally designed for tasks that required calculation such as accounting ledger sheets. Their primary function is to perform numerical operations on data, particularly mathematical and/or statistical functions. However, they have much greater potential in supporting both quantitative *and* qualitative research. Because a spreadsheet can be set up as a simple database, many people confuse spreadsheets with database applications. Databases are designed to handle and search large amounts of textual information and for outputting in very specific formats.

A spreadsheet is made up of rows and columns with the intersection between them forming a cell, as illustrated in Figure 2.1 below. Each row and column has a label; rows are labeled with numbers while columns are labeled with capital letters. Thus each cell (the intersection between a row and a column) has a name, e.g. A1, D5 etc.

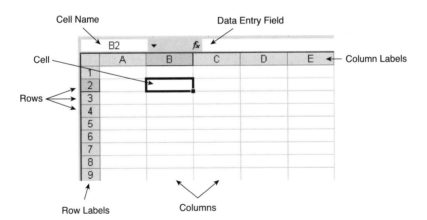

Figure 2.1 The general appearance of a spreadsheet, showing basic nomenclature.

While all spreadsheet applications vary slightly, they generally have these features. Example is from Microsoft Excel.

Words or numbers can be entered into cells by clicking into the cell and typing. As you type, the characters appear in the data entry field (although they may also appear in the cell). After typing in the cell you hit Enter/ Return or click "OK" (sometimes a tick is used) and the content is entered in the cell. You can move from one cell to another using the Tab key or the arrow keys on your keyboard. Alternatively, you can position your cursor each time with your mouse.

Each row and column will normally start with a label in the first cell which indicates what the data in that row or column relates to. The real strength of spreadsheets lies in their ability to perform mathematical calculations automatically.

- **Operations**. All operations begin with the = sign and use + for addition, – for subtraction, × for multiplication, or / for division. In the example in Figure 2.2, to find out the sum of John's responses to variables 1, 2 and 3, type into cell F2 the following mathematical operation: =C2+D2+E2.
- **Functions.** These provide a more efficient alternative to manually performing operations. They range from basic mathematical operations such as average, maximum, minimum or frequency, to more complex statistical or logical operations. All functions also begin with the = sign. For instance, to calculate the sum of John's three responses (C2, D2 and E2 above) you could type into cell F2 the following mathematical function: =SUM(C2:E2). The colon represents a range of cells including C2 and E2 and all cells in between. Similarly, to work out the average response to variable 1 and display the result in cell C9 you could type into cell C9 the following

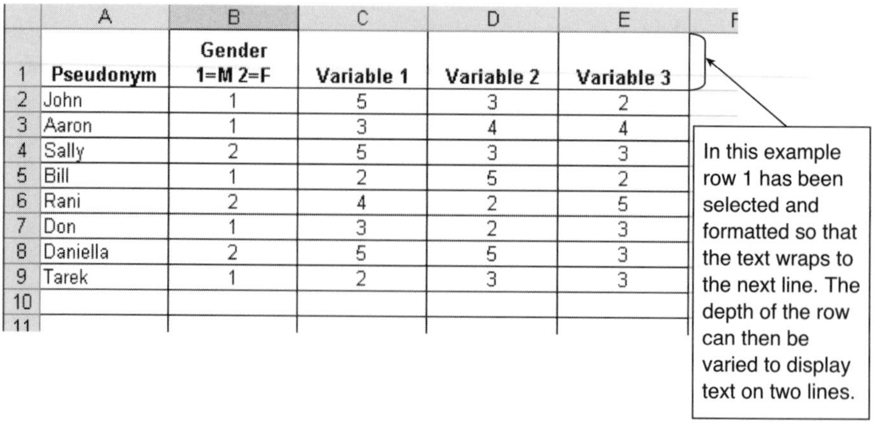

	A	B	C	D	E	F
		Gender				
1	Pseudonym	1=M 2=F	Variable 1	Variable 2	Variable 3	
2	John	1	5	3	2	
3	Aaron	1	3	4	4	
4	Sally	2	5	3	3	
5	Bill	1	2	5	2	
6	Rani	2	4	2	5	
7	Don	1	3	2	3	
8	Daniella	2	5	5	3	
9	Tarek	1	2	3	3	
10						
11						

In this example row 1 has been selected and formatted so that the text wraps to the next line. The depth of the row can then be varied to display text on two lines.

Figure 2.2 Entering data entry into a spreadsheet

Note that Row 1 and Column A contain labels describing the data. Example is from Microsoft Excel.

mathematical operation =AVERAGE(C2:C8) Your program will provide you with a list of available functions (see the Insert menu or Help).

The advantages of using a spreadsheet for mathematical operations is that if, for instance, you need to adjust one of the responses or scores, the sums or averages will automatically update. Spreadsheets enable you to sort your data based on the contents of any one or more rows or columns. Another useful feature of spreadsheets is their ability to create graphs and charts in a range of formats, as illustrated in Figure 2.3.

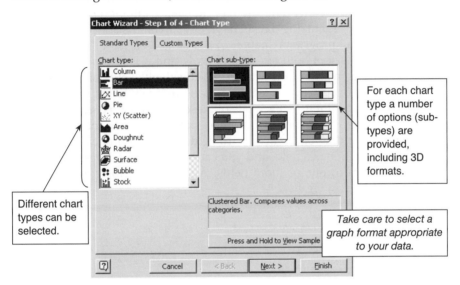

Figure 2.3   Examples of graph formats provided by spreadsheet programs

Some graph formats are more appropriate to particular data than others. For example, pie charts and 100% stacked bar charts display relative portions of a whole (suitable for nominal and ordinal data – see Chapter 11), while a simple bar chart displays and compares interval data. Example is from Microsoft Excel.

We provide further examples and details on how spreadsheets can be used to support your research throughout the book. In particular, Chapter 5 explores the use of spreadsheets to establish and manage a research budget; Chapter 7 provides an example of how a spreadsheet can help you to manage your literature searching; and Chapter 11 discusses their use in data analysis.

Databases

It is critical to have an understanding of what is meant by a database before you read this book as throughout we discuss a range of general, as well as very specific, database functions and programs. At one level, a database is just a collection of information (or data) that is stored in some orderly way. For instance, old library card catalogues and your pocket address book are both examples of databases. However, in a computer sense, database applications are programs designed to facilitate the storage of electronic data that can then be easily searched, sorted and accessed.

Databases can be customized for a wide range of research purposes. You are probably familiar with library databases, those designed to provide access to journal articles, conference papers, reports etc. (discussed in Chapter 7). Others include databases for managing bibliographic references (Chapter 9) or for organizing data (Chapter 10). Even the address book function of your e-mail program (Chapter 6) is a database.

Databases consist of both *records* and *fields*, and it is important to understand these terms in order to use databases effectively. Think of your address book (electronic or hardcopy). Within it you are likely to have an entry for each friend or acquaintance. Each one of these entries is a record. For each of these people you will record certain pieces of information, name, address, phone number and so on. In an electronic database each one of these categories of information is a field, and you can search your address book using a particular term in one or more fields. A typical electronic address book database is shown in Figure 2.4.

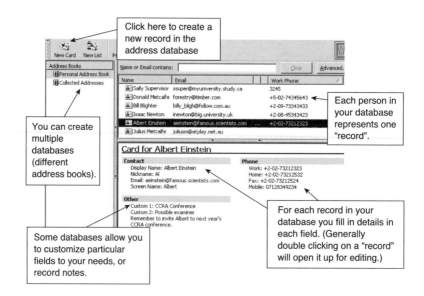

Figure 2.4   Address book database showing records and fields

Each person in your address book represents one "record" while the types of information that you record (name, work number, e-mail address etc.) represent the fields. Example is from Mozilla.

Databases are also very valuable for finding sets of data, sorting them in a particular order and displaying or printing them out in particular formats. For example, you might use the information in your address book to search for all records marked "CCRA Conference" and use this found set to e-mail out a conference invitation or call for papers. A range of strategies can be used to refine database searches, which we consider in more detail in Chapter 7.

Graphics and photographic applications

Throughout your research process there may be times when you want to present your ideas, data or planning processes visually. A range of graphics applications make this easy to do. In other sections of this book we mention mind mapping and visualization software (Chapter 3), software for creating Gantt charts (Chapter 5), how to use images or photos as a source of data (Chapter 10), and graphs and charts (see the section on spreadsheets in this chapter, and quantitative data analysis software in Chapter 11). There are two main types of graphics applications for creating and modifying images:

- **Drawing programs** create vector images which are made up of lines, curves, rectangles and other objects. You can edit, move or rearrange individual lines or shapes. You can also group and ungroup objects, so that if they are resized they will retain their original definition and perspective. Many commonly used word processing or presentation programs include a basic drawing facility within them. There are also drawing programs available as freeware, shareware and commercial software.
- **Paint programs** create or manipulate bitmap pictures (including photos) which are made up of a series of small dots. All scanned graphics and photographs are bitmaps. When they are enlarged, they lose definition and the individual dots that make up the picture become visible. Computers with Windows installed include a basic Paint program (Windows Paint), but again freeware, shareware and commercial programs are available.

Which graphics program should you use?
This decision will depend on the type of images you are creating, what you want to achieve, and your level of interest and skill in learning to use the software.

- **For simple diagrams or flowcharts,** the drawing tools within programs such as Microsoft Word or PowerPoint may be sufficient.

- **For more advanced diagrams, logos and complex images including scanned components** you will probably need more professional level software and will face a decision as to whether you do it yourself or have someone do it for you. There are many advantages in learning to create and modify images yourself, since you can continue to refine them as your research progresses.

With knowledge of just a few basic concepts and understanding you can start creating and modifying basic graphics. The following should get you off and running:

- **Creating layers**, which are different levels of an image built up over a period of time. Most of the more advanced graphics programs allow you to work with multiple layers, enabling you to edit, change, move or delete components of the overall artwork without disturbing other components.
- **Creating a text box** into which you can put words *or* use it simply as an object (such as a square or circle). These are used to position each element of your diagram on the page (like using layers) by dragging and they can be grouped or set to display in front or behind other objects. Modify the text box by exploring group, ungroup, order, align, rotate and crop functions found on the drawing toolbar.
- **Using appropriate file formats**. Each program has its own proprietary image format, but will also allow you to save images in standard formats. Graphics Interchange Format (.gif) is generally used for vector images such as line art, logos, cartoon images or Web art such as buttons and backgrounds, while jpeg format is generally used for photographs. When creating your own images, save working versions in the program's proprietary format which retains information about the layers and development process. When the image is finished, you can then convert it to a widely accessible format if you need to distribute it or insert it into another document.
- **Screen grabbing** is a particularly useful skill if you want to represent in a document an image of something on your screen. Many keyboards have a Print Screen key (sometimes it requires the function key to be used) which copies your computer screen to memory so that you can paste it into your word processing document or graphics program. A range of utilities also provide more sophisticated screen grabbing functionality, as do most graphics programs.

You can also access software that creates very specific types of images such as timelines, molecular structures, architectural drawings and laboratory equipment.

Want to know more about...

Graphics applications?

To locate other graphics software, search a software download site. Try searching for these common programs: GIMPshop (Open source freeware), ConceptDraw, CorelDraw, PaintShop Pro, PhotoShop, Timeline Maker or Visio.

PDF documents

Portable Document Format (PDF) is a special proprietary file format that displays an image of a document on a screen exactly as it would look if printed. PDF (file extension .pdf) is widely used for the distribution of journal articles, books, reports, manuals and other research documents. While using Acrobat Reader to view and print documents is fairly straightforward, we consider PDF here in some detail because, in our experience, few people understand how to use such documents effectively.

The most commonly used program to *create* PDF documents is Adobe Acrobat *Writer*. There are, however, other shareware and commercial programs available and the Mac OSX operating system has PDF functionality built in. Adobe Acrobat *Reader* is a free program used to simply *view* PDF documents. Most computers will already have it installed as it usually comes bundled with other programs such as Web browsers (discussed below). Note these particular issues when using PDF:

- **PDF documents can be very large** in terms of file size and can take a long time to download if you have a slow Internet connection.
- **You cannot change PDF documents, but you can copy and paste from them**. To do so, however, you must select the text tool ⯈ Select or Tₐ before you highlight blocks of text.
- **Some PDF documents are created with security features** so that functions such as saving, printing or highlighting to copy and paste are blocked. This is usually because the author or distributor does not wish to allow such functionality.

Adobe Acrobat Reader also incorporates e-book viewing and management functionality (see Chapter 7 for more information about e-books). There are also various utilities available which make it much easier to view PDF documents on palmtops.

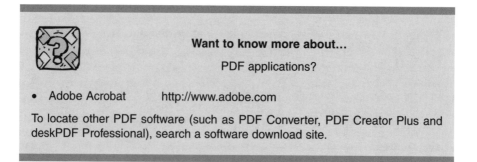

Want to know more about...

PDF applications?

- Adobe Acrobat   http://www.adobe.com

To locate other PDF software (such as PDF Converter, PDF Creator Plus and deskPDF Professional), search a software download site.

Networking fundamentals

Are the Internet and the World Wide Web the same thing? While many people have this impression, in fact they are not. While no doubt all researchers have at least some experience using the Internet and Web, we provide a little historical information for background.

The Internet, known originally as ARPANET, was conceptualized in 1962 as a global network of computers and became a reality in 1969. As a product of the Cold War, one of its key design concepts was to provide a communications network that would work even if some sites were destroyed by nuclear attack. From its initial implementation across four university sites, it quickly spread to other universities and research organizations, then to commercial organizations and finally into the home. Thus the Internet is a network of computer networks that enables a variety of functions, including the World Wide Web, electronic mail, mailing lists, chat rooms and file transfer. This is achieved by a set of international agreements or protocols to ensure that computer files and programs can be transferred among different computers running different operating systems.

The World Wide Web (WWW or the Web) was conceived in 1989 by two engineers, Robert Cailliau and Tim Berners-Lee, at CERN, a physics research facility in Geneva. Its initial purpose was to aid communications between physicists working on large global collaborative projects. The Web is essentially a hypertext system. This simply means that you navigate by clicking on links (known as hyperlinks) which then display another document. The Web uses the Internet as its transport mechanism but it also relies on international standards and rules for communication, also known as protocols.

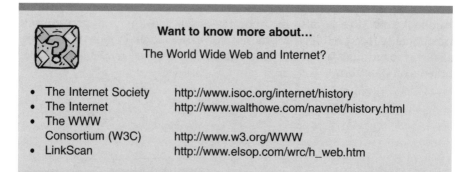

Want to know more about...

The World Wide Web and Internet?

- The Internet Society   http://www.isoc.org/internet/history
- The Internet   http://www.walthowe.com/navnet/history.html
- The WWW
  Consortium (W3C)   http://www.w3.org/WWW
- LinkScan   http://www.elsop.com/wrc/h_web.htm

Connecting to the Internet

There are various ways to connect to the Internet, all of which use different technologies (copper wires, optical fiber, wireless signals) and vary in speed and reliability. Indeed, your connection will almost invariably involve several or all of these. For example, in your home you might connect via wireless signal to a small base station, which connects to an ADSL modem that is connected to your telephone line which consists of a copper wire connection to the local exchange at which point the connection changes to optical fiber.

A second way to describe your Internet connection is in relation to its bandwidth or "speed." Bandwidth, an old term from electrical engineering, refers to the *capacity of the connection* (i.e. how much data the network can transmit). It is commonly measured in bits per second (bps).

The following briefly describes the common types of Internet connection and the range of speeds you can expect from each.

Dial-up modems (originally stand-alone devices but now built into most computers), allow you to connect to the Internet via your standard telephone line. Such connections involve copper phone lines and are relatively slow, usually in the range of 33–44 kilobits/second (kbps). They are prone to disconnecting if the signal quality on your line is poor.

Broadband refers to data transmission where multiple pieces of data are sent simultaneously to increase the effective rate of transmission. A number of technologies deliver broadband services:

- Digital Subscriber Lines (DSL) are a family of technologies (one of which is Asymmetrical Digital Scriber Lines, ADSL) that provides digital transmission over the last few kilometers of the local telephone network. Such services are not available in a local area until the local exchange has the required specialist equipment. Conventional ADSL download rates (the speed at which you can bring files and programs from the Internet to your computer) start at 256 kbps and can go as high as several thousand kbps. Upload rates (the speed at which you can send files or programs from your computer to another) start at 64 kbps and can go up to around 512 kbps. DSL is a connection that is "always on," which means you do not have to dial-in each time you want to use the service. What's more, it also allows normal phone operation so you don't need a special line to connect.
- Cable modems are a special type of modem designed to modulate a data signal over optical fiber infrastructure (typically used for cable television). They are usually rated at 1500 to 3000 kbps for downloads and 400 to 600 kbps for uploads.

Wireless connectivity allows connection without cables and can be achieved in a number of ways. A personal digital mobile phone can provide a slow 14.4 kbps connection. Wireless base stations used in libraries, downtown coffee shops or in the home can run between 11 and 54 megabits/second (mbps), but keep in mind that, as with all shared systems, this rate drops as more users are added to the system. Wireless LANs (Local Area Networks) that are set up to cover downtown and suburban areas are able to deliver high bandwidth (speed) connections even when there are many simultaneous users. Satellite Internet systems are really a special form of wireless base station but usually involve relatively low speeds (around 400 kbps).

Institutional connections, the type used in universities and research laboratories, usually involve Ethernet networks that provide local data transfer speeds varying from tens to hundreds of mbps. Outside connections to the Internet or other research institutions will also be in the mbps or gigabits/second range, or even higher speeds. Extremely high speeds are needed for projects involving massive amounts of data (such as particle physics or weather prediction).

Want to know more about...

Your current Internet connection speed?

You can test the speed of your connection for free at:

- Bandwidthplace   http://www.bandwidthplace.com/speedtest
- Speakeasy   http://www.speakeasy.net/speedtest

Accessing information on the Web

In this section we provide some definitions and easy-to-understand explanations of a few terms related to accessing information on the Web. We use these terms throughout the book and know that for many researchers clarification of the terms will be useful.

Web browsers
To access information on the Web you need a client application called a browser. This allows you to interact with a Web server to download and view or listen to text, graphics, digital video and sound files. Web browsers essentially facilitate the process of hyperlinking. In other words, clicking on a hyperlink (usually underlined in blue) causes the computer to display the linked document. You could think of a Web browser as providing point and click file transfer.

Examples of browsers include Mozilla Firefox, Opera, Safari, Camino, Netscape, Fast Browser Pro and Internet Explorer. As website technology continues to evolve, we advise you to keep up-to-date with the latest version of your preferred browser.

Proxy settings
Most commercial Internet Service Providers (ISPs), universities and other institutions require you to enter what is called a "proxy setting" into the preferences/options area of your Web browser in order to access websites. The proxy settings decrease the amount of long-distance Internet traffic by storing a local copy of a webpage on the ISP's server (for a short time) once someone has

looked at it. This means that the next time the page is viewed (within this time) it is loaded from the local server. Your institution or ISP will generally provide you with step-by-step directions on how to configure your proxy settings.

Plug-ins

A plug-in is a small additional program that operates within your browser to enable it to read, view or listen to particular types of material on the Web (such as graphics or video material). Plug-ins need to be installed separately and most have to be updated regularly as well, as newer versions are made available. Examples include Java, JavaScript, Shockwave and Flash. You may be prompted to download a plug-in when viewing some webpages.

HTML and XML

Hypertext Markup Language (HTML) and Extensible Markup Language (XML) are parts of the established international standards for information distributed on the Web. In other words, they are the coding systems that contain the information displayed on webpages, the rules for displaying it and the nature of the information being displayed. The average computer user doesn't need to know the technicalities of either HTML or XML because if you choose to create a website, there is software that creates the coding for you (see Chapter 6). However, as we make mention of HTML and XML throughout this book, we provide here a brief, simplified explanation.

HTML is coding that lies "behind" a webpage, telling your Web browser *what* to display and *how* to display it. For example, to start a new paragraph the code <p> is used; to display something in bold you start and end the bold coding with **bold text**. XML, on the other hand, allows you to give your data meaning i.e. to describe what data on your page refers to, for example <item>Mac powerbook</item> or <price>$2100</price>. In XML, unlike HTML, you create your own "tags" (the words that appear inside the triangular brackets) and you can hence customize them to your own needs.

By way of example, a popular music application, iTunes, uses XML to store data about each song. This data can then be used to search for and build a play list of a particular music genre or artist. XML is an important component of the Semantic Web.[1]

Want to know more about...

XML?

A range of books are currently in publication (and more appear all the time) on XML. Try a search in your local or online bookshop. The following websites are also useful:

- The World Wide Web Consortium   http://www.w3.org/XML

- An Introduction to XML   http://www.xmlfiles.com/xml

Having covered some of the fundamental technical information that should assist you in reading this book, we now turn to ways in which you can become more efficient in how you use your computer.

Increasing your technical efficiency

There are various ways of increasing your technical efficiency, ranging from purchasing new equipment or software to learning new skills. In this section we focus on typing skills, voice recognition software, customizing your software, recording macros, pasting links and special formatting.

Developing your typing skills

The standard QWERTY keyboard was designed in the 1800s for mechanical typewriters to slow typists down to avoid jamming the keys. Despite this historical legacy, one skill that can enhance your computer efficiency is fast and accurate typing. While some individuals become very proficient at typing with two fingers, for most people becoming more efficient means learning to use all their fingers on the correct keys. There are ergonomic and efficiency reasons for decreasing hand movements and for associating particular keys with particular fingers. There is a wide range of software available which teaches and reinforces typing skills, however ultimately there is no substitute for consciously trying to use correct fingers while you are typing up your research. There are, of course, other types of keyboard layouts (and shapes) that are designed to increase typing efficiency, which you might want to investigate (for example, do a search for Dvorak).

Using voice recognition software

While typing skills will continue to be important, voice recognition software has the potential to dramatically decrease the need for typing and reduce the incidence of repetitive strain injuries. Essentially these programs allow you to speak into a microphone plugged into the computer and the software will interpret your speech and turn it into text. While this might sound like the answer to all your typing problems, there are a few issues to consider when using this software:

- The software has to be "trained" to recognize your voice. While this can be quite quick initially, you need to keep training it when it makes a mistake, rather than making the corrections manually.
- You need to speak at a steady pace, preferably not too slowly. As the software uses both speech and language data, it needs you to talk in your natural speaking voice to make an assessment of what it is you are saying. This is easier when you are reading something, but more difficult when you are thinking and dictating.
- Voice recognition can prove more time consuming, particularly since considerable checking and correcting is required. Editing your work can be slower than using a mouse until you are used to it, as you need to keep giving instructions about where you want to go in your document and what you want to do.
- While it does not make any typographical errors, the software does *not* eliminate the need for careful proofreading. It is easy to miss small words (in, at, of etc.) that the software has added as you dictate. It is most likely to do this if you pause frequently while you are speaking.
- It can be distracting for others if you are working in a shared work area to hear you speaking to the computer and you may not want them to hear what you are writing!
- The most important thing to remember is that accuracy will improve with time and practice. Perseverance through the initial frustrations is essential and could save you much time and typing discomfort in the long run.

Examples of voice recognition software include Advanced Recognition Technologies; Dragon Naturally Speaking; Fonix; Philips Speech Recognition; Sensory Fluid Speech; Speech Works; Via Voice and iListen.

Text to speech software

As well as voice recognition software, there is also software that does the reverse, converting text to voice. Voice synthesis software converts text into spoken audio which you can then listen to on your PC or create MP3 or WMA files for use on portable devices like MP3 players, palmtops and CD players. Text to speech software can be used to listen to articles read aloud (perhaps while you go for your morning walk or while commuting), to proofread your own writing and for translation into different languages. It is also invaluable for people with visual impairments. Many programs provide a range of "voices" to choose from, with different genders and accents. Examples include TextAloud, Natural Voice Text to Speech Reader, 2nd Speech Center and SmartRead.

Customizing keyboard shortcuts, toolbars and menus

Using **keyboard shortcuts** can save time and effort, particularly when performing repetitive tasks, as they keep your fingers on the keyboard rather than having to shift your hand to the mouse. There are many standard shortcuts that are consistent across most programs such as:

- Control-C for copy;
- Control-V for paste;
- Control-X for cut;
- Control-F for find;
- Control-S for save;
- Control-Z for undo;
- Control-Y for repeat.

Most programs list shortcuts next to menu items, or you can look up a list in Help. Many also allow you to customize the keyboard shortcuts, allowing you to add your own to particular functions or change those already assigned. You can also customize toolbars (the rows with the small image-based icons which perform set functions) and menus (the text-based lists that drop-down at the top of the screen to provide functionality), as illustrated in Figure 2.5.

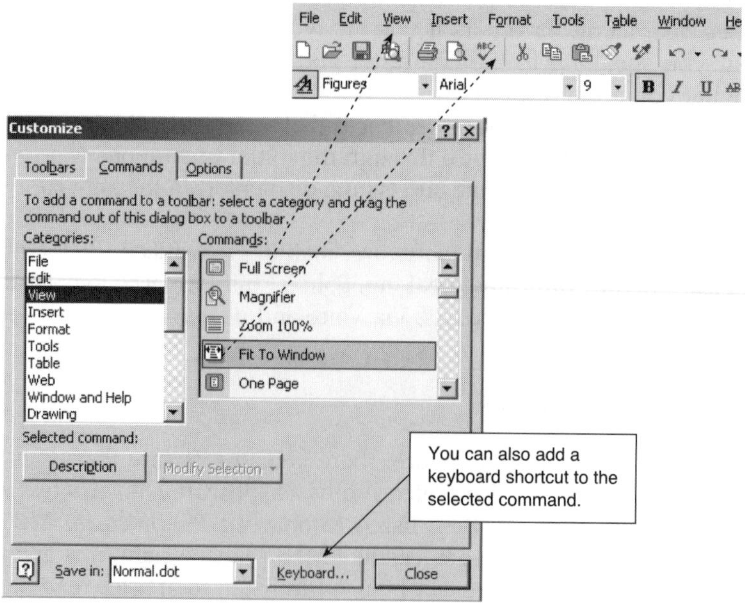

Figure 2.5 Customizing toolbars in your word processor or other program

If there are particular functions that you perform repetitively, you can increase efficiency by customizing your toolbars and menus. In this example, the "Full Screen" function is being added to the View menu and the "Fit to Window" icon is being added to the toolbar by dragging and dropping. Example is from Microsoft Word.

Using macros

A macro is a simple way of programming a series of commands or instructions which are grouped together as a single function or action. If you find yourself performing a task repeatedly, a macro can make this more efficient. When word processing, for example, you might want to speed up a series of actions such as inserting a table with a specific number of rows and columns and then formatting its borders and text. See Figure 2.6 for an example of how macros are recorded.

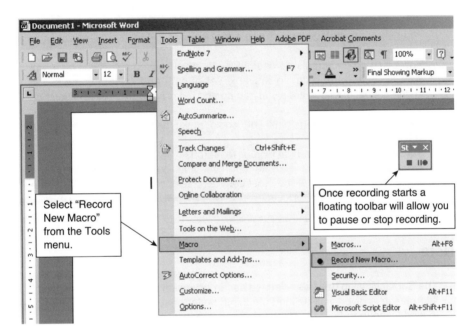

Figure 2.6   Recording a macro

Many programs allow you to record a sequence of steps and allocate these to a single button or function. In this example from Microsoft Word, "Record New Macro" has been selected. Recording of your current actions has started and the recording toolbar allows you to pause or stop recording when your action is complete.

Pasting links and special formatting options

"Pasting a Link" (part of the "Paste Special" command in the Edit menu) enables you to include data in a document that you may wish to keep updating as your research progresses. For example, imagine you have some data or a graph that you have created in a spreadsheet program, which you want to include in a word-processed draft of your research report. However, you know that some of the data will continue to change as you update your figures. Rather than having to redo the graph each time you update the spreadsheet, you can copy the graph from the spreadsheet and paste a link to it in your report. Then when the data changes and the graph updates in the spreadsheet, so will the graph in your research report.

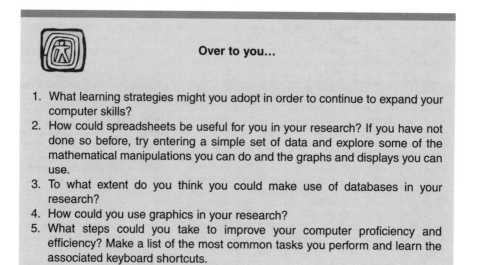

Over to you...

1. What learning strategies might you adopt in order to continue to expand your computer skills?
2. How could spreadsheets be useful for you in your research? If you have not done so before, try entering a simple set of data and explore some of the mathematical manipulations you can do and the graphs and displays you can use.
3. To what extent do you think you could make use of databases in your research?
4. How could you use graphics in your research?
5. What steps could you take to improve your computer proficiency and efficiency? Make a list of the most common tasks you perform and learn the associated keyboard shortcuts.

Note

1 The Semantic Web has been defined as "an extension of the current Web in which information is given well-defined meaning, better enabling computers and people to work in cooperation" (Berners-Lee et al. 2001).

Chapter 3

Managing Yourself, Your Ideas and Your Support Structures

We all know people who seem to have their life well organized. Their houses and offices are neat and tidy; they arrive on time for meetings; they meet their deadlines; they pay their bills on time; they can always lay their hands on the things they need. And we also know those whose lives appear chaotic. They always seem to be running late for appointments; their books and papers are piled up everywhere; they never seem to find what they want without a lot of searching around; they ask for extensions to deadlines. The chances are you lie somewhere between these two extremes and, if you are like us, you probably find yourself wishing at times that you were just a bit better organized. This is an area where your values, attitudes and beliefs about yourself and your research practice are critical. While no one would expect you to change your personality or your personal preferences about how you like to live your life, we are nevertheless confident that devoting a little attention to some basic organizational systems that we describe will pay huge dividends.

In this chapter we look at how being personally well organized and actively managing your relationship with your supervisor and support structures can contribute to the overall effectiveness of your research practice. We offer tips on:

- getting to know yourself and your work preferences;
- managing time, including using software for generating to-do lists;
- using diaries, logbooks and journals;
- using software for generating ideas;
- managing your relationship with your supervisor;
- setting up a peer support structure.

Know thyself

There are benefits for all of us in taking some time out to examine our personal work practices, particularly those that are inhibiting our capacity to do good research. Only you know how you best work, and only you know how organized you want to be and feel. And only you know your own context and motivations with regard to how you organize and manage yourself. Take a moment to consider the following questions:

- What other work and personal commitments do you need to balance with your research project?
- Are you working on just one research project or several at a time?
- How confident do you feel about using computer technology to assist your organization?
- When and how do you work at your best? Is it early in the morning or late into the night? Do you prefer to work in short bursts with frequent breaks or do you need longer stretches of time to concentrate? Does music distract you or focus you?
- How do you deal with interruptions? For instance, do you always answer the phone when it rings and respond to e-mails when they arrive? Do you make yourself available to people by leaving your door open or keep it closed and ask people to make appointments?
- Are you a visual person or more text-focused? Do you think best in images or words? Does it help you to mind map your ideas?
- Do you find that ideas come to you easily when you are in your work environment or do you find that your best thoughts happen when you are in the garden or falling asleep?
- How important is the design and ambience of the environment in which you work?

Having identified your main work habits and preferences, you may like to reflect on which ones you want to change and which you don't (or can't). If you are ready to take the plunge into a more organized life, you might find the following case study inspirational and helpful. This experienced academic researcher has found that putting time and thought into the way she organizes her workspace and work practices has produced considerable efficiencies in her research output (and she says it makes her life happier as well).

 Feature Researcher: Setting up efficient workspaces

Lyn Carson, University of Sydney, Australia

Carson (as she is best known) organizes her daily office routine with an underpinning philosophy of "if you touch it, deal with it." Every e-mail, piece of paper or phone call that she receives, she acts on immediately. Carson advocates the "5 Ds" approach to efficient work practice (which she derived from a personal effectiveness training course). When a piece of information comes her way she will either:

(Continued)

- *Do it now* (if it takes less than a few minutes);
- *Deposit it* (if it only needs to be filed in her paper filing system or e-mail files);
- *Discard it* (for example, if someone else has a copy or it is of no further use);
- *Delegate it* (someone else can deal with it and it can then be trashed); or
- *Develop it* (if it requires further attention she will allocate a time in the diary to do the task).

Carson also actively uses a to-do list and methodical filing processes which we hear more about in Chapter 4.

Managing your time

While understanding a little about your own work practices is the first step towards more effective research, a crucial skill is to learn how to manage your time efficiently.

> In one sense time is a finite, objective measurable commodity. In another sense it is better thought of as subjective. Time working on a PhD can have a very different feel about it depending upon whether a student has chosen a topic of genuine and continuing interest.[1]

While motivation and passion for your research topic will certainly take you a long way, no matter how motivated you are, you will probably feel as though you never have enough time. All of us devise time management strategies of one form or another and, in our experience, a good researcher will be constantly refining and improving these. While there are no fail-safe solutions or magical answers to this perennial problem, we suggest here some strategies that may assist.

Prioritizing your activities

Writing "to-do" lists should be one of your main time management strategies (see below for tips on these). At one level, a constantly updated list of things to do is essential. However, writing a long list of tasks without prioritizing or categorizing can feel overwhelming and may mean you don't get to many of them. One helpful strategy is to create a separate list for the different areas of your research (e.g. writing, literature, data collection and so on) and rate each task as high, medium or low priority. You might use a word processed document which you can print out, say once every week or month and update. There is nothing like the sense of achievement you get as you acknowledge all the things you have crossed off since your last update.

Another way to prioritize your work is to adapt a model suggested by Stephen Covey in his popular book *The Seven Habits of Highly Effective People*.[2] Tasks can be divided according to importance and urgency, revealing a four-quadrant matrix as shown in Figure 3.1.

	Important	Not Important
Urgent	I: Important and urgent	III: Urgent and not important
Not Urgent	II: Important and not urgent	IV: Not urgent and not important

Figure 3.1   Covey's four-quadrant matrix for prioritising tasks

According to Covey, we often spend far too much time in Quadrant III, attending to tasks which appear urgent (to other people) but are not important to us, and not nearly enough time in Quadrant II, where the lack of apparent urgency for important tasks means they don't get priority. Much of the organizational and management strategies we cover in this book fall into the Quadrant II category. These are activities that Covey refers to as "sharpening the saw," strategies that will ultimately save you time, energy and resources. Remember, however, not to completely disregard Quadrant IV as this might be where you decide to be frivolous, for the sake of a break or just to have fun.

As research is multidimensional, tasks you need to initiate or follow up will constantly come to your attention, often at inconvenient times. E-mails in particular can be a major distraction and we address strategies for managing these in Chapter 6.

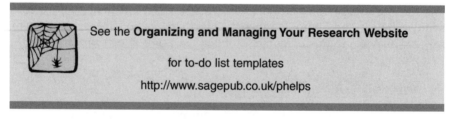

See the **Organizing and Managing Your Research Website**

for to-do list templates

http://www.sagepub.co.uk/phelps

Day-to-day time management

In Chapter 5 we consider ways to manage time over the life of a research project. Here, however, we offer some tips for managing your time on a daily basis:

- **Become aware of your preferred ways of working**. Answering some of the questions we asked in the previous section will help you identify your work preferences.
- **Build on the strategies that work**. Do work that requires concentration at ideal times of the day when you are most focused and are likely to be free from distractions.

- **Work towards self-imposed deadlines.** They should also form part of your day-to-day work routines (see Chapter 5 for tips).
- **Have different tasks running concurrently**. Divide your tasks into those that feel heavier or require lots of concentration (such as writing up theory or thinking about data) and those that are less demanding (such as reading or literature searching). When you feel stale on one task you can continue with the other.
- **Jot down ideas as they pop into your head** and return to them later rather than letting them distract you (see the next section for ways to manage notes, ideas and jottings).
- **Estimate how long something will take and then double it.** Most tasks take longer than you think.
- **Block out slots in your diary** for your research, including whole days, part days or even an hour. Rule lines through those times. Better still, clearly state the specific task you intend to do. If someone asks, you *are* busy that day and not available.
- **Don't fret if you have to reschedule**. Plans are always only a guide and are meant to be revised, not slavishly adhered to.
- **Aim to work in the most conducive environment**. Three hours at university away from the kids may be more productive than 6 hours at home – and that leaves 3 quality hours to spend with the family.
- **Reward yourself** with breaks or (healthy) treats when you have finished a task.
- **Maintain a balance** in your day between research work, social contact, rest and exercise.

To-do lists

You can use a range of techniques for managing your to-do lists and other similar notes. The first decision you face is whether to keep notes primarily in electronic or paper format. In our experience, minimizing the number of to-do lists you maintain is important, although you may have two or three different systems for different purposes.

- **Your diary** is a good place for to-do lists which have to be completed on set days. Use a tick box ❑ to monitor completion. Alternatively, you might consider a PDA, providing both diary and notes functionality (see Chapter 2).
- **A phone call log** is a methodical and permanent record (date and time) of any messages that you receive on your answering machine, as well as a place for notes from discussions you may have. A single note book or diary, left beside the phone, enables you to refer back to a record of calls received, issues discussed and people's contact details. Again, if action is required, use a tick box ❑ to monitor completion. Cross out entries if no action is required.
- **Notes or "sticky notes" utility software** enables you to attach notes to your computer's desktop in the way that you might write yourself notes and leave them on your real desktop. Notes can be set to either "roll up" (for longer term reminders) or display in full (for immediate priorities). Colors allow you to code or prioritize and some programs provide a reminder function, which can be set to sound at regular intervals to (say) remind you to get up and have a break (see also the section on health and safety in Chapter 4). Such software is particularly useful for recording "to-dos" electronically and monitoring short-term reminders. It is useful:

  - when you find yourself copy and pasting to-do information from e-mails, such as tasks that might be e-mailed to you from colleagues;
  - to remind you of websites or articles of interest that have been mentioned in e-mail alerts. This will save you from being sidetracked at the time of reading the message and allow you to file the e-mail immediately, so it doesn't clog up your in-box; or
  - to provide a running record of standard responses you are making to a batch of e-mails.

Want to know more about...

Notes utilities?

Some software which you may already be using will have basic notes or tasks functions incorporated (for example Microsoft Outlook). However, there are also more specifically designed note-taking utilities available online and many are either freeware or shareware. To locate other notes software, search a software download site. Examples include TurboNotes, Two Notes, Magic Notes and Express Notes.

Managing your ideas

As time goes on, it is amazing how you can forget key aspects of your research. Decisions which you thought were etched in your mind, such as why you selected particular participants to interview, or how you arrived at a particular approach to your data analysis, can feel like distant, hazy memories. Being a good researcher means being disciplined in your recording of notes, summaries and insights and having systems in place to organize these. In this section we suggest some strategies and tools that will improve how you manage and organize your ideas, including using journals and mind mapping.

Diaries, logbooks and journals

Maintaining a diary, logbook or journal allows you to record notes and reflections on meetings with your supervisors, conversations with your colleagues, engagement with literature, as well as random thoughts and insights that arise during day-to-day activities. Maintaining a reflective diary can prove extremely useful when it comes to writing up your research process, as in our experience students often forget key stages or events that shaped their research. Such diaries are of most value to your research when they are dated and entered in frequently and systematically.

You will need to decide whether to maintain an electronic or paper diary. The main advantage of a paper diary is its immediacy i.e. the ability to make jottings at any time and in any place. Advantages of keeping an electronic journal are that it is readily searchable (e.g. by date or keyword) and you can use notes either immediately as data or as part of the write-up of your research. While you will no doubt have your own preferred method, you might find the following ideas helpful:

- **Diary and journal software** is specially designed for journaling and diarizing, or can be adapted for that purpose. Features range from quick accessibility (such as with other "notes" programs discussed above); calendar structures (to prompt daily reflections); to database structures that enhance searchability.

- **The hypertext journal** allows you to link your notes and ideas as they arise and as relationships between them emerge. Hyperlinks can also be made to other media, including audio recordings and concept maps (see later in this chapter), allowing a train of thought to be conveniently documented and reaccessed.[3] In this sense a hypertext journal, in contrast to a traditional journal, can be a closer representation of the way you think.

- **Blogs** (derived from the term "Web logs") are a dynamic way of journaling your thoughts and, if you choose, allow you to easily make them public on a website. There are circumstances where this can actually form part of the research itself, such as in some forms of ethnographic and self-research. Blogs are discussed further in Chapter 6.

- **Video journaling.** You may have seen television shows which have been produced based on researchers' video journaling (such shows are common in areas of cultural studies and biology). If you are comfortable talking into a camera, or think your research might have potential as a Hollywood (or Bollywood) blockbuster, this might be for you!

- **A word processed table** can be a good scaffold to guide and formalize your reflections. The example in Table 3.1 is drawn from Kosnik's research[4] and demonstrates using a table for critical incident reflection. As soon as she recognized an event or situation as significant, Kosnik would begin an entry in the table:

Table 3.1   Example of a table to guide diarizing and reflection on research

Date and context of critical incident	**Description** of the event	**Analysis** is guided by two questions: What is my response to the event saying about me? What are the values inherent in my decision and the situation?

Want to know more about...

Journaling and diarizing software?

To locate examples of freeware or shareware journaling and diarizing software search a software download site (see Chapter 2). Start by searching for Alpha Journal, My Personal Diary, Tdiary or Advanced Diary.

Mapping your ideas

In the course of any research project, but especially in the early stages and during data analysis, you will generate ideas and thoughts in a way that is often difficult to capture in a linear fashion. A mind map is a "picture" that traditionally combines the use of words, images, numbers, color and spatial relationships in order to promote, facilitate and represent thinking. A mind map helps you explore and organize your thoughts and make connections between them. Terms used for similar processes include concept mapping, visual mapping, decision mapping and knowledge mapping. A mind map usually starts in the middle of the page with a series of "nodes" branching out from the center, representing concepts and relationships between concepts, as illustrated in Figure 3.2.

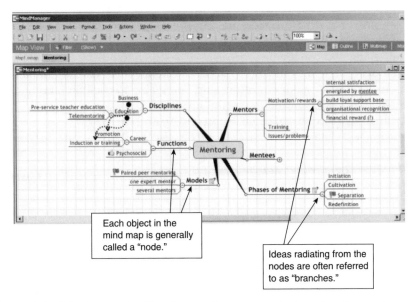

Figure 3.2   Mind map of a literature review on mentoring showing nodes and branches

Example created using MindManager.

Of course, you can mind map by hand on a large sheet of paper, using a variety of colored pens. Some people put ideas on sticky-notes stuck on their office wall so that they can easily move concepts around. You might remember that Brad's story in the Preface to this book illustrates this technique. You can also use the simple drawing tools provided within word processing, presentation and graphic applications (see Chapter 2). However, there is also a whole family of software specially designed to facilitate mind mapping and similar visualization processes. These programs provide flexibility and enhanced functionality, allowing you to focus on the thinking rather than spending time and effort getting the drawing right. Moreover, they can produce much more professional-looking graphics, enabling you to use these diagrams for presentation or publication.

How can mapping your ideas be useful in research?
You could use mind mapping strategies for:

- brainstorming and generating ideas and organizing those ideas;
- developing a structure for data analysis or writing;
- charting links between theoretical concepts;
- remembering information through word association;
- exploring a metaphor you intend to use in your research;
- recording, prioritizing and ordering tasks and subtasks (see Chapter 5 for more on project management);
- providing an overview of a large quantity of information (such as a literature review);
- planning or tracing decision-making processes (for instance in developing your methodology);
- presenting and conveying ideas in your research to others, either at a conference or seminar, or in your thesis or research report (see also Chapter 13);
- indexing files on your computer and being able to click on a node to go directly to a relevant file (hyperlinking);
- facilitating group discussions or processes; and/or
- using it as a data collection technique (as discussed further in Chapter 10).

Mind mapping and visualization software
Keep these points in mind when selecting mind mapping or visualization software:

- the diversity of diagrammatic formats (see Figure 3.3);
- the ability to enter ideas in outline mode (dot point or similar format) such that the software generates the visual diagram for you;
- whether you can drag and drop nodes to move them around;
- the ability to attach icons or graphics to particular nodes, for instance to flag tasks in progress, or differentiate between types of ideas;
- the number of "undo" operations available;
- the capacity to edit images once created;
- the ability to attach more detailed notes to particular parts of the diagram;
- the use of shortcut keys to perform commonly conducted actions;
- whether you can condense (collapse) and expand your diagrams (e.g. hide away particular branches);
- the availability of a search facility and spell checking;
- the ability to create hyperlinks to other files or external websites;
- the ability to export to other programs or save in recognized file formats (such as .gif, .jpg or .pdf). Some programs allow diagrams to be exported as a webpage and/or as a clickable image map, meaning that hyperlinks are maintained as part of the webpage. Other programs will export to a word processor, creating an outline structure which can become the basis for your document;
- Also see our general tips on selecting software in Chapter 2.

Examples of mind mapping and visualization software are listed in the software table at the end of this chapter.

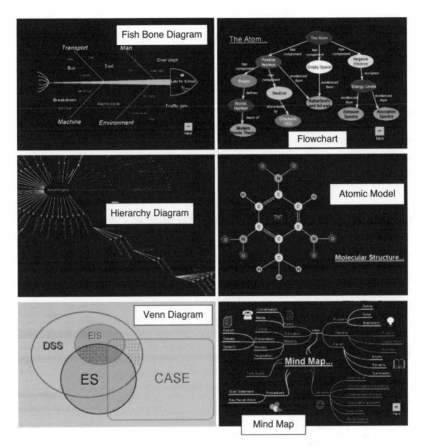

Figure 3.3   Diversity of graphical formats produced by visualization software

Examples are drawn from Axon Idea Processor.

Managing your supervisor

Doing research, particularly as a student, requires you to manage not only yourself and your ideas, but also your collegial and professional relationships. Over the period of your candidature, one of the most important relationships is the one you have with your supervisor. Getting off on the right foot by being proactive and clear about what this relationship entails could well make all the difference to the progress of your research. The most common issues that students report experiencing with supervision are:

- supervisors being unavailable or inaccessible;
- not getting appropriate guidance, especially in the early stages;
- not getting enough feedback on writing;
- having different approaches to work (e.g. structured/unstructured);
- communication barriers.

The first four issues (and to a certain extent the fifth as well) often result from a mismatch of expectations between student and supervisor about what supervision should entail. Clarifying these expectations, and negotiating differences where they arise, may go a long way towards avoiding some of these problems.

Negotiating expectations

One strategy for negotiating possible differences in expectations is for you and your supervisor to independently fill in a questionnaire, such as those provided in Tables 3.2 and 3.3 below.[5]

Table 3.2 Student questionnaire for negotiating expectations with supervisors.

Student questionnaire					
I would prefer my supervisor to:	**Priority (1=low; 5=high)**				
Be well informed about grants & scholarships I can apply for	1	2	3	4	5
Help me with selecting my topic	1	2	3	4	5
Inform me about where I can go for help with resources and expertise	1	2	3	4	5
Keep me informed about what the department/school expects of me in terms of my performance and progress	1	2	3	4	5
Monitor and provide feedback on my work to ensure adequate progress	1	2	3	4	5
Treat me fairly and equitably in terms of time and effort put into supervising their students	1	2	3	4	5
Give me new ideas for research	1	2	3	4	5
Help me to identify my key goals	1	2	3	4	5
Provide a lot of detailed supervision	1	2	3	4	5
Maintain regular contact/meetings on a pre-arranged schedule	1	2	3	4	5
Keep records of all meetings and indicate action taken or advice given	1	2	3	4	5
Require written work on a pre-arranged schedule	1	2	3	4	5
Be available and easy to approach on any problem	1	2	3	4	5
Give me strong encouragement in my research	1	2	3	4	5
Answer my specific questions	1	2	3	4	5
Have general expertise in supervising research	1	2	3	4	5
Be an expert in my area of research	1	2	3	4	5
Share their knowledge with me	1	2	3	4	5
Support me with technical issues and problems	1	2	3	4	5
Be interested in my research project	1	2	3	4	5
Listen to and respect my existing knowledge and skills	1	2	3	4	5
Introduce me to scholarly networks	1	2	3	4	5
Encourage me to explore issues for myself	1	2	3	4	5
Make available regular discussion groups for both myself and other students	1	2	3	4	5
Suggest ways I can make the most effective use of my time	1	2	3	4	5
Give me support and guidance in preparation of my written thesis	1	2	3	4	5
Comment on the content and drafts of my thesis	1	2	3	4	5
Offer detailed editing of my final thesis draft	1	2	3	4	5
Help me to develop my academic writing skills	1	2	3	4	5
Assist me to publish my research	1	2	3	4	5
Help me with my personal and employment issues	1	2	3	4	5

Table 3.3 Supervisor questionnaire for negotiating expectations with students.

Supervisor questionnaire					
My current supervision style and practice is to:	**Priority** **(1=low; 5=high)**				
Be well informed about grants & scholarships my students can apply for	1	2	3	4	5
Help my students with topic selection	1	2	3	4	5
Inform students about where they can go for help with resources and expertise	1	2	3	4	5
Inform students about department/school expectations of student performance and progress	1	2	3	4	5
Monitor and provide feedback on student work to ensure adequate progress	1	2	3	4	5
Treat all students fairly and equitably in terms of time and effort put into supervising students	1	2	3	4	5
Give students new ideas for their research	1	2	3	4	5
Help students to identify their key goals	1	2	3	4	5
Provide a lot of detailed supervision	1	2	3	4	5
Maintain regular contact/meetings on a pre-arranged schedule	1	2	3	4	5
Keep records of all meetings and indicate action taken or advice given	1	2	3	4	5
Require written work on a pre-arranged schedule	1	2	3	4	5
Be available and easy to approach on any problem	1	2	3	4	5
Give students strong encouragement in their research	1	2	3	4	5
Answer students' specific questions	1	2	3	4	5
Have general expertise in supervising research	1	2	3	4	5
Be an expert in the student's area of research	1	2	3	4	5
Share my knowledge with the student	1	2	3	4	5
Support students with technical issues and problems	1	2	3	4	5
Be interested in the student's research project	1	2	3	4	5
Listen to and respect the student's existing knowledge and skills	1	2	3	4	5
Introduce the student to scholarly networks	1	2	3	4	5
Encourage the student to explore issues for themselves	1	2	3	4	5
Make available regular discussion groups combining my students and other's students	1	2	3	4	5
Suggest ways the student can make the most effective use of time	1	2	3	4	5
Give the student support and guidance in preparation of their written thesis	1	2	3	4	5
Comment on the content and drafts of the thesis	1	2	3	4	5
Offer detailed editing of the final thesis draft	1	2	3	4	5
Help the student to develop academic writing skills	1	2	3	4	5
Assist the student to publish their research	1	2	3	4	5
Help the student with personal and employment issues	1	2	3	4	5

Once each of you have completed the questionnaire, go through and identify where there are differences in expectations. These then form your agenda for negotiation, which may need to occur over an extended period of time. The next section provides advice on how you can manage your relationship most effectively.

Managing your relationship with your supervisor

This is not always an easy task, particularly given the power and status differences and you may discover that you have very different personalities and communication styles. The following strategies are things that *you* can do over time to contribute to the quality of the relationship.

- **Negotiate agreements.** Have a clear understanding of what is expected of you and what you can expect from your supervisor. Use the questionnaires in Tables 3.2 and 3.3 as a starting point. Some institutions have formal supervisor/student contracts. If yours doesn't, consider drafting your own agreement as part of your negotiations.
- **Meet and communicate regularly.** In any negotiations, ensure you agree on how often to be in contact, even if this just means a quick "check-in" on how you are going. Contact can be face-to-face, by e-mail or by phone.
- **Take the initiative and be proactive.** It is usually a mistake to assume that your supervisor will contact you. Most supervisors are very busy people who are more likely to respond to communications than initiate them.
- **Respect your supervisor's time.** Be careful not to overtax their patience. In your initial negotiations, find out what is reasonable to expect in terms of response times.
- **Prepare an agenda for meetings** and forward it to your supervisor ahead of time so that you have a shared understanding of the meeting's purpose.
- **Keep your appointments and stick to your agreements.** This is a relationship that will flourish in an environment built on reciprocity and respect, so be reliable and conscientious.
- **Be clear about what you want from your supervision meetings.** The more prepared you are, the more productive your sessions are likely to be. If you let your supervisor know in advance what you want to discuss, they can be similarly prepared and offer you the best support.
- **Don't be afraid to ask questions.** You are in training to be a researcher and asking questions is the best way to learn. However, if you *can* find out answers from people other than your supervisor (e.g. on resource or IT matters), it will free up your supervision time for important content and methodological issues.
- **Be willing to question, but avoid arguing.** If you disagree with what your supervisor is suggesting, seek clarification and put your case as clearly as you can, but don't argue. Seek other opinions and discuss with your peers (see peer support groups below).
- **Record your conversations.** Consider taking an audio recorder to your supervision sessions. It frees up time from note-taking, allows you to revisit and reflect on important points and serves as a reminder of what you and your supervisor have agreed to.

- **Read your supervisor's thesis and publications.** Coming to know and appreciate your supervisor's work, how they write, the questions they are tackling in their own research and their preferred methods, will not only be helpful in informing your early and ongoing negotiations, but will also help to build mutual respect.
- **Work to your supervisor's strengths.** Like most human beings, your supervisor will be stronger in some aspects of supervision than others. As in any partnership, it is unrealistic to expect him or her to meet all your needs and expectations. Make the most of their strengths and seek help elsewhere in their areas of weakness.
- **Seek support and advice when difficulties arise.** It is unlikely to be a completely smooth ride, even if you follow all our tips. Be alert to difficulties and act early. Find out where you can get confidential and impartial support and make use of skilled mediators if communication with your supervisor breaks down. If all else fails, remember that divorce is not only possible, but may be best for all concerned.
- **Form a support group.** Read on…

Setting up a peer support structure

As well as being one of the biggest projects you are likely to undertake in your life, doing a research degree can also be one of the loneliest. If you are doing your research in the humanities and social sciences, where collaborative research is less common than in the experimental sciences, your main sources of support will probably come from your supervisor and your family, and it can be unwise to burden these relationships inappropriately. The issue of feeling isolated will be even more acute if you are studying at a distance from your university. In our experience, establishing peer support groups early in candidature can significantly ameliorate the isolating effects of postgraduate research.

A peer support group is a small group of three to five candidates who meet regularly (face-to-face or online) to discuss the content and process of their research projects, preferably for the duration of candidature. Ideally, your group should have a strong process that allows each person to have equal time to focus on and discuss his or her project. While such a group is definitely *not* a substitute for supervision, it can significantly enhance the relationship with your supervisor.[6]

Why form a peer support group?

- **To counteract isolation.** While the ultimate responsibility for your research rests with you (and your supervisor), the fact that others know what you are doing, are interested in your topic and are willing to put time into thinking through your challenges can keep you going even when it might seem that it is all too much.

- **To share ideas with other research students.** Being part of a group of people engaged in a similar level of intellectual endeavor allows ideas to be tested and thrown around without fear of judgment or ridicule.
- **To offer ongoing accountability.** One of the biggest challenges in doing postgraduate research is how to maintain momentum and self-manage your time in an environment often lacking a clear accountability framework. The act of setting goals that your peers witness and follow up can remedy any sense that deadlines can elapse without consequence.
- **To assist with publication during candidature.** A support group can be an excellent vehicle for trying out ideas about the papers you want to write and getting feedback on your writing.
- **To enhance and "add value" to supervision.** A support group can offer a place where you can voice concerns, doubts, frustrations and speculations that may not be appropriate to take into a supervision session. If your supervisor knows you are involved in such a group, they may suggest ways that you can use support group time in order to maximize the productivity of supervision meetings.
- **To maintain passion and interest in your research.** Having peers who are vitally interested in your inquiry can help you gain a fresh perspective at times when you may feel uninspired and weighed down by the enormity of the task before you. You also have the opportunity to be part of others' research processes, to be excited by what they are discovering and the terrain they are traversing, to contribute positively to their progress and to be delighted by their achievements.
- **To develop skills in networking.** A support group can provide a non-threatening "training ground" for developing collegial and networking skills. You have an opportunity to try out your conference presentations, get critical and supportive feedback on your work, learn how to ask the key questions that help others to reflect more deeply on their inquiry and develop skills such as active listening and giving constructive feedback, so essential for good collegial relationships.

Setting up an effective process

Whether you are planning a face-to-face or electronic group process, getting the right mix of people is crucial to ensure your group maintains momentum. It is less important to form a group with researchers from the same discipline area than it is to meet with people who share an interest in offering and receiving support and feedback and, to a certain extent, share similar values. The following guidelines have proven (in our experience) to be effective for support groups that want to use their time for concentrated, focused work.

If you are meeting in person choose venues where there are no distractions such as offices, meeting rooms or private houses. Avoid cafes and other public places. If face-to-face meetings aren't feasible, consider using one of the voice-based synchronous communication systems described in Chapter 6. Select times when participants don't have other distractions such as childcare or cooking dinner. As a rough guide, allow at least half an hour per person (i.e. a 4-person group would need a 2-hour initial meeting). Meet regularly, preferably every 2–3 weeks. Make sure that someone takes charge of the group process each meeting. This facilitation role means ensuring that: everyone knows when the meeting is on and where; the meeting starts on time; the group stays on track and keeps to time; and that everyone sets goals at the end of the session.

Try the following process structure for your meetings:

- Start with a 2–5-minute "check-in" per person that allows everyone to say how they are traveling, particularly in relation to their goals.
- Have an agreed-on process that allows each person to have equal time as a "focus person" either at each meeting (e.g. 30 minutes per person) or across meetings (i.e. taking turns to be the focus person at each session).
- Make sure that each focus person has the full attention of the rest of the group. The facilitator should remind others to maintain focus if they are tempted to talk about their own research or other unrelated issues.
- Structure in time for reflection on the process. Look at what is working well and what might need to change.
- Finally, make sure the sessions are recorded or documented, particularly in terms of problems expressed, suggestions made, goals set and achievements and progress gained. Online sessions can often be recorded.

Guidelines for group members

Being an effective member of a support group not only means being prepared for the session and working towards your own goals, it also means being able to offer the sort of support that will really make a difference – the sort of support that you would want to receive yourself. While this will vary with each person and change depending on their needs at any particular time, a number of general guidelines may be helpful to keep in mind:

- **Offer encouragement and affirmation** whenever possible. Validation for what they are doing well is often all someone requires to keep them motivated and on track with their tasks.
- **Learn to give constructive feedback** when asked for. Start with what you think is positive about their work and then *speculate* on how it could be improved.

- **Avoid giving advice**, unless it is specifically asked for.
- **Focus more on listening** carefully than being too quick to speak.
- **Ask open rather than closed questions** (how and what rather than why or why not).
- **Ask questions that help the person identify obstacles** (e.g. what is stopping you from achieving your goal?).

While the processes that make a successful group are relatively simple and straightforward, they are not always easy to sustain. Challenges that can impair success include:

- the time commitment may feel onerous;
- lack of commitment by just one member has a demoralizing effect;
- meetings that become conversational and chatty feel unproductive and wasteful;
- a group getting too "cosy," where encouragement and validation are not balanced with critical feedback and strategic questioning;
- group members developing dependence on the group for support.

Support groups should always be seen as an adjunct to, and not a substitution for, supervision. Keep your supervisors informed about what you are doing in your support group (assuming they are interested) and get the most appropriate type of support from both sources as you need it.

While the discussion in this section has focused on the experience of postgraduate students, many of the principles apply in any collaborative research environment and will be useful to you throughout your research career, as a team member or as a graduate student supervisor.

 Over to you...

1. What are the main "organizational weaknesses" that you need to overcome to become more personally efficient?
2. What are your main issues with time management?
3. What is one strategy you could adopt that could make an immediate difference in how you use your time?
4. What is your preferred format for keeping your notes?
5. To what extent would mind mapping software be useful to you in your research?
6. What are your supervisor's main strengths? How can you make the most of them?
7. What could you do to improve communication with your supervisor?
8. What would be the main benefits for you in being part of a support group?

Examples of brainstorming and visualization software.

Software	Manufacturer/ developer	Platform	Website	Licensing	Demo on website?	Special features
Axon Idea Processor	Axon Research	Windows	http://web.singnet.com.sg/~axon2000	Commercial	✓	Sophisticated program for generating and organizing ideas, concept mapping and simulation modeling. Includes basic simulation module and lots of templates
ConceptDraw MINDMAP	Buzan Centres	Windows, Mac	http://www.conceptdraw.com/en	Commercial	✓	Easy to use program. Provides a "wizard" to step through creating mind maps, concept maps, thinking maps, decision trees etc. Able to brainstorm in outline view
Decision Explorer	Banxia Software	Windows	http://www.banxia.com	Commercial	✓	Supports cognitive, causal and concept mapping. Contains a of range analytical and investigatory. tools Support for XML export. Free "viewer" available
Free Mind	VA Software	Windows, Mac and Linux	http://freemind.sourceforge.net	Freeware	✓	Uses a node structure and makes use of icons as visual markers. Allows hyperlinking to local files or websites. View the file structure on your computer as a mind map
Inspiration	Inspiration Software	Windows, Mac	http://www.inspiration.com	Commercial	✓	Designed primarily for use in class rooms (K6-adult). Version available for Palm OS and Pocket PC
Mind Genius	Buzan Organisation	Windows	http://www.mindgenius.com	Commercial	✓	Creates map diagrams, trees and other layouts such as affinity diagrams. Business, education and home versions. Can export to Microsoft formats and HTML

(Continued)

Software	Manufacturer/ developer	Platform	Website	Licensing	Demo on website?	Special features
Mind Manager	Mindjet. I and A Research	Windows	http://www.mindjet.com	Commercial	✓	Brainstorming and visual thinking. Contains a Gantt chart module. Maps can be exported in outline format or as HTML. Version available for Tablet PC
Mind Mapper	The Bosley Group	Windows	http://www.mindmapper.com	Commercial	✓	Brainstorming and visual thinking software available in different versions. Also contains a Gantt chart module
Map It!	Brain Power	Windows	http://www.mapitsoftware.com	Commercial	✓	Easy to use program. A mini-map viewer allows you to see the whole image while working on a zoomed in section of the whole. Has a brainstorming mode
Nova Mind	NovaMind	Windows, Mac	http://www.nova-mind.com	Commercial	✓	Operates in free layout, assisted and controlled mode. Creates free-flowing lines of text. Suggests words/phrases which relate conceptually or linguistically to the selected branch of a mind map
Smart Draw	SmartDraw.com	Windows	http://www.smartdraw.com	Commercial	✓	Produces mind, concept and knowledge maps, decision trees, Gantt charts, process documentation and more. Templates and wizards guide the design process

Notes

1 May 1997.
2 Covey 1989.
3 For a discussion on the use of hypertext journals, see Brown 2002.
4 Kosnik 2001.
5 Adapted from SPORS (Student Perceptions of Research Supervision) developed by the Centre of Staff Development at the University of Western Australia 2001, accessed from the fIRST website (http://www.first.edu.au).
6 For a more detailed description of the process of setting up a support group, see Fisher 2006.

Chapter 4

Organizing Your Work Environment

The space in which you do your research can impact significantly on the efficiency and effectiveness of your research time. Yet at some stage all researchers find themselves overwhelmed by "infoclutter."[1] Surprisingly, taking time to organize both your physical and virtual work environments can have a remarkably pleasing and reassuring effect. An uncluttered work space, where everything is stored systematically, provides minimal distraction and enables you to locate your relevant paper *and* your digital resources quickly and easily. Not only that, a functional work space will enhance your physical comfort and safety.

In this chapter we:

- provide tips on organizing your physical work environment, including the layout of your office and ergonomic considerations;
- suggest ways to manage shared physical and virtual work environments;
- discuss the value of establishing a universal schema for all your filing;
- explore issues to consider when making choices between print and electronic storage;
- offer strategies for storing and filing paper resources;
- provide tips on managing electronic files, including risk management.

Organizing your physical environment

What does your work space look like? Do you have a designated research area or do you have to share a space with other researchers or make do with the kitchen table? Does your physical workspace help you focus on your work or distract you from your priorities? Is it physically comfortable? Do you move between various office environments such as home and work? How easy is it for you to find the document you are after at any time? Are you a "hoarder" or a "spring cleaner?" In this section we provide guidance on organizing your physical environment to ensure you are comfortable, efficient and safe while working on your research.

Organizing your desk

The best way to manage your desk space is to aim to have as little as possible permanently or even temporarily stored on its surface. You will be guaranteed to cover the desk soon enough with your day's work and resources related to upcoming priorities. Here are some suggestions for uncluttering your desk:

- **Move paperwork as quickly as possible to your current working file** (see section on filing below). Only leave out current priority work.
- **Use a single rack of files on your desk** if you prefer some paperwork within eyesight.
- **Use a shelf above your desk** to keep frequently used resources within easy reach but off your main working surface.
- **Put pamphlet boxes on the shelf above your desk** for note-books, phone directories etc.
- **Keep all small items such as paper clips, staplers, hole punchers and note pads in drawers**, and use sorter trays or small boxes to keep them organized.
- **Get a riser stand for your laptop** which will lift it off the horizontal surface. Combined with an external keyboard and mouse this may prove invaluable ergonomically and as protection from external hazards (e.g. spilt coffee). Investigate a cordless keyboard and mouse to provide added flexibility.

Taking care of your health and safety

The place where you do the majority of your research work needs to be one which will not impact adversely on your health. Unfortunately, prolonged computer use is implicated in a number of health problems, including musculoskeletal problems (particularly of the shoulders and upper back), stiffness, headache, backache and eyestrain. Repetitive Stress (or Strain) Injury (RSI) results from doing something over and over in ways that impose stress or strain. For instance, typing is a highly repetitive act; an average speed of 60 words per minute means you will be striking the key board 20,000 times per hour.

There are two sources of stress imposed on you when you are typing at a computer: environmental (external) stress and behavioral (internal) stress.[2]

- **Environmental stress** comes from the world around you. It can include badly designed furniture, inadequate lighting, excessive work schedules; poor organization of your workstation and so on. This is what the science of ergonomics deals with and we give some ergonomic tips below.
- **Behavioral stress** is what you impose on yourself by the way you work and the way you organize your body as you work. This could include the strain you put on yourself by holding yourself rigid or by typing with your wrist bent and too much tension in your arms. Changing the height of your chair or the type of keyboard you use will not necessarily mean that you are putting less strain on yourself as you type.

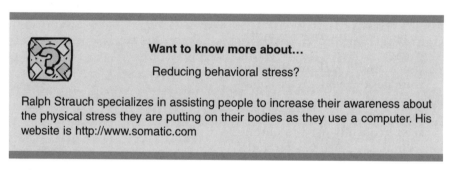

Want to know more about...

Reducing behavioral stress?

Ralph Strauch specializes in assisting people to increase their awareness about the physical stress they are putting on their bodies as they use a computer. His website is http://www.somatic.com

Unfortunately, it is much easier to change environmental factors than it is to change habits that have built up over the years, which is why there is such a focus on ergonomic factors in "treating" RSI, rather than addressing longer term self-awareness. It is beyond the scope of our discussion to suggest ways in which you can change these habits, but if you are experiencing chronic pain in your neck, back, shoulders, arms or wrists, despite having the "correct" furniture and workstation design, we strongly recommend focusing some attention on how you use your body while working.

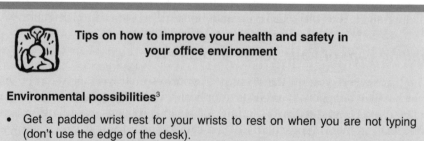

Tips on how to improve your health and safety in your office environment

Environmental possibilities[3]

- Get a padded wrist rest for your wrists to rest on when you are not typing (don't use the edge of the desk).
- Keep your keyboard at a height where your elbows can bend at right angles and your wrists can remain level.
- Position your monitor to reduce glare (i.e. not in front of or next to a window or directly under a light).

(*Continued*)

- Use a stable, adjustable chair or a straight-backed chair at the correct height for your comfort (your legs should touch the floor and form a 90° angle). You can also try kneeling chairs or gym balls.
- Try an adjustable desk that allows you to adjust the keyboard and monitor height or you could retrofit a slide-out shelf for your keyboard.
- Adjust your monitor height so you can look straight ahead or slightly downwards.
- Try an ergonomic keyboard.
- Try out a "joystick" mouse which allows you to move your arm in a way that puts less pressure on your wrist.
- Position a document holder at the same height as your monitor when reading documents while typing.
- Consider lighting levels to prevent eye-strain but also minimize glare.
- Ensure that leads and cords are not trip-hazards. Strong tape can secure cords on a temporary basis.
- Ensure rooms, particularly photocopying and printing rooms, are well ventilated.

Behavioral possibilities

- When you type, let your wrists float above the wrist rest and keep them level.
- To prevent eyestrain, look away from your monitor frequently, preferably out to the horizon (see below and Chapter 12 for reading on screen).
- Take frequent breaks, move around and intersperse your writing session with other activities.
- Do frequent stretching exercises during long writing sessions (see below for software that can help you do this).
- Try voice-recognition software to reduce keyboard use (see Chapter 2).

Want to know more about....

Ergonomic software?

Programs have been developed to assist you in taking breaks and giving you exercises to do while at your computer. Some count the number of times you touch the keyboard, the distance your mouse moves and how often you press the mouse button. You can indicate how often you want to be reminded to take a break. Some actually "freeze" what you are doing when the time is up. You'll be surprised at how quickly 20 minutes passes!

Ergo Break   http://www.ergohealth.com
Work Pace   http://www.workpace.com

Managing multiple offices

If you work in both your university and/or organizational environment and from your home then you will need to make decisions about where your resources are stored and how you move them between locations. You may also need to organize a "mobile office" that you can take into the field. Having some sound strategies in place will save you much stress and angst and ensure that the resources you need will be at hand without lugging around a filing cabinet on a trolley! The following tips might prove useful if you are the type of researcher (like us) who likes to take your work out beside the pool, to the beach or just to bed.

- **Use your mobility as part of your goal-setting process.** Rather than carrying resources for five or six different tasks with you at once, be more decisive. Commit yourself to completing one or two tasks only in any one place.
- **Use a plastic sleeve folder or cardboard envelope** to collate material that you know you need to keep close at hand in all your work contexts. These might relate to your current priority tasks (perhaps not just related to your research) or your short-term goals. This works well for daily travel between home and work. Include one to two articles in this folder just in case the opportunity arises to do a little reading while waiting for the kids' bus or a doctor's appointment. Perhaps include your to-do list in the first sleeve and go through the folder every 4–5 days to keep work circulating and not stagnant.
- **Leave your laptop behind (sometimes).** Not only is this good for your sanity but having your whole computer with you doesn't help you focus on a defined goal, such as to read two papers a night.
- **Give yourself variety.** While it is important to have a stable work environment that is well organized and functions well for serious work, take advantage of the flexibility that a laptop and paper-based reading allows. On a sunny day work under a tree.

Ensuring physical security

Depending on the type of research you are doing, you will need to secure your physical equipment, samples and data, both at the building in which they are housed and in your own office. Your university will probably provide building security via master keys or swipe card access and/or the building itself will be patrolled by security staff. Within your office (at home and work) you might need to lock up your hardcopy data and backup media. Don't overlook such things as locking windows and using smoke alarms. If you have a laptop, use a security chain. Popping out of your office for 1–2 minutes to run to the photocopier may be all it takes to lose your precious research tool. We discuss security of digital data later in this chapter.

Working in a shared workspace

One issue that researchers frequently face is having to share a workspace, such as an office and/or laboratory. This has both upsides and downsides, as the following comments from our research with students reveal[4]:

> While it can sometimes be distracting and drain time (via coffees etc), this loss is negligible in relation to the gain incurred by having a support network surrounding you through the day-to-day slog.

> I am very privileged to have my own office ... However, it also detracts in the sense that it can get very lonely and I forget to socialise with others... I wish that I had someone to work with, that I could talk to about the good and bad things about PhD research and teaching at university.

Shared workspaces can be both physical and virtual. For instance, you may be sharing computer equipment, backup or storage space with someone you may never meet in person. Here are some general tips for maintaining harmonious shared workspaces.

 Tips on managing shared workspaces

- Have a diary or logbook where you can note down when individuals expect to be at the office to identify opportunities for solitude. It can also assist in taking messages.
- If you are sharing a computer, use different user profiles to ensure you can't/don't access or (worse still) delete each others' files.
- If you are working on a common project and share a common file storage area (virtual or physical), explicitly discuss guidelines for filing. Preferably, develop a shared filing schema (see below).
- Have a loans book where you record any items (readings, books, equipment) passed on to anyone else. Date the loans and use it as an opportunity to discuss and record an expected return date.
- If you are sharing digital cameras or recorders, take care to delete your files after copying them to your computer, so the memory card is empty for the next user.

 Feature Researcher: Catching up with Carson

University of Sydney, Australia

In Chapter 3 we met Carson, and her "5 Ds" approach to managing herself and her time. Carson also provides some excellent tips on organizing a physical

(Continued)

(Continued)

research environment. What strikes a visitor to Carson's office is its sense of spaciousness, beauty and order. There are no piles of paper lying around, there are clear surfaces, lovely wall pictures, comfortable and welcoming seating, and shelves files are clearly labeled. Visitors receive a relaxed and friendly welcome from someone well in control of her working environment. And not surprisingly, Carson is a very efficient researcher.

To work to the principle "if you touch it, you deal with it" Carson has organized her workspace accordingly. Under her desk she has a filing drawer for things she needs to use or refer to everyday:

- an "in" file, which only has today's work in it;
- a "pending" file, which has work that needs to be done within 48 hours;
- an "out" file, which has material to be filed or to go to someone else;
- a "reading" file, which contains material to be read within the next week.

She also keeps her frequently used files close at hand, which for her are current research projects, current writing projects, current teaching schedules and current accounts (research budgets etc.). At the front of these files is her "to-do" list, which has two columns, headed "urgent and important" and "not urgent and important" (based on Covey's principles discussed in Chapter 2). Carson reviews this list at the end of each week and updates it for the following week.

Another aspect of Carson's filing system is a hanging rack that sits on her desk with files numbered from 1 to 31. Each of these files represents a date for the current and following month and in that file goes material she will need for anything that happens on that date (such as meeting agendas, reading for meetings etc.). As each date passes, the file represents a date in the following month (e.g. once April 10th passes, that file becomes May 10th and so on), and the used material is filed or discarded.

The other feature of Carson's information storage is that both her electronic and paper files use the same filing structure, so that if she wants to find a particular paper copy of an article recorded in her EndNote library for instance, it will be filed according to the same system, making the paper copy easy to find.

This last tip from Carson is the particular focus of the following section.

Constructing a universal filing schema

As your research progresses, you will be astounded at how rapidly the quantity of both your paper and electronic resources expands. The time it takes to sort out a massive pile of print or electronic files is likely to be much greater than small ongoing investments of time to maintain order. Even worse, searching for a lost file can cost a frustratingly large amount of your precious research time.

At the very least, you will need to store, file or organize the following types of resources throughout your research:

- hardcopies of printed or photocopied documents;
- books and other bound documents;
- electronic documents/files;
- e-mails;
- Internet bookmarks (favorites).

Developing one consistent, overarching filing schema means you can use it to file all these resources.

To begin, take time to reflect on your personal context and list the categories that your various commitments fall into. Don't limit yourself just to your work or research activities; include all areas of your life. Developing a logical and reasonably comprehensive schema and applying it fairly consistently across all your filing domains can streamline your work practices considerably. For instance, as a postgraduate research student you might do some undergraduate tutoring and perhaps be involved in one or two other small projects as a research or administrative assistant. You also have a life outside your research that might involve family commitments, hobbies and other interests. Your schema might look something like the one illustrated in Figure 4.1.

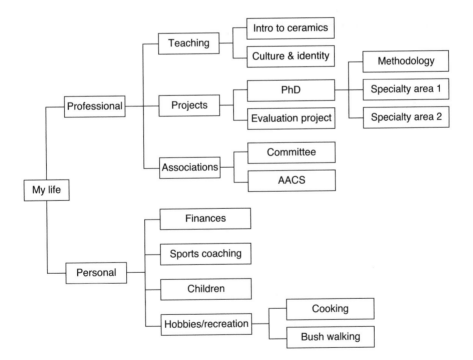

Figure 4.1   Example of an organizational schema for a research student

Note that all broad areas in which resources are received or collected are represented.

Having identified the areas of your life that generate resources you can then set up your storage systems to reflect these categories and try to be consistent in using it for all your filing. There will be some categories that aren't relevant to some of your filing domains. For example, you may not have books in your office related to your personal interests but you will no doubt have e-mails and bookmarks to file which *are* related to your children or hobbies. Applying your general framework as comprehensively as possible will make all the difference to your overall efficiency.

In Chapter 9 we focus specifically on how your filing schema can be effectively used to organize your literature.

Electronic or hard copy?

Organizing your physical work space is only half the story. Organizing the electronic information and resources that come your way is even more critical. Before we examine strategies for managing your electronic work environment, we explore some of the issues you need to consider when deciding whether to store resources electronically or in hard copy format as well as some tips for reducing your paper use.

Practical, technical and ethical considerations

It has been sardonically suggested by the occasional wag that PhD stands for Photocopying Degree. As you become more technologically savvy, you will be looking for ways to reduce the need for all that photocopying and what to do with the resulting mountains of paper. While you will inevitably be led by your personal work preferences, it is important to think critically about your habitual practices (such as automatically printing e-mails) and weigh up the relative advantages and disadvantages of each format.

- **Hardcopies can be read virtually anywhere, any time.** This allows you to continue your work while waiting for a bus, sitting at the beach or reclining in bed.
- **Highlighting, annotating and making notes on hardcopy** may be more familiar and comfortable in a text environment. However these can be done electronically as well (see Chapter 12).
- **It is easy to copy and paste summaries or quotes from electronic sources**, but scanning segments of hardcopy text to digital format is also possible (see below).
- **Searching for key words or phrases** is automated and instantaneous with electronic files.
- **Breaks away from the computer screen are important** both physically and psychologically. Reading on screen can be more tiring. At the same time, working in bed may not be that ideal either.

- **Carting around large wads of paper can be inconvenient**, especially if you work in a mobile environment (see above), but lugging around a laptop can be equally tedious.
- **Both paper and electronic resources need to be filed and stored,** but electronic storage, of course, takes up virtually no physical space.
- **Large quantities of printing and photocopying** raise ethical concerns about excessive paper consumption. Use recycled paper wherever possible and employ some of the paper-saving strategies we suggest below.

Reducing paper use

A common reason people give for printing papers and e-mails is that they find it difficult to read large volumes of text on screen (see also Chapter 12 on this issue). Some strategies for overcoming the disadvantages of screen reading and making the most of electronic formats include:

- **using the biggest and best quality monitor you can**, or even using two monitors to maximize screen area;
- **zooming-in on text** to overcome issues of font size, for instance, enlarge your document to 130% (or more) or display it at screen or text width;
- **cutting and pasting content** (for instance, from a PDF document as described in Chapter 2) into a word processor to allow greater customization and interaction as you read and the ability to summarize by cutting extraneous text as you go;
- **highlighting and annotating on screen** using your word processor (see Chapter 12);
- **using e-book formatting options** to enhance text presentation, including fitting text to the available screen size, eliminating the need for scrolling;
- **saving and reading a document off-line** to minimize connection costs, which also means you have an archived copy (although note copyright issues).

Of course not all references are available in electronic format and there will always be a role for hardcopy printouts and photocopies. Try the following strategies to keep your paper use to a minimum:

- Skim read articles before printing or photocopying and be selective about what you *really* need to print or copy. Only print or copy the range of pages you need.
- When photocopying, reduce size so that you can fit a double page spread of a book on a single page and copy back-to-back (one-sided to two-sided).
- When printing, stipulate two pages to the sheet or print two-sided. Your ability to do this will partly rest on the type of printer you use and also the application you are printing from. Note that some printers require you to click on Print Properties and change the printer options as well.

- Consider printing and copying on the back of used paper. This can work well providing you are meticulous about not using stapled pages or crumpled or damaged sheets.
- Scan print into digital format (see below).

Photocopying features

While all researchers no doubt know how to use basic photocopier features, we have watched many students and research colleagues creating inefficiencies for themselves because they weren't aware of the more advanced features available on their copier, which may include the following:

- **Margin shift, border erase and book edge features** allow you to control how the margins of your original are dealt with, either removing the risk of black smudges when copying thick books or enlarging text to fill more of the available paper size.
- **Booklet creation** reduces the size of each page by 50% and prints two pages per sheet, in correct order, so that the document can be folded and stapled.
- **Bound document copying** allows you to lay a bound book on the glass plate and the copier automatically copies one page and then the next.
- **Cover sheets.** This feature will feed the first page of each document from a different tray (containing, for example, colored paper or letterhead).
- **Watermarking.** Some photocopiers print text such as "draft" or "confidential" in the background of each page, without it appearing as part of the original document.
- **Collation and binding.** Not everyone is aware of the ability to staple in different page positions and that some copiers even hole punch.
- **Job interrupt** allows you to put through a more urgent or quick copy if a long photocopy job is running.

Scanning and optical character recognition

Scanning offers a useful alternative to photocopying but it is important to note that in many countries digitization of copyright material breaches copyright laws. There are two main types of scanners: flatbed scanners and "pen" scanners.

Flatbed scanners allow you to place a document on a flat glass surface or to feed a series of loose pages through a document handler (like a photocopier). Such scanners come with software that leads you through a series of steps, roughly as follows:

- A preview function shows the document on screen, allowing you to confirm which part of the document or image you wish to capture.

- Adjust the setting to specify the required resolution (image quality) in dots per inch (dpi). The higher the resolution the larger the file size but the clearer the quality. Try to select the appropriate resolution, e.g. 72 dpi for images displayed on screen and 300+ dpi for printed images. The software will normally guide you through this.
- You then click to scan the document. The scanner and software captures what is on the flatbed or document handler. Note that words, pictures and graphics are all treated as image files.
- If you wish to convert the words that are within the document to real text you need to run the scanned image through an Optical Character Recognition (OCR) process. OCR software attempts to identify what letter each symbol in the scanned document represents. This is a complex process and the accuracy of the resultant text is highly dependent on the quality and layout of the original document. In most cases the OCR process is only partially successful and you need to check the document for recognition errors. Using a spell checker is rarely sufficient since translation errors can create completely different words which are still recognized by a dictionary. Such errors can drastically change the meaning of text and are particularly problematic in the case of quotes.

Pen scanners are handheld "pens" that you run over text line by line, as if you were using a highlighter. It is important to go slowly, smoothly and accurately. Pen scanners generally have an OCR function built in and they process the symbols into text as they go, storing the resultant text in a small built-in memory which can then be transferred to your computer at a later stage (by USB or wireless connections). While most claim to be 98 or 99% accurate, like other scanners and OCR software this is not always the case. Pen scanners are particularly useful when traveling to a library or reading literature away from your computer.

Managing your paper resources

One of the first things you notice when you walk into an office is whether the person residing there has good systems in place for managing their paper resources. If you have sound processes in place for storing your hard-copy files (such as literature, data, records and administrative documents), you will be well on the way to efficient research practice.

Filing cabinets

One of the best places to start your organizational routine is with your filing cabinets. A few hours invested here can pay huge dividends. Many of us view our filing cabinets as places where we store all those old documents and archives that we (perhaps subconsciously) know we will never look at again. This means many researchers start out on a new project with much of their prime office storage space already spoken for. Yet filing cabinets are perhaps one of the most effective forms of storage for current and active documents. Here are some tips to prompt you to take a fresh look at your filing cabinet space:

- **Aim to decrease your stored paperwork by at least half to one-third.** This is easier than you might think. Methodically go through all the documents you currently have stored. At least start with one drawer. How essential is it to keep each document? Be ruthless. If you haven't referred to it for 2 or more years it should definitely be either ditched or archived. Financial and legal papers need to be kept. However, if there is a low probability that you will need to access them regularly, move them to longer term storage such as document storage boxes, transferred to a cellar, attic or storage room. Label archived boxes clearly.
- **Think about your universal filing schema** (see earlier in this chapter). Consider different drawers (or cabinets) for each section of your life, or at least different sections of the same drawer.
- **Allocate one drawer for "current working files,"** preferably in the most accessible location in your office. If you are short on cabinet space invest in a rolling hanging file holder which can slide under your desk. Include lots of loose, empty hanging files for new entries. Each time a new project, issue, commitment or topic arises, label one of the blank hanging files and pop all relevant paperwork inside. Aim to start with the drawer at least half empty. It will fill up soon enough.
- **Use one or more other drawers for medium-term storage.** Files will move down from your "current working files" drawer as they become less current.
- **Allocate separate drawers for literature.** Chapter 9 provides tips specifically on how to manage and organize your literature.

Other paper storage options

Apart from filing cabinet storage, other options include ring-bound folders, plastic sleeve folders, cardboard envelopes, pamphlet boxes and archive boxes.

Ring-bound folders offer mobility and maintain the ability to annotate or highlight documents. In our experience, ring-binders are most appropriate where sequences in documents need to be maintained, for example for primary data (e.g. survey responses or interview transcripts) from respondents who are numbered sequentially or for minutes of meetings.

Plastic sleeve folders provide mobility and protection since documents don't need to be hole-punched and are protected from moisture and wear and tear. In our experience plastic sleeve folders are most appropriate for carrying around current reading or current work (see the previous section on managing multiple offices) where sequence or structure is not important.

Cardboard envelopes are another good way of moving your current reading material from place to place. An advantage here is that you can include a pen, highlighter and some scrap paper in the envelope. Grab the folder and you are off and running. If you don't have the specially designed cardboard envelopes, try stapling down the sides of a regular manila folder.

Pamphlet boxes are most useful when you need rapid sorting. For instance, when sorting out hardcopy literature you might use three pamphlet boxes to collate them before reading and filing.

Archival boxes can be most useful for long-term storage, such as for data that has to be kept for a set period of time after a research study, and which you know you won't refer back to.

For long-term archiving you might want to consider converting documents into electronic format and managing them in ways we suggest in the next section.

Managing your electronic resources

Just as important as organizing and managing your physical environment is organizing and actively managing your electronic workspace, i.e. the files and other information that are stored on your computer. We have worked with many beginning (and even experienced) researchers whose work practices are solely affected by poor file management practices; they spend unnecessary time locating documents, mistakenly working with older versions or files, deleting files by accident, or keeping in their main file storage area every electronic document that has passed their screen, without ever doing a "spring clean" and deleting unnecessary files. In this section we consider the essential skills of managing your computer's desktop and files, reducing file size, managing risk and using file management utilities. Also see the following for organizing your electronic environment:

- organizing and managing your e-mails (Chapter 6);
- managing your Web bookmarks/favorites (Chapter 8);
- managing and filing electronic copies of literature (Chapter 9);
- collecting, handling and analyzing data (Chapters 10 and 11).

Managing your desktop

Your computer's desktop is a very useful working space, however it shouldn't be used as a "digital dumping ground."[5] If you don't file documents immediately, you *can* use the desktop as a temporary saving location and it can serve as a visual reminder of work to be done. Note that on some networks (such as in a computer lab environment) and on some shared computers, saving to the desktop will mean that your files are deleted when you shut the computer down, so take care when working in an unfamiliar computer environment.

If you do use your desktop, here are some tips for managing it more effectively:

- Create folders on your desktop to store related files. That whole folder can then be filed away in one go.
- Learn to create shortcuts (aliases on a Mac). These are a special type of file that points to another file, folder or program. They can be created and moved to the desktop or to any place in your filing structure to assist you in maintaining a logical and efficient file structure. Opening the shortcut is the same as opening the actual file.
- If you move between offices but only print in one location, consider creating a "To be printed" folder on your desktop and use it to store a document, or better still create a shortcut to the properly filed document.
- When you install new programs you will often end up with shortcuts to programs on your desktop and these can really clutter up your virtual workspace. If you don't use them, delete them (this doesn't delete the program itself, just the shortcut). You can always open the program directly from your programs menu. Another strategy is to drag the shortcut to your taskbar to place a copy there, before deleting the shortcut from the desktop.

Filing your electronic documents

Filing electronic documents is essentially a process of creating folders, and then creating folders within folders before moving files into those folders. We recommend that you use your universal filing schema (see earlier in this chapter). Have one single location where all your files are located, typically "Documents" or "My Documents." There are several ways to create folders and sort your files. On a Windows platform you can use Windows Explorer [Click the Start button – Programs – Accessories – Windows Explorer] or alternatively you can drag and drop (on a Mac or PC). This intuitive approach involves opening two windows, one that contains the file you want to move and one where you want the file to go, and dragging and dropping it from one location to another.

There is also an argument put forward by some that with the growing storage capacity of hard drives and the fact that technology can provide advanced search facilities, which look at every word within a file, electronic file management may not be as essential as it once was. Again, your decisions in this respect will be influenced by your personal work preferences.

Tips on filing your documents

- Use your filing schema to guide your folder structure.
- File electronic copies of literature in a single folder (see Chapter 12).
- Give all files meaningful names that will help you retrieve them at a later date (not stuff1.doc, stuff2.doc).
- Consider creating a folder of multipurpose, frequently used documents such as letterheads, stationery, logos, your research templates and to-do lists.
- Create archive folders, within other subfolders. These can be a useful place to put older versions of documents you think you may not need again. If you practice good archival backing up (see below) these files can be deleted after a certain time.
- Avoid saving large files that don't need backing up (e.g. software installers) in your main folder structure.
- Regularly "spring clean" your files and readjust your filing structure as your research progresses. Do delete files that have been archived and which you are fairly confident you won't need again (e.g. earlier versions of a document).

Managing file sizes

Part of the skill of file management is being aware of file size. To find out your file's size on a Windows platform, right click on the name of the file or folder and select "properties" from the menu. On a Macintosh, select the file and choose "Get Info" to display the file size. Knowing the file size is important in determining whether the files will fit on your backup medium (CD-ROM, DVD, USB stick etc.), or whether it is wise to compress a file before e-mailing it to a colleague.

Compression is the process of reducing the size of computer data so that it takes up less disk space and/or so that a whole folder of files can be condensed into one file. Most software found on the Internet, for example, is compressed so that it can be more quickly and easily downloaded. Compression is useful if you want to send a large file or a collection of files to another person via e-mail, or if you want to archive your old files so that they do not take up as much disk space.

Most computers come with compression/decompression programs already installed. Macintosh computers commonly use Stuffit Expander and PCs use WinZip, PowerZip or a similarly named program. If you do not have a compression program installed, download one from one of the many software download sites (see Chapter 2). Compressing a file or folder is generally a process of:

- right clicking on the file;
- selecting "Add to Zip" (or similar, depending on your specific program);
- giving the new compressed file a name;
- indicating where to save it (for instance onto your desktop).

Note that compressing files does *not* delete the original files. It simply creates a new compressed version of the original. Decompressing files is basically compression in reverse. Usually it is as easy as double clicking on the compressed file, indicating where you would like to save the uncompressed files and clicking "unzip."

Managing risk

While most people who use computers are aware of the need to back up their files, many still don't employ sound risk management strategies. Threats are many and varied and each risk raises its own need for protection. Having multiple copies of data in different locations is critical, provided the sites are secure. Your research data may need to be kept strictly confidential and in some contexts changes to the original data need to be authorized and a secure audit trail maintained. Software utilities can be used to automatically record any changes made to a file, who made them and when. Ask yourself:

- What barriers are in place to secure my research data?
- Does my project data have any specified security requirements?
- What are the weak points?
- How could my risk management be improved?

In this section we consider management strategies for a range of risks common in computer environments.

Encryption
Based on the science of cryptography, encryption involves encoding information in such a way that only the computer (or person) with the key can decode it. If your research involves highly confidential or classified information you may want to include encryption as your initial security measure. This is a confidentiality security measure only and should be used in conjunction with other risk management strategies.

Most computer encryption systems belong to one of two categories: symmetric-key or public-key encryption. In symmetric-key encryption the computer uses a secret key (code) to encrypt information before storage or transmission across a network. To access encrypted data you need the same key. Public key encryption uses a combination of private and public keys with the private key being known only to your computer while the public key is given out by your computer to any computer that needs to securely communicate with it. Pretty Good Privacy (PGP) (http://www.pgpi.org) is a popular freeware public key encryption system compatible with a range of operating systems.

Backing up your work

The importance of backing up your computer files cannot be overstated, not only because of potential computer failure, but also because of the risk of burglary, fire or file corruption. You will need two types of backing-up systems.

- **Day-to-day backup** needs to be quick and easy so that you can back up your work several times a day.
- **Archival backup** involves periodically making a backup of *all* your data, dating it, and keeping it as a reference point to your files at a designated period of time. The frequency with which you do archival backups is a personal decision, related to the nature of data you are creating. You might prefer to delete older versions of files, or little used work after at least two or three archival copies have been made. Alternatively you may prefer to keep all files on your computer regardless.

You have a number of backup options to choose from. Keep in mind that transferability of data from one medium to another is an ongoing issue when archiving data as storage technologies continue to change.

- **Floppy disks** were the first removable backup medium and have been superseded, illustrating the point above.
- **Flash memory sticks** (also called USB sticks or thumb drives) are great for day-to-day backups of relatively large files (the more you pay, the more storage space you get). They have wide readability on all computers with a USB port, but they are easily mislaid, damaged or stolen and are thus not so good for archiving.
- **CD-ROMs and DVDs** are good for archiving and have wide readability. They are durable, inexpensive and are easily labeled, dated and stored. They have an advantage over other media that are magnetic in that the latter can be corrupted by strong magnetic fields. They do, however, require a CD/DVD writer or burner.
- **External hard disk drives** are available in various capacities, as desktop or portable pocket-sized units.
- **Network backups** are useful, particularly if you use a desktop computer at work or within your university. Automatic backup software can be run so that backup occurs at a set time each day or week. However, keep in mind that if the backup server is in the same building you are still at risk in the case of fire. You should always find out what versioning is performed (e.g. how long data are kept before being overwritten). Issues can include lack of personal control, limited space and difficulties getting backups retrieved.

Tips on using "Save As."

BEWARE! If you use "Save As" to save a file you are working on to your backup medium, be aware that the version of the document you are then working on is not the original. If you continue to make changes to the document you will be saving the new work on the backup medium only, not on your computer's hard drive. You thus run the risk of having multiple versions, not a backup version. The drag and drop method is preferable for moving, copying and backing up files.

Version control

Version control (or versioning) is the process of progressively creating copies of a file (with different names) as it develops over time, with each file being labeled with a date, e.g. Chapter1_Mar06, Chapter1_July06 (and so on) or other differentiating schemes such as Draft1, Draft2 or ACSTPaper_PreEdit, ACSTPaper_TyposFixed. Versioning ensures that you can always go back to an earlier version if either:

* you accidentally or on purpose delete something which you later realize you need; or
* you find that your file has become corrupted (unreadable), enabling you to track back through earlier versions until you find one that is readable.

Some programs (such as Microsoft Word) can automate the versioning process, but take care when using this facility as it can increase the size of files considerably. Also be aware that saving different versions of a file on your own computer is not enough on its own. You must also back up one or more versions on separate media and preferably archive your versions, as described above.

Malicious programs: viruses, worms and spyware

One threat that is specific to computers and digital data is "malware" or malicious software, the most prevalent of which are computer viruses. Put simply, a virus is a program that causes your computer to perform differently. It might reveal itself through anything unusual, from an annoying pop-up advertising screen that occurs on a particular keystroke to your entire hard disk being erased without warning. Viruses are self-replicating in that they spread by inserting copies of themselves into other programs or files. A "worm" is a self-contained virus that does not need to attach itself to another program to replicate. Another category of malicious software is spyware. These programs work in various ways to intercept your data flow or take control of your computer's operations without your knowledge or consent.[6]

Malware can be difficult to detect, easy to propagate, hard to remove and devastatingly destructive. You can pick up a virus, worm or spyware through:

- **Disks or other types of storage media.**
- **E-mail:** viruses cannot be transmitted by just reading your e-mail but they can be attached to files such as word documents or .exe (program) files. You do, however, need to be careful when using e-mail programs that automatically open attachments when reading your messages.
- **Downloading programs** from a website. Basically, if it's a file you can execute (a program), then it is possible for a virus to attach itself. Pictures are safe because you are only viewing the file, not running it.

To guard against receiving or sending viruses and worms:

- **Have antivirus software installed and running on your computer** (your workplace probably provides them free). Most antivirus programs run in the background all the time and so if you download and open a file or insert a disk, the program will check it automatically.
- **Update your virus software frequently.** As new viruses are detected antivirus software manufacturers release updates that counter the new viruses (check the date of the last update to ensure they are installing correctly).
- **Don't open any files received by e-mail or click on any links to websites that you have suspicions about**, even if you have antivirus software installed and even if they are from a trusted source.
- **Learn how to set your Web browser's security settings** (in the options section of the program).
- **Do not click on any unsolicited pop-up messages** when browsing the Web, particularly if they suggest that your computer has a virus.
- **Ensure your operating system is kept updated** with patches.
- **Ensure you have firewall protection**. Most organizations provide this, but if you are working outside this protected environment, you may need to install firewall software (sometimes, but not always, a component of virus protection software).

Hoaxes

Hoaxes are e-mails that circulate alerting people to nonexistent viruses. Some, for instance, provide directions on how to delete a so-called virus off your computer, and in the process you can end up deleting essential files. To avoid being taken in by a hoax, ask yourself the following:

- **Is the e-mail from a genuine computer security expert?** Hoax e-mails are often forwarded from a friend, who got it from a friend, who got it from their daughter, who got it from her friend who supposedly received it from IBM's virus experts ... you see the problem.

- **Does the e-mail urge you to forward the message to everyone you know?** Genuine virus alerts will not ask you to do this.
- **Does the message contain a link to an authoritative page?** Valid e-mail alerts rarely go into detail but rather summarize the threat and provide a link to a well-known computer security website.
- **Has someone asked you to provide your password or other ID?** NEVER provide any private information over a network unless it is securely encrypted.

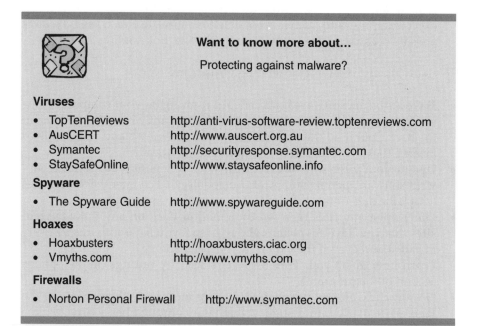

Want to know more about...

Protecting against malware?

Viruses

- TopTenReviews   http://anti-virus-software-review.toptenreviews.com
- AusCERT   http://www.auscert.org.au
- Symantec   http://securityresponse.symantec.com
- StaySafeOnline   http://www.staysafeonline.info

Spyware

- The Spyware Guide   http://www.spywareguide.com

Hoaxes

- Hoaxbusters   http://hoaxbusters.ciac.org
- Vmyths.com   http://www.vmyths.com

Firewalls

- Norton Personal Firewall   http://www.symantec.com

Tips on managing risk

- Always have at least two copies of valuable files in two different locations. This provides a significant level of security.
- Always have your master/main copy of your work saved on your hard drive (never on a disk). Only ever back up to disk, never work directly from it.
- Back up every day or several times a day, before the risk of losing what you have been doing becomes too great.
- Keep archival backups as well as day-to-day backups.
- Always take the time to verify that your files have been successfully copied to your backup media. A corrupted backup is no back up at all.
- Check if your research contract or ethics approval requires specific security measures.

Data management utilities

If your research involves a combination of text, still images, sound or video files, it may be helpful to catalogue or otherwise organize your files using specially designed software and utilities. The types of tools we describe in this section may prove useful where your files are a main source of data. This information is thus directly relevant to the data collection, management and analysis processes we discuss in Chapters 10 and 11.

A range of freeware, shareware and commercial file management software (sometimes referred to as asset management databases) are available, allowing you to better organize, manage, index and annotate your files. While databases that actually *contain* all the data soon become too large to work with (particularly in terms of backing up or file sharing), *cataloguing databases* do not actually import or alter the original files. Data can still be saved and stored elsewhere (e.g. on a CD-ROM, DVD or other networked computer) and the software will link to them. Some programs make small images (thumbnails) of each file within the database to represent rather than recreate the file. This is most useful for images and video files. There are a number of advantages provided by data management utilities[7]:

- **Files can be catalogued automatically** by the computer, or manually indexed by you.
- **Search facilities** allow you to easily locate specific files or groups of files. Adding keywords allows you to create defined sets of documents, facilitating searching (e.g. "interviews," "diary entries," "observations," "literature quotes").
- **Annotations (either text or audio) can be added** to the files to organize and manage notes or metadata, thus further facilitating searchability.
- **Cataloguing files on a network** can assist research teams to collaborate.

Some data management databases (for example, AskSam) are "unstructured," meaning that they impose very few structural restrictions on how data is managed, thus providing more flexibility in indexing and handling data i.e. they do not use the same strict record and field structure described in Chapter 2.

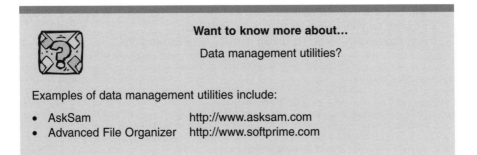

Want to know more about...

Data management utilities?

Examples of data management utilities include:

- AskSam   http://www.asksam.com
- Advanced File Organizer   http://www.softprime.com

(*Continued*)

- Scribe SA — http://www.scribesa.com
- Library Master — http://www.balboa-software.com
- InfoRapid — http://www.inforapid.de

Some qualitative data analysis software and bibliographic software provide similar or enhanced functionality (see tables at the end of Chapters 9 and 11).

Over to you...

1. What is the first step you could take towards organizing your physical work environment?
2. How could you change your filing system to take account of all aspects of your life, not just your research?
3. How could you improve the way you manage your computer files?
4. What are the main security risks you face in your research, both physical and electronic?
5. What are the most important steps you could take to protect your work?

Notes

1 "Infoclutter" is a term used by Ormiston 2004, and one which we think is most appropriate.
2 Material in this section is based on Ralph Strauch's *Low-Stress Computing*, available from http://www.somatic.com
3 Adapted from Palmquist and Zimmerman 1999.
4 Phelps et al. 2006.
5 Ormiston 2004.
6 Note that there are legitimate programs that provide remote control of one computer by another (e.g. Timbktu Pro or Apple Desktop Remote) and these can be useful in certain circumstances, such as when an IT person is assisting to rectify a problem on your computer from a remote location.
7 Information in this section is drawn partially from Brown 2002.

Chapter 5

Planning and Overseeing Progress of Your Project

In Chapters 3 and 4 we discussed the importance of analyzing your own personal work practices and putting in place good processes for managing yourself, your ideas, and your work environment. Your responsibilities don't end there, however. You also have to plan and manage the overall progress of your research project.

While our focus throughout the book is primarily on single-researcher studies, the processes discussed in this chapter are also relevant for managing larger projects, involving multiple employees or researchers and large budgets. We cover techniques that involve both commonly available software and dedicated project management applications, leaving it to you to judge the relevance of these systems for your own research context.

In this chapter we cover:

- tools to support development of a research plan or proposal;
- how to establish timelines and milestones;
- tips to keep your project on track and completed on time (as distinct from the every-day time management strategies we addressed in Chapter 3);
- the use of project management software;
- financial issues, including locating sources of funding, applying for grants, writing budgets and monitoring expenditure.

Developing a research plan

Developing a research plan or proposal is an important first step in any research project. This process requires you to think through (in some detail):

- what you want to do or find out;
- why you want to do the research (or better still, why it is important to do it);
- how you intend to collect your data;
- what informs your project (e.g. a literature review identifying other relevant research and showing your understanding of your chosen methods and theoretical framework).

Most postgraduate research students will be required to produce a proposal early in their candidature. This can take a significant amount of time, particularly if you have not enrolled with a clear research focus. We have seen many a student stall at this point and become unnecessarily disillusioned, sometimes changing their entire research focus several times over the course of one or even several years. You will also require a thorough research plan if you intend to apply for funding for your research. Experienced researchers know how competitive such grants are, and how detailed and accurate their proposals must be. It can take months of laborious work to develop such a proposal.

It is beyond the scope and focus of this book to provide guidance on how to write a research proposal, and many texts already do this well.[1] Rather, we focus on software that can assist you to plan and design your research, in particular, "expert system" software.

Planning your research using expert system software

Expert system programs guide you through a decision-making process. As such, an expert system acts like a peer or critical friend, asking key questions, making suggestions based on your responses, ensuring you make all the required decisions, critiquing your work, giving you feedback, pointing out areas which might be strengthened and identifying inconsistencies or missing details. We are not suggesting that expert system software can replace advice from your supervisors, other experienced researchers or statisticians, or that it can write your proposal for you. It will, however, help you think through your project and make informed decisions and thus also performs a valuable research training function.

In this section we focus on one particular piece of software, as to our knowledge there is not (at the time of writing) an equivalent program that provides support for both qualitative and quantitative research.[2]

Methodologist's Toolchest[3] utilizes expert systems and decision support technology to provide step-by-step guidance through the creation of research proposals. Various modules of the program prompt you to think through and write your research aim, background and significance, content, researcher experience, research design and methods as well as ethical and management aspects of the project proposal. The software then creates the first draft for you.

The program consists of nine different modules:

- **The Peer Review Emulator** guides you step-by-step through the research proposal writing process, identifying key decisions that must be made, ensuring that you address all relevant areas, pointing out weaknesses or inconsistencies, and advising on areas for improvement. If you make a change in one section of the proposal, it reminds you which other sections might require updating.
- **Ex-Sample** assists you to determine your appropriate sample size, particularly for quantitative studies. It can assess the effects on your project of response rates, contamination and other factors and utilizes formulas based on over 60 types of analyses including survival analysis, logistical regression, stepwise regression, path analysis and so on.
- **Statistical Navigator** helps you make decisions regarding appropriate statistical analyses from information provided about your objectives and assumptions. It can work in "consult mode," asking you a series of questions (much like a human expert might) and, based on your responses, suggesting and ranking appropriate statistical processes. In "browse" mode it provides descriptions of statistical techniques organized into the major analysis approaches and you can examine each in your own order.
- **Designer Research** guides you through a process of constructing your experimental, quasi-experimental or nonexperimental research design. It helps you to identify potential threats to validity (internal, external, construct and statistical), reliability, subjectivity and researcher bias and to minimize these while avoiding contradictory design strategies. The module takes account of particular disciplinary and methodological contexts. This module also includes guidance on creating your budget and a Gantt chart (see later in this chapter) for managing your research schedule.
- **Measurement and Scaling Strategist** supports you to construct your questionnaires. It recommends how concepts should be measured and explains the reasoning behind these recommendations. You can identify whether there is an existing scale available for measuring the concept through references to the literature. It can also guide you through decisions such as whether to use open or closed questions and scaling strategies such as Likert scales. A built-in editor helps compose the questions and a checklist prompts you to consider common problems.
- **Data Collection Selection** asks you a series of "if-then" questions (again, like a human expert might) and, based on your answers, rates various data collection procedures according to their suitability for your research problem, explaining its reasoning so that you can confidently make your

final decisions. It includes considerations of cost, access, response rate, data sensitivity, time availability, and other factors.

- **Ethx** is relevant to research involving humans and will help you create your ethics proposal, making sure key issues aren't overlooked. It will even guide you through writing an informed consent letter.
- **WhichGraph** assists you to make better decisions about which graphic display will best present your data. Like the Statistical Navigator it has a consult and browse mode.
- **Hyper-Stat** is a hypertext dictionary of statistical, graphical and methodological terms. It works across all of the Methodologist's Toolchest modules to provide readily accessible definitions and explanations at all stages throughout the proposal writing process. When you are required to consider particular research strategies or methods, a simple click will provide background information to inform your decisions. Hyper-Stat can also be used as a stand-alone program. The qualitative research strategies and concepts integrated into Methodologist's Toolchest (v.3.0 onwards) are backed up with descriptions, definitions, explanations and references so that you can justify your decisions with reference to the literature.

Figures 5.1 and 5.2 are illustrative screen grabs from the program.

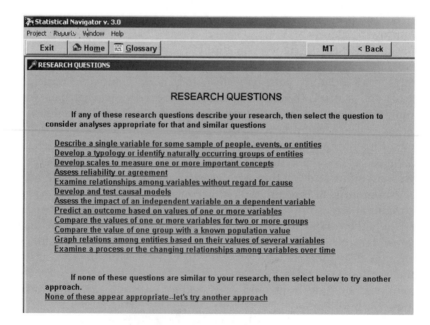

Figure 5.1   Planning research using consult mode in an expert system software program

In this example the software is posing a series of questions so you can select the most appropriate options before being guided further in your planning process. Example is from Methodologist's Toolchest.

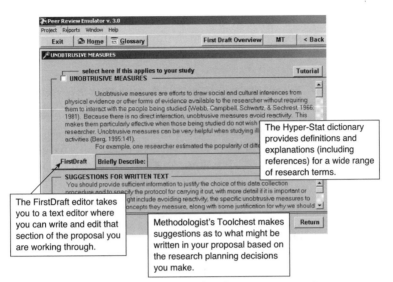

Figure 5.2   **In context support for planning in an expert system software program**

The hypertext dictionary of statistical, graphical and methodological terms provides definitions and explanations relevant to each stage in the planning process. In this example, suggestions are also provided as to what might be written in the proposal. Example is from Methodologist's Toolchest.

Timelines and milestones

To what extent do you need to work to a strict timeframe? If you are on a scholarship or salary you might see your research as being like a regular job and maintain a 5-day, 9–5 commitment. If you are on an industry-funded scholarship, your funding body may require regular reporting on progress. On the other hand, you may be undertaking research for personal fulfilment and enrichment and may not be under pressure, financial or otherwise, to rush towards completion. If this is the case, your research may take on the character of a *magnum opus*, a lifetime achievement that you pour your heart, soul and limitless hours into with no restraints. Or you may lie between these extremes, seeing the timely completion of your research project as a stepping-stone to further research or career advancement.

Whatever your personal situation and goals, pressures on universities and research institutions dictate timely completion of research degrees and substantial research output from staff. In this environment, we suggest that learning to efficiently and effectively manage research timelines is as important a part of postgraduate research training as deepening disciplinary knowledge and developing methodological skills.

The relationship between timelines and milestones

A project milestone is a significant event, outcome or "deliverable" that has a set date. You can work backwards from milestones to determine what has to be done and by when, to achieve your goals. Project milestones thus form the basic elements of a project's timeline. An effective research timeline operates at several levels:

- **The overall project timeline** maps the entire course of your research (usually framed in years rather than months) and accounts for such milestones as ethics clearance, progress report deadlines, conference presentations or paper submission dates, time to be spent in the field and, of course, your final thesis or report submission date.
- **Mid-term timelines** include more detail and are usually framed in months and weeks. They might account for scheduled interviews, meetings with supervisors, appointments for data collection, or completion of specific sections of your thesis or report.
- **Day-to-day timelines** are more related to personal time management and to-do lists, as discussed in Chapter 3, but are still part of your overall project management.

We strongly advise you to map out your overall project timeframe with your supervisor or research colleagues from the very beginning of your project. In fact, this is generally a requirement for the research proposal you submit to your university or funding body. Mid-term timelines often evolve as you progress, allowing you to flesh out the details of your overall timeframe. You might add details and review mid-term timelines every 3–4 months. You will, of course, be revisiting your day-to-day timelines on a daily basis. We would advise integrating your overall and mid-term timeframes into a project plan while using alternate strategies for day-to-day goals.

Tips for Managing Timelines and Milestones

- **Be realistic about your submission date.** Identify your ideal date and add on 10–30% to allow for unforeseen circumstances. It is far better to meet your deadline than overrun it.
- **Work backwards from your submission date.** If you are truly committed to that date then everything else must come before it.

(Continued)

- **Set milestones and stick to them.** While you may experience a little slippage from time to time, your milestones are what push you to complete on time. Aim to be uncompromising with them.
- **Be realistic with your milestones.** Let them push you, but not too much or you will quickly find yourself becoming stressed and disillusioned.
- **Build in rewards such as holidays or breaks.** Try to set milestones that you must achieve before you take your reward.
- **Ask your supervisor to help you stick to your timeframes.** While many supervisors see this as the candidate's responsibility, asking them to hold you to your timelines may give you that additional push you need (see also Chapter 3 on managing the relationship with your supervisor).
- **Set goals that are tangible and observable.** It is important for your morale to be able to step back and show someone (including yourself) what you have achieved, no matter how small that achievement might be. Even a goal of drafting a four paragraph section or organizing your office can be cause for celebration (see also Chapter 3).
- **Be more flexible with your writing timelines.** Writing is a creative process and does not always fit the demands of a schedule. However, many writers argue that writing something every day is essential for maintaining discipline. Consider scheduling concurrently challenging writing tasks (such as writing up theory) and lighter tasks (such as editing or describing your methods). See Chapter 12 for more writing tips.
- **Remain flexible but tough.** Realize that you can't anticipate all the things that will impact on your research. While it is important to remain flexible to accommodate the unforeseen, you also need to be tough to ensure your overall timeframe isn't compromised. For example, if your data collection phase is delayed, bring forward activities such as writing up your relevant literature.
- **Involve your peer support group** (see Chapter 3).

Documenting timelines and milestones

Designing a research project timeline might be as simple as writing a list of dates and events on paper or typing them using word processing software. It helps to format the timeline so that it can easily be revisited, modified, added to and adjusted (not so easy if it is handwritten). If you use a word processor, create a table so that it is easy to insert, delete or move rows. This enables you to start with the overall timeframe when you first begin your research and insert mid and day-to-day goals as you progress, as shown in Figure 5.3.

There are also a number of readily available programs that can assist. For instance, a spreadsheet program (see Chapter 2) can be used to establish a visual Gantt chart[4] by simply shading the cells of the spreadsheet, as illustrated in Figure 5.4.

Date/month	Tasks	Complete?
February 5 2006	Draft of ethics application to supervisor	✓
February 14 2006	Ethics application complete and signatures obtained	✓
February 15 2006	Submit ethics application	✓
February 17 2006	⊠ Ethics applications due	✓
March 20 2006	Ethics meeting date	
April 1 2006	Responses to ethics committee	

Figure 5.3   Simple word processed timeline constructed using a table

By using tables, rows can be easily inserted, cut or moved, providing flexibility when revising your timeframe. Milestones can be marked by bolding or using a symbol. This example shows mid-term timeframes.

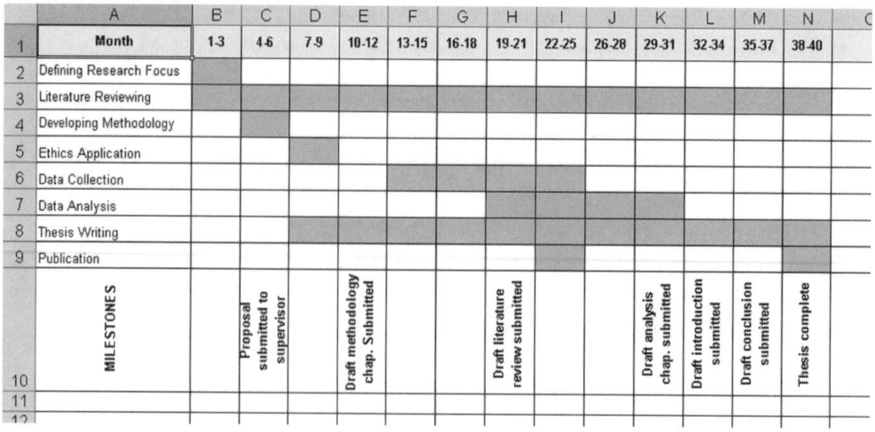

	A	B	C	D	E	F	G	H	I	J	K	L	M	N	
1	Month	1-3	4-6	7-9	10-12	13-15	16-18	19-21	22-25	26-28	29-31	32-34	35-37	38-40	
2	Defining Research Focus														
3	Literature Reviewing														
4	Developing Methodology														
5	Ethics Application														
6	Data Collection														
7	Data Analysis														
8	Thesis Writing														
9	Publication														
10	MILESTONES		Proposal submitted to supervisor		Draft methodology chap. Submitted		Draft literature review submitted			Draft analysis chap. submitted	Draft introduction submitted	Draft conclusion submitted	Thesis complete		
11															
12															

Figure 5.4   Simple spreadsheet Gantt chart, showing overall project timeframe

The cell shading function is used to highlight when tasks need to be undertaken. Note that the font alignment in the final row is formatted to change the direction of the text. Example is created using Microsoft Excel.

See the **Organizing and Managing Your Research Website**

for templates to set out time lines.
http://www.sagepub.co.uk/phelps

Mind mapping and visualization software (described in Chapter 3) can also be used to create a flowchart of tasks and milestones. Some other graphics applications provide specific functionality for producing Gantt charts (see Chapter 2). With a little skill and knowledge it is also possible to use generic database applications to meet your needs, as illustrated in the following case study.

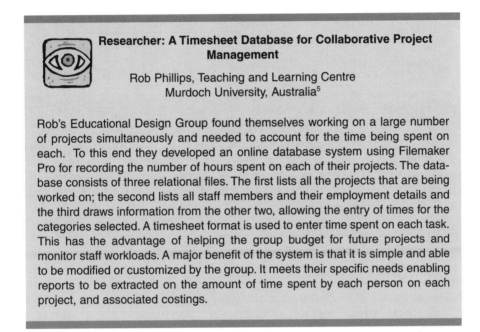

Researcher: A Timesheet Database for Collaborative Project Management

Rob Phillips, Teaching and Learning Centre
Murdoch University, Australia[5]

Rob's Educational Design Group found themselves working on a large number of projects simultaneously and needed to account for the time being spent on each. To this end they developed an online database system using Filemaker Pro for recording the number of hours spent on each of their projects. The database consists of three relational files. The first lists all the projects that are being worked on; the second lists all staff members and their employment details and the third draws information from the other two, allowing the entry of times for the categories selected. A timesheet format is used to enter time spent on each task. This has the advantage of helping the group budget for future projects and monitor staff workloads. A major benefit of the system is that it is simple and able to be modified or customized by the group. It meets their specific needs enabling reports to be extracted on the amount of time spent by each person on each project, and associated costings.

A range of other readily accessible software can be adapted for both long-term and short-term time management. For instance, personal organizer software (such as Microsoft Outlook) allows you to establish calendars, make task lists, schedule events and have reminders that alert you to upcoming priorities. There is, however, a range of software specifically designed for the management of projects, and we address these in the following section.

Project management software

While project management software (also called process management software) is particularly suited to projects involving a team of people, significant numbers of resources, or detailed reporting requirements, it can be adapted well to smaller-scale research projects. In general, the more complex the project, the more appropriate it is to use project management software.

Of course, project management software does not manage the project for you and does not substitute for sound planning and organization. As project manager or leader you still need to identify what needs to be done, plan the order in which things need to occur and assess and monitor progress on goals. The software is just a tool to assist you in these processes.

Most project management software is based on Critical Path Method (CPM)[6] and broadly involves:

- entering all the tasks (goals) and subtasks (subgoals) necessary to complete a project;
- stipulating the order in which tasks need to be done;
- associating resources with tasks, including material, financial and human resources;
- indicating (sometimes using a calendar) when specific resources such as people or finance are available.

The software will then generate a schedule of who needs to do what and when. Many programs prompt you to save one or more baseline schedules which represent your initial plan. The software then allows you to track the project's progress, which can be compared with the initial plan. In larger and more complex projects the software can be used to analyze optimum timeframes by experimenting to determine consequences of hypothetical occurrences, for example, the impact of accelerating timeframes or the consequences of a task not being completed on time.

How can project management software support your research?

- **It supports the planning phase** by prompting identification of tasks and subtasks necessary to meet milestones and deadlines.
- **It can schedule tasks** for you, based on parameters such as start and end dates, relationships between tasks (such as the order in which they have to occur) and available resources. It can also reschedule your tasks based on any changes or slippage. For example, if your ethics application is not approved at the time you originally envisaged, the software will assist in rescheduling your data collection tasks.
- **It will produce a timeline** that traces activities running in parallel over time. This is often visually presented as a Gantt chart (see Figure 5.5) and/or a calendar.
- **It allows monitoring of progress** on tasks, ensuring that prerequisite tasks are completed before other tasks and warning of any slippage on overall deadlines.
- **It will monitor time spent on the project by people involved**, which allows reporting on workflow and project costing, and is particularly valuable where staff work across multiple projects.
- **It will record financial aspects of research**, including logging expenses, producing invoices and costing out salaries based on time taken to complete tasks.
- **It facilitates communication** between a team of researchers about what needs to be done by when and by whom.

- **It supports collaborative access to documents** through check-in and check-out functions or by monitoring access to documents on a network.

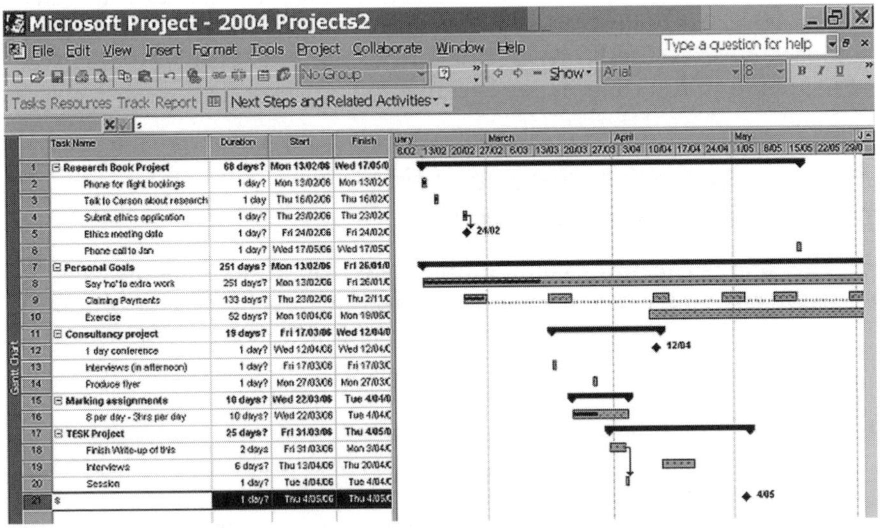

Figure 5.5   Example of a Gantt chart created using stand-alone software.

The various types of bars indicate when in the timeline tasks are planned, the time allowed for each, and when work is completed. Diamonds represent milestones. Example is from Microsoft Project.

Types of project management software

Stand-alone project management applications are programs that operate on your own computer or (in some instances) on a local network. They are generally commercial software and, if you are involved in team research, you will require multiple copies or a site license.

Web-based project management applications are accessed through a Web browser and to use the software you generally need to subscribe or register. There is often a fee associated with registration, although some applications provide free but limited trial use. Pricing is generally determined on the number of registered users. During project set-up you register the various users, allocate them access rights to the project and stipulate what actions they are or are not able to perform (for example, whether they can add tasks or vary completion dates). Web-based project management environments provide similar functionality to stand-alone applications, however they also often provide enhanced online communication e.g. via discussion boards and/or automatic e-mail notifications. Some also support document sharing i.e. the ability to check-in and check-out file versions, such that two people cannot accidentally make changes to the same document at the same time.

Web-based applications have the advantage of (generally) not requiring users to install additional software. However, users need to be online at all times during use. Web-based projects are generally hosted on the server of the company that produces the software or, alternatively, the software can be purchased and installed on your organization's server. While the former approach is easiest for the average researcher, the latter enables greater security of data and full control over backing up.

Points to consider when selecting project management software

- **The range of features you require.** Many applications are designed for use in business and contain advanced features less likely to be of value to the average researcher (e.g. invoicing and advanced finance management). The cost of such additional features may not necessarily bring corresponding benefits.
- **Your level of Internet access and whether you need to work offline.** This will be a consideration if you spend considerable time in the field or if your Internet connection is slow or unreliable.
- **Your level of collaboration with others**. Choose software that has features that may benefit that collaboration.
- **The range of "views" on the project data.** These might include Gantt chart formats (with varying levels of detail), PERT charts,[7] task sheets or resource allocation sheets. Some programs provide pre-setup forms for data entry.
- **Compatibility with other software.** Examples include calendar or diary systems, e-mail programs, spreadsheets or word processing programs.
- **Report and display formats.** Some information such as time usage or budgetary matters can be displayed as graphs or charts, which can assist the planning process. Schedules might also be productively displayed and/or printed as calendars.
- **Risk management, security and backing up.** This is particularly critical for Web-based applications where the data related to your project might reside on the computer of the manufacturing company. You need reassurance that your data is safe and secure.
- **PDA compatibility.** This can be useful if your research involves field work or traveling.
- **Also consult the general tips on selecting software in Chapter 2.**

Examples of project management software are listed in the software table at the end of the chapter. Note that Methodologist's Toolchest (mentioned earlier in this chapter) also provides Gantt chart functionality.

Budgets, grants and resource management

Unfortunately, the classic stereotype of the impoverished research student struggling to make ends meet without adequate funds to live, let alone do their research, is still a reality for the majority of PhD candidates. The notion of "resource management" may seem ludicrous if you don't have any resources to manage!

Financial issues, including those relating to your own personal budget and cash flow, can have a considerable impact on the successful completion of your research. Unless you are on a well-funded scholarship, you will have to weigh the need to seek paid work to survive and pay the bills against the consequent loss of time and focus on your research project. It becomes a stressful and difficult balancing act. In this section we not only suggest how you might manage the resources you do have, but also offer some tips on how to locate resources which you would like to have.

Beg, borrow ... but don't steal

Tips for making do with what you have.

- **Find out what your institution can/will and cannot/will not provide.** This includes hardware, software, grants, conference funding, access to printing and photocopying and so on. Knowing the right people to ask is the trick.
- **Make friends and discuss your research** with as many people as you can. Experienced researchers will often have equipment such as tape recorders, transcribers or field equipment that they are not currently using. Providing you look after it, they may be happy to lend it to you.
- **Team up with other postgraduate students** to make collaborative purchases and/or share resources and advice. Multiuser software licenses are an economical approach.
- **Make the most of freeware and shareware** software (see Chapter 2 and tips throughout this book).
- **Make the most of library resources**, rather than purchasing texts or taking out subscriptions to journals.
- **Consult the licensing arrangements on software.** A stand-alone license is generally for use on one computer at one time. If it is uninstalled from one computer it can sometimes (legally) be reinstalled on another. Again, this can be useful if a colleague has purchased software but isn't currently using it.
- **Use technology to reduce the need for travel.** Traveling for the purposes of networking or data collection can be a major expense. Synchronous and

(*Continued*)

asynchronous communication environments (discussed in Chapter 6) can greatly reduce project costs. Consider, for example, conducting interviews or focus groups online (see Chapter 10).

- **Involve your family.** Older children can perform all sorts of useful roles from photocopying, labeling, typing, scanning and entering data to transcribing and filing. It is a good way of involving them in what you are doing and they will no doubt appreciate some extra pocket money!

Locating funding sources

The Web can help locate sources of funding including scholarships and research grants, tenders, prizes and awards. While these are usually very competitive to win, and probably require a long-term vision, it is important to be aware of these potential sources of support.

- **Internal funding.** If your institution offers funds for research students, you will find their application forms and guidelines on their website.
- **National research funding.** Sometimes these are discipline specific while many countries' governments provide a central register of their funding schemes.
- **Professional organizations** often have funding aimed specifically at supporting developing researchers and their members.
- **Philanthropic organizations** can be good sources of potential funding. Some websites listing grants (or the more comprehensive databases) allow you to subscribe to regular e-mail announcements about funding opportunities in your area of interest.

Want to know more about...

How to locate funding?

The following websites provide information about funding sources. The list is indicative only. Try a Web search of your own for more specific requirements.

- The Foundation Centre (U.S.)   http://fdncenter.org
- Grants.gov (U.S. Federal)   http://www.grants.gov
- GrantsNet (biomedical   http://www.grantsnet.org
  research & science)
- International Scholarships   http://www.internationalscholarships.com

(Continued)

• National Endowment for the Humanities (US)	http://www.neh.gov
• British Academy (humanities & social sciences)	http://www.britac.ac.uk
• International Researcher & Exchanges (IREX)	http://www.irex.org
• Spencer Foundation (education)	http://www.spencer.org
• The Science Portal (Australian)	http://www.science.gov.au
• Arts and Humanities Research Council (UK)	http://www.ahrb.ac.uk
• American Philosophical Society (U.S.)	http://www.amphilsoc.org/grants
• Community of Science	http://www.cos.com
• Australian Research Council	http://www.arc.gov.au
• The Leverhulme Trust (UK)	http://www.leverhulme.org.uk
• American Educational Research Association	http://www.aera.net/grantsprogram
• International Education Research Foundation	http://www.ierf.org
• JASON (Australian Postgraduate Scholarships)	http://www.jason.unimelb.edu.au
• CIES (administers the U.S. Fulbright Scholar Program)	http://www.cies.org

Databases requiring subscription:
(Check with your institution's library for access to these.)

SPIN from InfoEd	http://australia.infoed.org/spin/spinmain.asp
Grantsearch	http://www.grantsearch.com
Grant$elect	http://209.61.189.163/gs/about.htm

Applying for grants

The art of writing grant applications (known as "grantsmanship" or "grantspersonship" in more politically correct circles) requires a range of skills and strategies in its own right. No matter how groundbreaking your proposed research, if you don't present your ideas appropriately, and target the appropriate funding body, you won't get funded. The following list provides some pointers for writing successful applications:

- **Weigh up your chances of success against the time and effort it takes to apply.** This is not meant to be a discouragement – you have to be in it to win it. However it is important to be realistic. There is no point applying to funding schemes which offer little chance of success. Make sure your project objectives match the scheme's aims. If possible, find out the average success rates, so you don't get your hopes up too high. Once you decide to go for it, be positive, focused and determined.

- **Seek opportunities for industry collaboration and co-funding.** Many research grants are easier to obtain if you can demonstrate that you have a contribution from industry or another organization. Having a research focus that attracts interest from business and industry, or that has some prospect for commercialization, is certainly an advantage.
- **Demonstrate that you are already very capable of conducting research.** Conducting a pilot study is generally a good move, and even better if you have that pilot written up and published before applying for the grant.
- **Attach yourself to an experienced researcher.** Perhaps the number one predictor of success with a research grant is prior success. Unfortunately this makes it hard for beginning researchers to be in the running. A good strategy, therefore, is to link up with an experienced researcher who has a good track record in winning research funding. Although they will put their name first on the application, or sometimes (for pragmatic reasons) be the only researcher named, you stand a better chance of being directly involved in a funded project that will contribute to your future success.
- **Make sure you have the most current application forms.** Guidelines and forms vary from year to year. Don't be caught out.
- **Be methodical when reading the funding guidelines** and follow them to the letter. Check and re-check that you have provided all the required information. If the structure of the application is flexible, then use the selection criteria as headings and address each in detail.
- **Sell yourself and your ideas.** Not everyone is good at this, but it is an important aspect of being a top researcher. A grant application is really a sales pitch. You need to convince the funding body that yours is the best proposal. Again, get advice from experienced researchers or your supervisors on how to do this.
- **Presentation is important.** Think of the assessors reading their 145th application. What makes yours stand out? Use an attention-grabbing title and clear, concise language, free from jargon. See Chapter 12 for tips on typography.
- **Stick to the word limit.** If it says five pages, only present five pages. While you may be able to use narrower margins or smaller font, keep it readable (again, see Chapter 12).
- **Aim to have your application completed well ahead of time** and ask for feedback from as many people as you can, particularly those experienced in grant writing. Knowing who is likely to be on the selection committee and what their particular interests are can be beneficial.
- **Make sure your proposal makes it there in time.** Don't leave submission too late as things have a way of going wrong at the last minute. Allow time for printing, collation and postage (if electronic submission isn't accepted). Obtain proof of dispatch and receipt, just to be sure.

- **If you aren't successful, don't be discouraged.** You've now done most of the hard work. Learn from the feedback, refine your application and apply again to the same scheme or another funding source.

Methodologist's Toolchest, mentioned earlier in this chapter, is a valuable tool to support the development of your grant application.

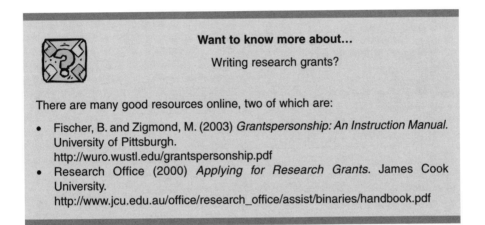

Want to know more about...

Writing research grants?

There are many good resources online, two of which are:

- Fischer, B. and Zigmond, M. (2003) *Grantspersonship: An Instruction Manual.* University of Pittsburgh.
  http://wuro.wustl.edu/grantspersonship.pdf
- Research Office (2000) *Applying for Research Grants.* James Cook University.
  http://www.jcu.edu.au/office/research_office/assist/binaries/handbook.pdf

Writing budgets

Writing a budget for a grant application can be quite an exercise. Most funding schemes require you to cost all your expenses, provide detailed justification for each expenditure and show how you arrived at your figures.

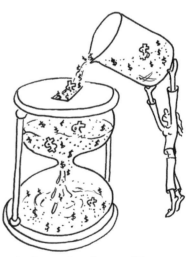

Calculating expenses

In writing grant applications you can rarely just list all the items you would like to operationalize your research. In most cases, the granting schedule will have a maximum amount available, requiring you to work backwards to determine what you can realistically expect for that amount of money. This becomes an iterative process as you continue to calculate what is possible. The larger the amount you apply for and the longer the period of time covered by the funding, the more complicated it becomes. Again, a spreadsheet can be an excellent tool for this process as it assists you to:

- automatically calculate totals using functions;
- play with various funding scenarios;

- make adjustments to salary rates (for instance to account for rising annual costs) through the use of "lookup tables" – it's best to create duplicates of the sheet you are working on;
- iteratively add or remove items to increase or decrease expenditure until you arrive at the appropriate total budget cost. Again, functions will automatically show current totals.

Figure 5.6 provides an example of how such a spreadsheet might look.

	A	B	C	D	E	F	G
1	YEAR 1 - SCENARIO 1 USING SALARY RATES						
2	Source of funds	Quantity	Base rates	Granting Body	In Kind Contribution	Total	
3	PERSONNEL (including on costs)						
4	Researcher	0.5	see B26		$ 31,473.12		
5	Admin.Assistant	0.2	see B28	$ 8,142.40			Function in cell D5 reads: =B5*B28*B25
6	Research Assistant	0.5	see B31	$ 29,417.92			
7	EQUIPMENT						
8	Laptop computer	1	2640	$ 2,640.00			
9	Video Camera	1		$ 3,000.00			
10	Digital Tape recorders	4	100	$ 400.00			
11	MAINTENANCE						
12	Data Analysis Software			$ 300.00			
13	Incidentals			$ 300.00	$ 2,000.00		
14	Stationary				$ 500.00		
15	Copying				$ 1,000.00		
16	Mobile phone			$500			
17	Phone costs				$ 200.00		Function in cell D19 reads: =B19*C19*B31
18	TRAVEL	no. of trips	kms				
19	Visits to location 1	3	250	$ 390.00			
20	Visits to location 2	5	140	$ 364.00			
21							
22	TOTAL DIRECT COSTS			$ 46,454.32	$ 35,173.12	$80,627.44	
23							
24	LOOKUP TABLES		Notes				Function in cell D22 reads: =SUM(D4:D20)
25	Oncost Multiplyer	1.12					
26	Researcher Salary Rate	$ 56,202.00	Level B, Year 3				
27	Admin Assistant Hourly Rate	$ 18.54	HEW3, Year 1				
28	Admin Assistant Salary Rate	$ 36,350.00	HEW3, Year 1				
29	Research Assistant Hourly R	$ 26.54	HEW5, Year 1				
30	Research Assistant Salary R	$ 52,532.00	HEW5, Year 1				
31	Kilometer rate	0.52	Based on 1600cc engine capacity				
32							

Figure 5.6   Example of a budget calculated using a spreadsheet program

Note: The use of lookup tables and functions allow for easy recalculation based on different scenarios. For instance, to calculate Year 2 salaries, the sheet could be duplicated and the ranges in cells B26, B28 and B30 adjusted for the annual increment. If an hourly rate is used instead, then the functions can be adjusted to record number of hours in cells B4, B5 and B6. In this case the function in cell D5 for example would read = B5*B27*B25. Example is from Microsoft Excel.

Justifying and explaining expenditure calculations

Justifying the amounts you think you will need to spend on salaries, travel, equipment etc. involves being quite detailed about your research methodology. If, from our example, you have asked for a research assistant half-time at $29,417, it is not sufficient to say "this is the award rate with on-costs." Rather, you must justify why you need a research assistant; why they need to be paid at this level; and why you need them half-time. Your justification might look like this:

I anticipate conducting 50 interviews, each of 1 hour duration. Each interview will require at least 1 hour in preparation (locating relevant interviewees, seeking initial informed consent, organizing appointments). Each interview will then require 2 hours follow-up time, which includes recording researcher notes and checking transcription. Coding of transcribed interviews using qualitative data analysis software will take approx. 4 hours per interview. Hence each interview will require 8 hours of research assistant time. Total time for interviews $=50 \times 8 = 400$ hours. Analysis of coded data will take a further estimated 200 hours [so on]. Preparation of data for paper writing will require another 150 hours [… and so on]. A Research Assistant, Level 1 appointment is required because conducting the interviews necessitates a high level of interviewing skills, content knowledge and professionalism. Furthermore, the research assistant will need to be familiar with qualitative data analysis software and have appropriate writing skills to prepare the data for the initial draft of the journal paper [and so on…].

Monitoring expenditure

If you are successful in your grant application, careful monitoring of your expenditure becomes an essential part of the research process. While income and expenditure will (in most cases) still be monitored by your institution, self-monitoring allows you to reconcile and confirm your calculations against their records.

The simplest way of monitoring your expenditure is again through the use of a spreadsheet with an income and expenditure column and some basic calculation functions to tally residual amounts (see Chapter 2). It is useful to include a notes column for comments on details as well as a checklist column that you might use to confirm that%each of your entries corresponds with centrally maintained records, as illustrated in Figure 5.7.

	A	B	C	D	E	F	G	H
1	Date	Item	Calculation Notes	Income	Expenditure	Running Total	Check	Notes
2	24-April-2006	Initial Grant		$ 14,000.00		$ 14,000.00	YES	
3	30-April-2006	Research Assistant	25hrs @ $20.50 +12%		$ 574.00	$ 13,426.00	YES	
4	16-May-2006	Biblio Software			$ 250.00	$ 13,176.00		
5	29-May-2006	Travel	250km at 52c/km		$ 130.00	$ 13,046.00		Reclaim car costs
6	30-May-2006	Accommodation			$ 200.00	$ 12,846.00		Sleepy Inn - Chicago
7						$ 12,846.00		
8						$ 12,846.00		
9						$ 12,846.00		

Function in cell E3 reads:
=25*20.5*1.12

Function in cell E5 reads:
=250*0.52

Function in cell F3 reads:
=F2+D3-E3 and is filled to cells below

Figure 5.7   Example of a simple budget managed using a spreadsheet

Running totals are automatically calculated using functions. Note also the use of specific columns to record notes or to cross reference with other finance systems. Example is from Microsoft Excel.

See the **Organizing and Managing Your Research Website**

for templates for calculating budgets and monitoring using expenditure using Excel and other spreadsheet programs.

http://www.sagepub.co.uk/phelps

There are also software products designed to manage personal budgets and expenditure that can be adapted for research purposes. As mentioned earlier, managing your own (probably limited) finances may be just as critical to your research success as getting a grant. Examples are provided below.

Record keeping

No matter what the size of your project, it may be worth giving some thought to keeping a formal set of records that document the various stages of the project. These records can include everything from your initial proposal, ethics application and approvals, to key correspondence and reports. In large projects, where there is a turnover of research staff, this is vital. It may be that your institution or organization has formal requirements that relate to accountability or auditing. A formal set of records for any project also provides a historical account of the work for future researchers to consult. In some organizations there may be a requirement for these records to be centrally archived.

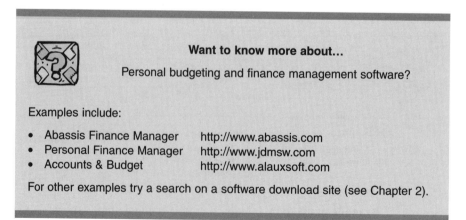

Want to know more about...

Personal budgeting and finance management software?

Examples include:

- Abassis Finance Manager   http://www.abassis.com
- Personal Finance Manager   http://www.jdmsw.com
- Accounts & Budget   http://www.alauxsoft.com

For other examples try a search on a software download site (see Chapter 2).

Over to you...

1. What are the most significant tasks you need to achieve over the life of your research project? Try converting these tasks into clear milestones with a date attached to each one.
2. What are the major mid-term milestones you need to complete in the next 6 months? Have a go at documenting your long- and mid-term milestones in a simple Gantt chart.
3. How would your project benefit from using project management software?
4. To what extent would your project benefit from further funding? Would it be worth the effort of applying?
5. What could be useful for you in setting up a personal and/or research budget management process?

Notes

1   For example, Rudestam and Newton 2001; Roberts 2004; Leedy 2005.
2   While we acknowledge that this may, in future, be one example among a range of similar products, we do not wish to imply that we are promoting it above or beyond any similar software.
3   Methodologist's Toolchest is produced by Idea Works, Inc. (http://www.idea-works.com)
4   A Gantt chart is a horizontal bar chart which shows tasks plotted along a timescale, and indicates start and finish dates. It was named after Henry L. Gantt, an American engineer and social scientist, who used the approach during World War One.
5   The database was developed from an initial concept by Alistair Campbell and Joe Luca of Edith Cowan University.
6   Critical Path Method (CPM) was developed by DuPont and Remington Rand in the 1950s.
7   A PERT chart is a flowchart format similar to that produced by visualization software, discussed in Chapter 3.

Examples of project management software

Software	Manufacturer/ developer	Platform	Website	Licensing	Demo on Website?	Notable Features
@task	At Task	Web-based	http://www.attask.com	Commercial	✓	Includes calendar, finance management, mail, timesheet and reporting. Ability to customise access rights
Ace Project	Websystems	Web-based	http://www.aceproject.com	Commercial (5 projects, 5 users for free)	✓	Manages multiple projects with Gantt charts, calendar, time sheet tracking, statistics, e-mail, discussion forums and document sharing
BPS Project	Business Propulsion Systems	Web-based	http://www.bpsproject.com	Commercial	✗	Integrated project planning, tracking and task management. Document sharing and online communication. Regulatory compliance, internal audit and operational risk functions
Faces	Reithinger GmbH	Windows and Linux	http://faces.homeip.net	Free (Open source)	✓	Promoted as the "Swiss Army Knife for Project Managers". Use as is or customize (uses python programming language)
FastTrack Schedule	AEC Software	Windows, Mac	http://www.aecsoft.com	Commercial	✓	Includes a range of templates and visual output formats. Exchanges data with Microsoft Project, Outlook and iCalendar
GanttPV	Brian C. Christensen	Windows, Mac and Linux	http://www.pureviolet.net/ganttpv	Free (Open Source)	✓	Defines tasks, task durations, dependencies and start dates to create Gantt charts. Use as is or customize (uses python programming language)

Software	Manufacturer/ developer	Platform	Website	Licensing	Demo on Website?	Notable Features
iTeamwork	iTeamwork	Web-based	http://www.iteamwork.com	Free	✓	E-mail notification of completed, outstanding and upcoming tasks. Pay to host multiuser projects
Microsoft Project	Microsoft	Windows, Mac	http://www.microsoft.com/office/project	Commercial	✓	Integrates with other Microsoft Office programs. Help files, user groups and support publications available
Mind Manager	Mindjet. I and A Research	Windows	http://www.mindjet.com	Commercial	✓	Brainstorming and visual thinking software with project management features including Gantt chart module. Produces a meeting agenda with hyperlinked documents. Standard and Professional versions, plus a reader
MJI Team Works	MJI Web Consulting	Web-based	http://www.mjiteamworks.com	Commercial	✗	Browser-based software solution for team collaboration and management of multiple projects. Includes resources and document management, incident management, timesheet management and cost control
Project Desk	Deskshare	Web-based	http://www.projectdesk.net	Commercial (4 users free)	✓	Online timesheet. Maintains a log of time spent on each task. File sharing, discussion board and e-mail alerts. Subscribe for more extensive projects

(Continued)

Software	Manufacturer/developer	Platform	Website	Licensing	Demo on Website?	Notable Features
Project Insight	Metafuse	Web-based	http://www.projectinsight.net	Commercial	✓	Time, expense and invoicing capabilities and reporting on resources across projects. Ability to re-use elements across different projects through copy and paste
Projistics	Projistics.com	Web-based	http://www.projistics.com	Commercial	✓	Includes project planning and scheduling, Gantt charts, resource management, time tracking and timesheets, collaboration tools, issue tracking and reporting features
Project.net	Project.net	Web-based	http://www.project.net	Commercial	✓	Includes document management, communication and tracking databases. Provides a range of templates or save your own projects as templates for later reuse
Projux	Projux Online	Web-based	http://www.projux.com	Commercial	✓	Manages time, expenses, invoices and collaboration on projects
ProjectPerfect	ProjectPerfect	Windows	http://www.projectperfect.com.au	Commercial	✓	Logs issues, risks and action items. Manages budget and expenditure and diary notes. Links to Microsoft Project. Requires users to have Microsoft Access installed
RIQ Tek Manager	RIQ Tek		http://www.riqtek.com	Commercial	✓	Provides visualization (mapping) of workflows through a Web interface. Generates notifications through e-mail

(*Continued*)

Software	Manufacturer/ developer	Platform	Website	Licensing	Demo on Website?	Notable Features
Taskland	Taskland.com	Web-based	http://www.taskland.com	Commercial	✓	Provides an interactive Gantt Chart. Synchronization with Microsoft Project and website integration
TrackerOffice	Automation Centre	Windows or Mac	http://www.trackeroffice.com	Commercial	DVD by mail	Extends Microsoft Outlook to include project scheduling, status reports, employee files, task assignment, expense reports, time cards and purchase orders. Requires a Microsoft Exchange server which many organizations will already have in place
TurboProject	IMSI	Windows	http://www.turboproject.com	Commercial	✗	Has three versions (Pro, Standard and Express) providing differing degrees of complexity. Varying price structure
VIP Team To Do List	VIP Quality Software	Windows	http://www.vip-qualitysoft.com	Commercial	✓	Creates, manages and sends to-do lists to team members by e-mail to plan and track progress of team tasks. Three versions available

Chapter 6

Communicating and Networking Electronically

Networking cannot substitute for effective research, and effective research cannot substitute for networking. Interaction with the broader research community is vital in developing both good research practices and your national or international profile as a researcher. While there is nothing like meeting with colleagues and fellow researchers face-to-face, an ever-increasing range of technologies can provide you with unprecedented opportunities for communication and networking from your office, your home or while you are on the move. Such technologies can provide an all important means of research training and for closer engagement in the broader research community.[1] Furthermore, they can provide you with the opportunity to establish and maintain communications and professional relationships with international subject experts, to keep up-to-date with developments in your field and to take advantage of opportunities such as online conferences. In our experience, however, new researchers often don't make the most of such opportunities.

In this chapter we consider some of the technologies that can be used to support communication and networking between researchers, including:

- Web-based resources that facilitate involvement in face-to-face and online conferences;
- the essential tool of e-mail;
- other forms of asynchronous communication, including mailing lists, discussion boards, blogs, wikis and podcasting;
- synchronous forms of communication, including both text and audio chat, video conferencing and Internet telephony;
- translation resources;
- establishing your presence on the Web.

Using the Web for professional networking

Tools such as e-mail, discussion boards, blogs, podcasts, chat and video conferencing can facilitate interaction not only between you and your supervisor, but also between you and other research students, between you and your research participants and between you and experienced researchers, no matter where they are located.

Of course the rich and often subtle environment of face-to-face communication at conferences, seminars and workshops (not to mention the tearoom or faculty corridor) cannot as yet be duplicated electronically. Those often unplanned discussions and digressions, which in hindsight can prove critical in solving a thorny problem or answering that perplexing question, often occur over a beer or a glass of red wine. While technology doesn't (yet) provide any substitute for these experiences, it can assist you to promote, locate and organize such events. And serendipity does happen in cyberspace as well.

The Web provides a range of very specific ways to support professional networking, allowing you to:

- **select appropriate postgraduate programs** and relevant supervisors using university websites;
- **contact other researchers** working in your area by locating researchers' personal/professional websites, which provide their contact details, current information about their research, publications and professional affiliations;
- **locate information about upcoming conferences**, including calls for papers, registration details and conference bookings;
- **organize, facilitate or join online conferences**, workshops and other gatherings such as "webcasts";
- **identify people who conduct research in your area** through databases of "research in progress," dissertations and theses (see Chapter 7).

Want to know more about...

Using the Web for professional networking?

National and international listings of experts:

- GENIUS   http://infoed.is.mcgill.ca
- Experts.com   http://www.experts.com
- Profnet   http://www2.profnet.com/enter
- Mind   http://www.lib.monash.edu.au/databases/1709042.html

(*Continued*)

Locating e-mail addresses or phone numbers

- The Global Yellow-Pages   http://www.globalyp.com
                             (Phone directories from around the globe)
- IAF (U.S.)   http://www.iaf.net
- WhoWhere (U.S.)   http://www.whowhere.com
- Europe on the Internet   http://people.yahoo.com
- IDEA (European Union)   http://europa.eu.int/idea

Other ways in which the Web can act to facilitate professional networking and communications

- NetText (send messages from the
  Web to mobile phones via SMS)   http://www.netspot.com.au/nettext.htm
- Faxaway (deliver e-mail or Web
  information to fax)   http://www.faxaway.com
- Webcasts (definitions and further
  information from Wikipedia)   http://en.wikipedia.org/wiki/Webcast

Organization of conferences

Open Conference Systems (OCS) (http://pkp.sfu.ca/ocs) is a free Web publishing tool that facilitates organization of conferences. It includes features for creating a conference website, sending a call for papers, managing submissions and the reviewing process, registering participants, posting proceedings to a website in a searchable format and enabling post-conference online discussion. OCS has been developed by the Public Knowledge Project at the University of British Columbia.

Asynchronous communication

Asynchronous communication refers to communication that does not occur at the same time, i.e. where one person leaves a message for others to read, hear or view at a later time. In this section we consider a number of specific asynchronous communication tools and their use in research: e-mail; mailing lists and discussion boards; blogs and wikis; and podcasts. We devote some length to our discussion of e-mail as, in our experience, most researchers do not take full advantage of the potential their e-mail program has to offer.

E-mail

E-mail is one of the most effective ways for researchers to communicate. It is, however, quite clear that some use it more efficiently and effectively than others. We all know people who have literally hundreds of messages in their in-box, and thus can miss following up on, or replying to, important communication; they may miss valuable workshops and seminars or simply not reply to people within a professional and courteous timeframe.

In this section we assume that you are familiar with at least the basic functions of e-mail and that you will already have an e-mail account. Like most users, you may not have considered the strengths and weaknesses of your e-mail system or have fully explored its features. In this section we consider a range of ways in which e-mail can be used to support research and address the omnipresent and increasingly critical issue of managing e-mails efficiently.

How can e-mail support your research?

The efficient use of e-mail can benefit your research by:

- **facilitating communication** between you, other researchers and/or your supervisor, including negotiating meeting times, forwarding agendas, exchanging document drafts and providing updates on progress;
- **assisting you to be part of the research community** within your institution, alerting you to seminars, training sessions, functions and administrative aspects of your candidature;
- **enabling you to contact other researchers** in your discipline, locally, nationally or internationally;
- **providing a vehicle for you to subscribe** to journal alerts or table of contents services (see Chapter 7);
- **allowing you to join mailing lists** which publicize or disseminate information relevant to your research topic, or which you can use to promote your own research;
- **providing a means of organizing interviews** or collecting data (see Chapter 10);
- **facilitating the writing of joint papers** with writers located anywhere in the world.

Feature Researcher: Using E-mail for Effective Supervision

Anne Graham, Southern Cross University, Australia

Anne is a very busy academic who is both a Head of School and a Director of a research centre – the Centre for Children and Young People. Anne supervises many research students and needs to be both efficient and effective with her time. She employs a strategy whereby students must e-mail her an agenda of issues they wish to discuss 24 hours before their fortnightly or monthly meeting. After each supervisory session, students send a follow-up e-mail to Anne with a summary and reflection on what they gained from the session including tasks to be completed or progressed before the next meeting. The benefits include:

- enhancing effectiveness of the student/supervisor partnership by providing continuity, routine and discipline;

(Continued)

- offering a structure for meetings, and enabling both student and supervisor to be prepared to discuss particular issues;
- providing an ongoing record of discussions, achievements and agreed outcomes;
- ensuring every student takes responsibility to identify and prioritize their research goals and tasks and feels well supported in achieving these.

Deciding which e-mail program to use

There are two types of e-mail systems, each with strengths and weaknesses, depending on your particular context.

- **Server-based e-mail** is accessed using client software installed on your own computer and configured according to e-mail account details provided by your ISP (Internet Service Provider). When using server-based e-mail your messages are stored on your ISP's server and the software downloads the messages to your computer when you go online. You can write and store messages on your own computer while offline and log on again when you are ready to send a batch of queued messages. Sending and receiving messages is straightforward when accessing the Internet through your own ISP account. However, when traveling with a laptop, you may find yourself needing to gain Internet access through a different ISP. Your institution may be able to set up a VPN (Virtual Private Network) or your ISP may provide global roaming (the ability to use your ISP account to access other local networks worldwide). You should check with your institution and your ISP regarding the services available to you.
- **Web-based e-mail** is accessed using your Web browser. Popular and free examples include Hotmail, Yahoo Mail or MailMate. You do not need to have an account with an ISP but can set up an e-mail account from any computer with Web access. Your account is generally established immediately. Writing and reading of e-mails must occur when you are online. While many of these e-mail systems are "free," there are inevitably issues with their use, such as unsolicited junk mail or spam.

Some ISPs allow e-mail accounts to be accessed using either system and there are also ways of accessing server-based e-mail from websites using services such as Mail2Web (https://mail2web.com).

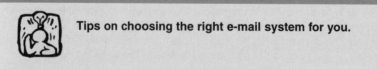 **Tips on choosing the right e-mail system for you.**

Server-based e-mail may be appropriate if you:

- already have an account with an ISP;
- want your e-mail address to be associated with your university or employing organization;

(Continued)

- are likely to stay with the same organization or ISP for a significant period of time;
- *do not* have reliable and fast Internet access;
- are traveling with a laptop or palmtop and wish to be able to work while off-line (e.g. in airport lounges and planes);
- want to minimize the risk of exposure to junk mail and spam.

Web-based e-mail may be appropriate if you:

- do not have an account with an ISP;
- want to set up an e-mail account immediately;
- want a second e-mail address for a specific purpose (such as survey responses);
- want to protect your main server-based address from spam, for example, when registering for software (see section on spam below);
- find yourself using multiple computers;
- are traveling without a laptop or palmtop;
- are likely to change ISPs or employment contexts regularly and want to maintain a stable e-mail address.

If you do choose to change e-mail systems, many programs will allow you to export your previously received messages from one program and import them into another.

Exploring the features of your e-mail program
Consider the relevance of these features for supporting your research:

- **Cc and bcc.** "Cc" means carbon copy, so if you send a message to person X and cc the message to Person Y, Person X will know that Person Y also received it, as Y's address will appear on the incoming message to X. "Bcc" means blind carbon copy. If you send a message to person X and bcc the message to Person Y, Person X will *not* know that Person Y also received it as Y's address doesn't appear on X's message. You might, for instance, consider sending a bcc to your support group when e-mailing your supervisor about an issue you have discussed in the group.
- **Attachments.** It is important to be aware of the hazards associated with sending and receiving documents as attachments to e-mails. Wise people do not open e-mail attachments unless they are confident that they know what they contain (see Chapter 4 on malicious software). Make this clear when sending attachments yourself. Also be aware of the size of the files (see Chapter 2 in relation to file compression and checking file size).

- **Address book**. This simple database contained within most e-mail programs is used to record information about individuals or groups of people (see Chapter 2 on databases). Once an address book entry is set up you no longer need to remember their full e-mail address(es). For example, instead of typing in peter.papperdopolous@e-mail.com.au, you can simply type in "peter." If you regularly e-mail a group of research colleagues or participants you can also create an address book entry which includes all their addresses. For example typing in "FGroup" might e-mail all participants in your focus group.
- **Mailboxes**. These folders within your e-mail program enable you to sort and file messages into categories with descriptive names. Most programs allow you to create folders within folders (as in Figure 6.1). See Chapter 4 in relation to using a filing schema.

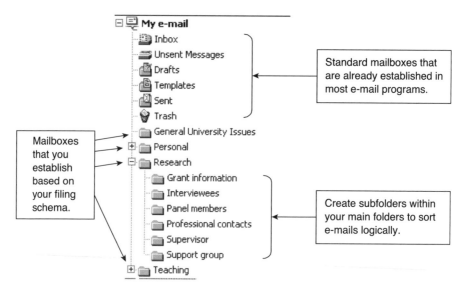

Figure 6.1 **Mailboxes created to correspond with your filing schema**

Note the use of mailboxes within mailboxes to enable filing within subsections (e.g. grant information is a subsection of research). Example is from Mozilla.

- **Find function**. This enables you to search through all your e-mails, based on particular criteria. For instance, you might remember receiving an e-mail about an upcoming conference in Hawaii. Doing a search on "conference" and "Hawaii" should locate it.
- **Signatures**. A signature is a brief message that is automatically added to the end of your outgoing messages. It would usually consist of a few

lines giving your name, contact details and your website address, if you have one. Some programs allow you to have more than one signature (e.g. an official signature and a less formal one) and to select the appropriate signature for each e-mail you send, with one set as the default. It is good practice to exclude the signature when doing routine e-mailing to colleagues as this keeps your messages to a minimum length.

- **Filters.** These automatically transfer e-mails that fulfill particular criteria directly to a specified mailbox on arrival. For example, if you are on a mailing list you might transfer all e-mails from that list to a special mailbox or you may want to send regularly received spam directly to the trash. Setting up these filters is essentially a process of defining logical parameters, as illustrated in Figure 6.2, but take care or you may find yourself missing important communications. Programs such as Hotmail and Outlook enable you to block or filter all messages from a particular sender with a simple click of a button.

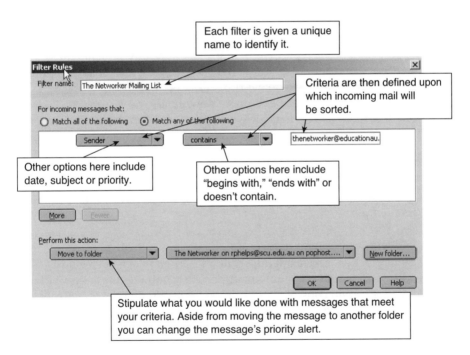

Figure 6.2   Setting up filters in an e-mail program

In this example all incoming messages which are from the Sender thenetworker@ educationau.edu.au are moved to a folder called The Networker Mailing List. Example is from Netscape Messenger.

- **Templates (or Stationery).** Many e-mail programs allow you to save a generic e-mail wording in a format which is easily retrieved, perhaps modified and then sent. This is particularly useful in research where you are using a standard wording to make contact with potential interviewees, follow-up with conference attendees, or to send a thank you message to individuals who have sent you resources (see also Mail Merge function in Chapter 12).
- **Auto-reply function** (also known as holiday/vacation messages). Many ISPs enable you to have an automatic response forwarded to anyone who e-mails you. This might, for instance, state that you are on leave, but will pick up e-mails on your return. Alternatively, you may decide to stop e-mails reaching you, and have the auto-reply tell the sender to resend their message (if important) to a different person or after a certain date. You can either contact your ISP for their assistance or set this up yourself if your system allows.
- **Options or preferences.** This area enables you to customize other features of your program, such as to:

  - change the folder where your attachments are stored;
  - ensure that when you delete an e-mail that any attachment is also deleted (important in minimizing storage space and ensuring potential virus risks are also deleted);
  - set how often you want e-mails to download;
  - (with server-based e-mail) leave the messages on the server for a set number of days so that they can be accessed again from another computer;
  - use a particular stationery as default;
  - prevent attachments over a set file size downloading until you specifically request them, which is very useful if you have limited Internet access time or slow line speeds.

Managing and controlling e-mail

As many researchers and academics will attest, e-mail can very readily take over your working and personal life. A goal that you need to keep working toward is to maintain control over your e-mail rather than let it control you. The following tips offer some useful strategies.

    Tips on managing your e-mails.

- **Manage your in-box.** Having 400 e-mails in your in-box can not only make you feel overwhelmed, but can also result in you overlooking important messages.

(*Continued*)

- **Use mailboxes** and use them well.
- **Try never to deal with an e-mail more than once.** When you read an e-mail decide there and then whether to delete it, file it or respond to it. Only if it is *really* necessary, leave it in your in-box, which can then work as a "to-do" list.
- **Avoid checking your e-mail at your best working time.** If you are freshest working in the morning, don't check your e-mails until after you've made good progress.
- **Don't let e-mail distract you.** Turn off sound alerts or automatic jumps to your e-mail program in preferences/options. Consider downloading your messages every 2–3 hours or longer so you can get on with other work in between times.
- **Decide if you really need to check e-mails every day.** There will be times when you should avoid e-mail all together, such as when you are focusing on data analysis or writing up.
- **Use auto-reply messages strategically.** As well as using these when you are on leave, consider such messages when you want to keep your head down without e-mail interruption for a longer period of time so you don't feel pressured to respond.
- **Skim read contents alerts** or mailing list contributions and copy and paste anything of relevance into a location you can return to at a convenient time. A notes program (see Chapter 3) can be useful for this.
- **Learn how to avoid spam**.

Controlling spam

Spam (a term derived from a famous Monty Python skit) is unsolicited e-mail, mostly containing illegitimate or unwanted content matter such as advertising, financial services or schemes, gambling, free holiday offers or pornography. Spam can be received from unknown or known sources (e.g. registration at conferences, vendors, product and other known companies). While there is no single strategy that prevents the proliferation of spam, try the following:

- **DO NOT reply to spam** and do not follow any directions to "unsubscribe" as this will frequently confirm your e-mail as valid and you will receive even more.
- **DO NOT click on website links** contained within unsolicited e-mails as this can register you for further spam or download a virus (see Chapter 4).
- **Use a temporary free Web-based e-mail account** when you register products or sign up for chat or other services.
- **Find out what your institution's policy is on filtering spam**, and be aware that in some instances it can mean that personal e-mails from some domains or containing some content (such as advertising) cannot reach you.

Mailing lists and discussion boards

Mailing lists (sometimes called "listservs") consist of e-mail addresses of people interested in the same subject. A group of people subscribe and then receive copies of all the messages sent to that particular list. A discussion board is like a mailing list, however, rather than messages being delivered via your e-mail address, they are displayed on a webpage.[2]

Mailing lists and discussion boards can involve as few as two people or as many as thousands. Some are announcement lists (one-way), where you receive messages but don't post any yourself (e.g. electronic magazine subscriptions or updates on professional news). Others are discussion lists (two-way), where everyone on the list can join the online conversation. Some mailing lists are "moderated," i.e. they have someone in charge who decides which material will be accepted and sometimes who can and can't join. Some mailing lists are of quite high academic or professional quality, while others are more informal.

Subscribing involves either sending an e-mail or filling out a form on a webpage. It only takes a few seconds and generally involves no inconvenience to anyone as mailing lists are managed automatically by computer programs. The main issue with joining mailing lists is that you might end up receiving a lot of messages which may or may not be useful. It is worth joining a reputable list just to see what sort of things are discussed. If you don't like it, you can follow the directions to unsubscribe.

How can mailing lists and discussion boards support your research?

- Given the huge range of groups available it is quite likely that there will be at least one focused on your general (and perhaps very specific) area of research which may well provide extremely relevant and current information.
- Don't just seek out groups focused on your content area. Some groups discuss methodology, specific research software, or act as postgraduate support networks.
- Mailing lists and discussion boards are not only a way of sharing your specific research interests, ideas and experiences or asking questions. They can also help you to become known in your field.
- Mailing lists are quite straightforward to establish and manage and if you can't identify one in your own area, consider initiating such a group. This is usually done using software such as Mailman (http://www.gnu.org/software/mailman) run from a server, so talk to your IT Department.
- Some mailing lists serve as current contents alerts, announcing new issues of journals and providing tables of contents, abstracts, and sometimes links to the full text of articles (see Chapter 7).

Want to know more about...

Locating mailing lists and discussion groups?

Try the following sites:

- CataList   http://www.lsoft.com/lists/listref.html
- Ozlists   http://www.gu.edu.au/ozlists
- Tile.net   http://tile.net/lists

To locate very specific groups, try a Web search similar to the following examples:

phytochemistry + discussion	OR	"action research" + discussion
phytochemistry + list	OR	"action research" + list
phytochemistry + group	OR	"action research" + group

Blogs and wikis

Blogs (derived from the term Web logs) are like journals or diaries that are maintained online and are publicly available. They usually are recorded by a single author and often take a "stream-of-consciousness" form of writing (or speech, in the case of audio blogs). However, they can allow readers to contribute, reply, or respond to issues raised, much like an online "guestbook." During the Iraq war, blogs became a way of individuals disseminating timely, personal views and perspectives as well as information that the regular media was not able to reach or willing to publish. In this way they can be seen as a powerful tool for supporting freedom of speech at a time when press freedoms are under threat. There are millions of blogs now available, their popularity probably due to the fact that creating and participating in one is free and easy to do.

A wiki (from the Hawaiian meaning "quick") is a piece of server software that allows a community of users to freely create and edit webpage content using a Web browser. The structure of a wiki is different from most communications options in that it allows "open editing," that is, both the content and the organization of the contributions can be edited by anyone (or almost anyone). This creates opportunities for collaboration as well as raising issues of trust and validity. The best known wiki site on the Web is Wikipedia, a free encyclopedia created by a whole community of contributors and is a site that is continually evolving. This is a superb example of the potentially high quality of information that is possible to build up through a wiki community.[3]

In summary, blogs are designed for individual use, while wikis are designed for collective use.

How can blogs and wikis support your research?
They could be:

- a source of information which reflects public or community perspectives;
- an opportunity for publicly documenting or disseminating your research;

- a way of keeping a research journal and sharing your reflections with others;
- a means of communicating across your research team;
- a way of updating participants on your research activities;
- a technique for gathering data from participants (in some contexts).

Want to know more about...

Blogs and wikis?

To learn more about blogs consult:

- How blogs work   http://computer.howstuffworks.com/blog.htm
- Weblogs compendium   http://www.lights.com/weblogs
- To create your own blog   http://www.blogger.com

To learn more about wikis consult:

- WikiWikiWeb   http://c2.com/cgi/wiki?WelcomeVisitors
- Wikipedia   http://en.wikipedia.org/wiki/Wiki
- Set up a wiki (JotSpot)   http://www.jot.com

Podcasts

Audio podcasting is a technique for providing access over the Internet to audio broadcasts, allowing you to download the sound files and listen to the broadcast at your leisure. As the sound files are typically in MP3 format, they are relatively small and easy to transfer to an MP3 player or iPod. You can download files selectively and individually, or you can install software that will automatically download any new podcasts provided on a certain site or on a certain topic (these use RSS Feed technology, as outlined in Chapter 8). Many radio stations are beginning to provide access to their programs in podcast format. Video podcasting involves preparing (essentially compressing) and sharing short video files in the same way as audio files are shared.

How can podcasting support your research?

- It can provide access to very current information, particularly that discussed in the media.
- Sound files can be listened to repeatedly, facilitating more thorough analysis. Some research that deconstructs media discussion, for example, may find this very convenient.
- Podcasting is relatively easy to do yourself. Essentially it involves recording an audio file electronically, converting it to MP3 format and making it available on a website. Researchers may (in some contexts) find it useful to distribute information in this format.

- If you or your colleagues do any media releases or interviews yourselves (see Chapter 13), you can keep a copy of the broadcast for future reference.

Want to know more about...

Podcasting?

Audio podcasting

- e-Learning Centre (U.K.)   http://www.e-learningcentre.co.uk/eclipse/Resources/podcasting.htm
- PodCasting News   http://www.podcastingnews.com
- ABC Radio National (Australia)   http://abc.net.au/rn/podcast
- iPodder.org   http://www.ipodder.org/directory/4/ipodderSoftware

Video podcasting

- Apple tutorials   http://www.apple.com/quicktime/tutorials (on using Quicktime on both Mac and Windows)
- Screencasting   http://digitalmedia.oreilly.com/2005/11/16/what-is-screencasting.html

---

Synchronous communication

Synchronous electronic communication is communication that occurs simultaneously; in other words, the people communicating need to be online at the same time. In this section we consider three forms of synchronous communication that have the potential to support research: text and voice-based chat; videoconferencing; and Internet telephony (VoIP).[4]

Text and voice-based chat

"Chat" refers to one type of synchronous communication between two or more users via networked computers. People access chat using either their Web browser (with an additional plug-in, such as for Yahoo chat) or a dedicated chat client program (such as for MSN or ICQ). The most common type of chat is text-based which means that, once a chat has been initiated, participants enter text by typing on their keyboard. Once they click submit (or hit "enter"), the text will appear on other participants' monitors almost immediately. Voice-based chat enables participants with personal microphones (usually part of a

headset) to speak, rather than type, and have other participants hear and reply. Chat rooms can be either open (anyone can join) or closed (only those invited in can participate). In either case, participants might be drawn from all over the world to participate and collaborate in the virtual environment.

Some chat software provides additional features such as:

- **interactive whiteboards**, where participants can collaboratively write, draw and display work on websites, open to all participants to view;
- **document and application sharing,** whereby one participant can open up access to their computer such that others in the chat room can view or interact with their programs or documents;
- **the ability to control who can or can't speak at any time**, for instance, participants may be required to electronically "put their hand up" to indicate they would like to say something and the moderator allocates turns;
- **polls, surveys or quizzes,** some of which provide instant feedback about the results.

How can text and voice-based chat support your research?

- Chat has the same potential as many of the forms of asynchronous communication, however it allows for more immediacy in the interaction.

While the telephone rivals voice chat in some contexts, it is much easier and cheaper to facilitate whole group, long-distance discussions using chat.

- Chat environments can be used for data collection, including for conducting interviews or focus groups. Polls and survey features can facilitate quantitative data collection. Often chat sessions can be recorded for future reference and analysis.
- Chat can support two or more authors to work on a document simultaneously and collaboratively. This could be useful, for instance, if a supervisor wanted to provide feedback on a thesis draft while geographically separated from their student.
- Application sharing can be a great way of gaining training, support or problem solving with software.
- Most (but not all) synchronous communication environments enable sessions to be saved and archived. Again this can assist when used for data collection. It also means that presentations or discussions can be revisited after the event.

Feature Software: Elluminate Live!

http://www.elluminate.com

Elluminate Live! (formerly vClass) provides an example of a real-time online classroom environment involving high quality voice reproduction and video, as well as a shared whiteboard and application sharing. It uses its own proprietary Collaborative Communications Framework (CCF) to ensure all participants are in sync, regardless of their Internet connection speed.

Elluminate provides an environment for discussion and collaboration and could be used where supervisors and students cannot meet regularly face-to-face or where a research team is geographically scattered and needs regular sessions to discuss the progress of a project. The shared applications feature means that a group of researchers can collaboratively view and interact with a document, a data analysis program or other research application. Various members of the session can take control and make adjustments to the document and other team members will immediately see and be able to comment on and discuss the actions or results. A recording can also be made of all discussions and decisions, and referred back to at a later date.

Elluminate has particular potential as a research support group tool, so that postgraduate students who reside at a distance from each other can benefit from the same group processes as were discussed in Chapter 3. Similarly, Elluminate provides great opportunities for research training and supervision, with the ability to demonstrate the use of software, to talk through a piece of literature or discuss editorial changes to a document.

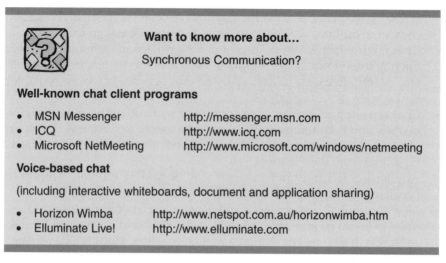

Want to know more about...

Synchronous Communication?

Well-known chat client programs

- MSN Messenger   http://messenger.msn.com
- ICQ   http://www.icq.com
- Microsoft NetMeeting   http://www.microsoft.com/windows/netmeeting

Voice-based chat

(including interactive whiteboards, document and application sharing)

- Horizon Wimba   http://www.netspot.com.au/horizonwimba.htm
- Elluminate Live!   http://www.elluminate.com

Internet telephony

Internet telephony (also known as Voice over Internet Protocol, VoIP) allows you to make local, national and international voice calls from your computer using the Internet. Calls can be peer-to-peer or you can conduct a multipoint voice conference, which is useful for focus groups. It enables:

- **Calls between two computers.** In this case, both you and your correspondent need to have the software installed and both use a computer with a microphone, in order to conduct the conversation.
- **Calls between your computer and a standard phone number**, for which you usually pay a small fee (the equivalent of a local call), even for a conversation to the other side of the globe.

VoIP, then, is very economic for conducting international calls and has the potential to replace conventional telephone services. Some programs (e.g. Skype and SkypeOut) also enable you to use a webcam and include video images with your call. To get started with Internet telephony you generally need to download a plug-in for your Web browser from one of the relevant websites.

Want to know more about...

Voice over Internet Protocol?

You might like to have a look at some examples:

- PhoneFree   http://www.phonefree.com
- Free World Dialup   http://www.freeworlddialup.com
- Speak Freely   http://www.speakfreely.org
- Skype   http://www.skype.com

Videoconferencing

Many organizations (particularly universities, large businesses and govern-ment organizations) provide room-based videoconferencing facilities which can be used by groups. Desktop videoconferencing, however, also provides a cost-effective means of communication for individuals. All each user requires is a personal computer, a small dedicated video camera (that con-nects via the USB or firewire port) and a set of headphones incorporating a small microphone and some software (either commercial or shareware). There are two basic formats for desktop videoing: direct connect (you con-nect directly to the IP address of another computer) and third party server (involves each user connecting via a server).

How can videoconferencing support your research?

Videoconferencing shares many of the advantages and potential applica-tions of text and voice-based chat while incorporating the many benefits of non-verbal communication. Video conferencing has potential for:

- conducting interviews at a geographical distance where non-verbal communication is important or critical;
- communicating with supervisors at a geographical distance, particularly where it might be beneficial to show or demonstrate something physically;
- conducting virtual conferences, presentations or workshops;
- using video cameras (webcams) for data collection (see Chapter 10).

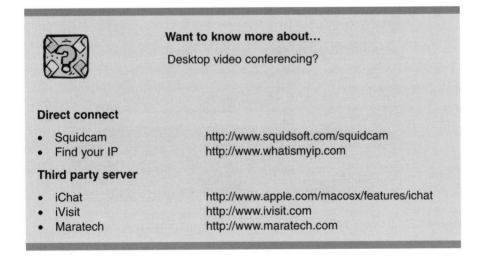

Want to know more about...

Desktop video conferencing?

Direct connect

- Squidcam   http://www.squidsoft.com/squidcam
- Find your IP   http://www.whatismyip.com

Third party server

- iChat   http://www.apple.com/macosx/features/ichat
- iVisit   http://www.ivisit.com
- Maratech   http://www.maratech.com

Translation resources

A number of resources are available on the Web to facilitate cross-cultural communication, in particular, translation of text from one language to another. These websites enable you to copy and paste a block of text written in one language into the text field, select your "from" and "to" language options and ask the software to translate. Enter "good morning" and ask for it to be translated from English to German and you'll get "guten morgen." Even more impressive, type in "good morning" and ask for English to Japanese translation and you get おはよう. Of course, any text should be checked for accuracy. Two examples are Altavista's Babel Fish (http://babelfish.altavista.com) and Google language tools (http://www.google.com.au/language_tools?hl=en). For the researcher working in cross-cultural contexts, this can create significant efficiencies by providing an alternative to finding a human translator (Figure 6.3).

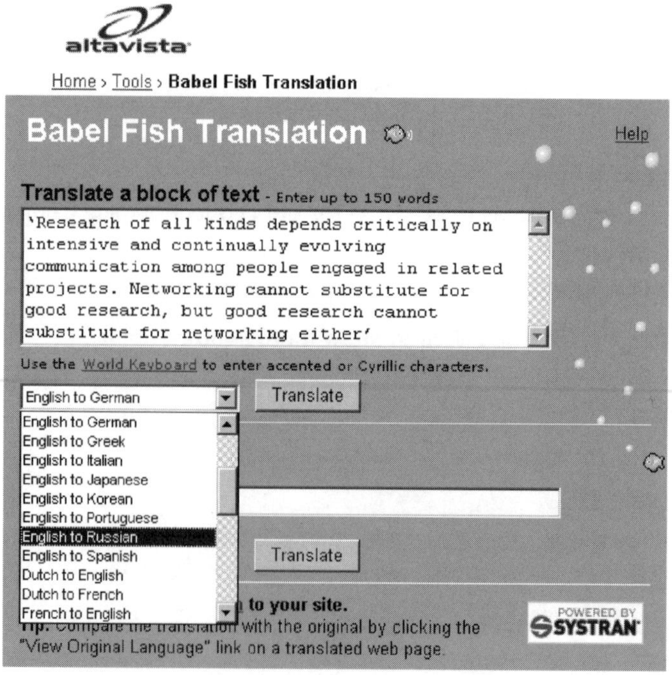

Figure 6.3   Using a Web-based translation site to translate a block of text

In this example a block of text has been copied and pasted into a text field and is being translated from English to Russian. It is also possible to enter a website address (URI) and have a whole webpage translated. Example is from Altavista's Babel Fish.

Establishing your own presence on the Web

If you search for yourself on the Web, what do you find?

Just as you might try to locate other researchers' contact details using the Web, other people may be trying to contact you in the same way. There are a number of ways you can establish your own presence on the Web:

- **Adding your contact details to relevant databases and directories.** Find out what contact databases exist in your discipline or country and add your own personal details.
- **Including your website address in the signature of your e-mail.** Also remember to include it and your e-mail address on all correspondence, including papers that you publish.
- **Capitalizing on the website facilities already existing in your organization.** Most universities, for instance, provide a space where both staff and postgraduate research students are encouraged to include information about themselves, their research interests and publications etc. In most cases someone in your organization will organize for information to be placed on the site.
- **Creating and maintaining your own website.** Sounds difficult? Not at all. The section below will get you started.

Creating your own website

There are many reasons why, as a researcher, you would want to create a website.

- **A website gives you a public profile**, making you and your research projects accessible to an international audience.
- **A website can be a great place to collate your research portfolio** or curriculum vitae (CV). You can use it to record your updated publications list, your employment and research experience and your contact details.
- **A website can promote your current research.** It can assist other researchers with interests similar to your own to become aware of your research in progress, and make contact with you if their own research is relevant or overlaps.
- **A website can be used to make contact with research participants or other stakeholders,** either providing further information, or acting as a means of data collection itself (see Chapter 10).
- **A website can be an adjunct to media coverage.**

Creating a website is nowhere near as difficult or complicated as many people think. In the early days of the Web, developers had to learn a coding language called HyperText Markup Language or HTML (see Chapter 2) which made the process tedious and slow. Now a range of software referred to as HTML editors make the process easy. If you can word process a document, you can create a website.

See the **Organizing and Managing Your Research Website**

for more information about creating your own website, including:

o   9 things to understand before you start;
o   11 easy steps to creating a basic website.

http://www.sagepub.co.uk/phelps

Planning the design and content of your site before you begin however is essential.

- **Look at other researchers' sites** and see what they include. Think about the information that you appreciate being able to find about other researchers on their sites. For instance, it is usual to have a picture, brief biographical information, qualifications, experience, research interests, publication list, online versions of papers (where copyright will allow) and so on.
- **Think carefully about the content and headings** on each page. Ensure all key words related to your research are included on your site so that search engines will retrieve it when someone is searching for those topics.
- **Take heed of the tips for nonlinear and on-screen writing** in Chapter 12.
- Most importantly, **draw a blueprint of your site on paper before you begin** (see Figure 6.4).

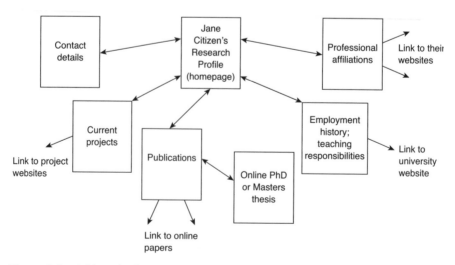

Figure 6.4   A blueprint for a personal research site

Note that we recommend the use of HTML editors, programs designed specially to assist people to produce websites, rather than HTML converters. The latter convert (or "Save As") a document produced for a different purpose, such as a word processed document into a HTML marked-up page. A list of freeware, shareware and commercial HTML editors is provided in the software table at the end of this chapter.

Over to you...

1. What features of your e-mail program could you start using to improve your e-mail management?
2. What mailing lists and discussion boards exist in your field that may be worth investigating and participating in?
3. How could your research benefit from starting a blog?
4. What forms of synchronous communication do you imagine would suit your research project?
5. What features would you include on your own research website?

Notes

1 Researchers at the University of Toronto are trialing a range of online technologies to "bring the research apprenticeship online," specifically for external and part-time students. Their project includes the creation of learning objects; and makes use of video and audio conferencing, document sharing and whiteboard facilities.

2 An older form of electronic group communication is newsgroups or usenet, which requires special newsreading software to access the messages.

3 A number of articles have been published that compare Wikipedia with other encyclopedia forms. One such article which appeared in the journal *Nature* (Giles 2005) evoked considerable debate. The article and references to other papers which dispute these findings are available online.

4 Other forms of synchronous communication such as MOOs and MUDs are less widely used in research, but for further information read the short article at http://www.usus.org/techniques/muds.htm

Examples of HTML editing software.

Software	Manufacturer/ developer	Platform	Website	Licensing	Demo on Website?	Special features
AceHTML	Visicom Media	Windows	http://softwares.visicommedia.com	Commercial and Freeware	✓	A wide range of basic and advanced website creation features. Visicom also offers website hosting services
Alleycode HTML Editor	Konae Technologies	Windows	http://www.alleycode.com	Freeware	✓	Real-time rendition, quick access to projects, an unusual real estate view of documents and a style sheet wizard
BBEdit	Bare Bones	Macintosh	http://www.barebones.com	Commercial	✓	A wide range of basic and advanced website creation features
CoffeeCup HTML Editor	CoffeeCup Software	Windows	http://www.coffeecup.com/html-editor	Commercial	✓	Drag-and-drop editor; wizards for frames, tables and forms; FTP client, image mapping, style sheets
Dreamweaver	Macromedia (now Adobe)	Windows, Macintosh	http://www.macromedia.com/ software/dreamweaver	Commercial	✓	Professional-level program. Can be purchased as part of Macromedia Studio, or separately. Wide range of features
Frontpage	Microsoft	Windows	http://www.microsoft.com/Frontpage	Commercial	✓	Similar interface to other Microsoft products. Comes with lots of templates
HotDog Professional	Sausage Software	Windows	http://www.sausage.com	Shareware	✓	Built-in Web site management tool, navigation viewer, HTML property sheet and FTP utility. Imports, creates and edits CSS style sheets

(Continued)

Software	Manufacturer/ developer	Platform	Website	Licensing	Demo on Website?	Special features
Mozilla Composer	Mozilla	Windows, Macintosh	http://www.mozilla.org/products	Freeware (Open Source)	✓	A simple program which has all the basic features
NVU	Linspire	Windows, Macintosh, Linux	http://www.nvu.com	Freeware (Open Source)	✓	Includes a site view feature. User forum for support
Trellion Internet Studio	Trellion	Windows	http://www.trellian.com/internetstudio	Commercial	✓	Includes button generator and support for eCommerce. FTP client and site management
SiteSpinner	Virtual Mechanics	Windows	http://virtualmechanics.com/products/ spinner	Freeware	✓	Drag-and-drop functionality and lots of templates. Includes image editing and creation modules. FTP client

Chapter 7

Effective Literature
Searching

A literature search is likely to be one of the first tasks you undertake in your research. Writing a literature review can be daunting, frustrating, confusing and time-consuming. You are expected to be familiar and up-to-date with all that has been written in your field and to write critically about that literature, in order to establish your credibility as a researcher and to argue for the relevance of your research. Our survey of research students[1] indicates that many feel moderately confident in their literature searching skills. In our experience, however, few are strategic, planned or methodical, leading to a scattered, random approach to literature searching. While they may find relevant papers, many students are left with a lingering feeling of doubt about how thorough their searches have been.

There are many good resources already available to help you to write up your literature review[2] and it is beyond the scope of this book to discuss the critical reviewing process itself. Rather, in this chapter we consider:

- the changing nature of information literacy;
- fundamental searching strategies and skills;
- tools for locating literature;
- advice on monitoring literature and keeping up-to-date.

This chapter should be read in conjunction with Chapter 9, which provides guidance on managing and organizing the results of your literature searches.

The changing nature of information literacy

Researchers who completed their higher degrees before the online information explosion (perhaps your supervisor is one), will have possibly used quite different strategies from those explored in this chapter. Their searches would have included card-based library catalogues, walking down rows of book shelves and traveling to libraries to search out important and relevant works. They would have perhaps had elaborate card systems for storing their references, with pages of hand-written notes to work through. They would have spent many hours compiling their references into a bibliography, a painstaking task involving hours of checking and proofreading.

Electronic catalogues and databases, together with the Web (considered in more detail in the following chapter), have greatly increased accessibility to literature locally and internationally. Increasingly, many databases are providing access to scholarly literature in full text. While this certainly provides many benefits to researchers, the exponential increase in available information has also brought with it the need for increasingly efficient strategies to search, sort and manage literature and the need to make judicious decisions about the quality of material on offer.

While there have been significant changes for researchers in the types of processes they engage in when conducting a literature search, there are also some fundamental behaviors and principles which continue to be relevant regardless of the changes brought by technology. We consider these in the following section.

Fundamental searching strategies and skills

What does it take to be an effective literature searcher? Think about how you search for information. Do you go straight to a library catalogue and search for a subject or specific title? Do you start with a bibliography from a useful source and follow-up the references listed by the author? Do you rely on references supplied to you by colleagues? All these strategies are useful and appropriate at different stages of the research process. Expanding your repertoire to include the range of strategies listed in Table 7.1[3] will undoubtedly enhance the effectiveness of your information searches.

In this and the following two chapters we consider a range of skills, techniques and tools that support these literature-searching strategies. Before you read on, however, it is important to understand the nature of databases and the terminology associated with them. We address these fundamentals in Chapter 2. If you have not yet read this section, now would be a timely point to do so.

Table 7.1   Characteristics of different types of information seeking strategies.

Information-seeking strategy	Nature and purpose of the strategy	Comments
Planning	A process of brainstorming key terms, synonyms and how these might combine, including use of search syntax. It is also important to plan which search tools are appropriate and relevant to consult	See later sections in this chapter
Reconnaissance	An initial exploratory search to identify key ideas or studies, provide an overview of the topic or identify some good terms to use in a more methodical search. For example, scanning the proceedings of a conference in your topic area	Useful to determine whether an issue is topical or a focus for a particular audience or discipline
Browsing	A process of searching by fairly broad subject or topic. One example of this is looking along the library shelves in a particular subject area. Electronic databases also allow browsing by subject or keyword	Useful to identify general references which might inform planning or methodical searching
Methodical searching	Once you have identified the most appropriate key terms (through planning, reconnaissance and/or browsing) a methodical search can be conducted both within and across relevant databases and catalogues	Keep a methodical record of your searches (see later in this chapter)
Citation chaining	A technique where you follow chains of citations which lead to other relevant material. Citation indexes are an important tool in this process, but Web searching can also prove useful	Highly valuable when you have located an ideal or seminal reference in your field
Limiting searches	A process of differentiating and narrowing search results in order to filter references and identify those most relevant and appropriate to your needs. Differentiating might occur on the basis of approach or perspective, by level, quality, currency or type of source	Useful to exclude references that are not peer reviewed or that have been published only after a certain year
Monitoring	Maintaining awareness of developments in a field or from a particular source. For example, you might set up a "table of contents" alert for new issues of a journal	See later sections in this chapter

Planning your search

When you conduct a literature search, do you go straight to a familiar or well-used search tool and enter the first terms or words that come to mind? While this is a common practice and can yield relevant resources, you will get better results from a more planned and organized approach. In particular it is important to: identify key terms; plan how key terms will be combined and entered; and keep records of your searches.

While planning will be iterative and initial strategies will continue to be refined and expanded, you should make this a conscious and considered process. Be aware of the differences between looking for specific rather than general information and between an exhaustive and a representative search. In planning your searches, always keep in mind your overall purpose.

Identifying key terms

In any large research project there will be a significant number of concepts or terms that will relate to your topic. The first step is to jot down the key terms, but don't stop there. Brainstorming to identify synonyms or related terms (including both more general and more specific terms) is also vital as different words or phrases may be used in the literature to describe very similar concepts. You may also want to consider how terms are used in different countries or how different spelling forms are used, including the use of plural and singular forms. We recommend setting up a table exploring all these possibilities, such as the one in Table 7.2.

Table 7.2   Identifying key terms relevant to your literature search.

This example relates to research on "the influence of women's self-perceptions on career advancement".

Search strategies	Examples of search terms/key words
Synonyms for "women"	females
Synonyms for self-perception	self-esteem; self-confidence; self-understanding
Synonyms for "career"	profession; vocation; work; employment
Synonyms for "advancement"	progress; promotion; success
Related concepts	women and management; women and business; women in organizations; gender stereotypes; glass ceiling
Terminology variations	corporations/businesses/companies
Spelling differences	organisation/organization
Singular/plural forms	Woman/women; company/companies; profession/professions

As you locate relevant references, you may find that alternative terms are used by different writers or by the database producers. Keep jotting these down and re-running your searches based on these terms (see also the section below on keeping a record of your searches).

Planning how terms will be combined and entered

Identifying key terms to search for is only the first step towards developing efficient searching strategies. The real skill comes in knowing how to refine your search in a way that gives you the best chance of finding the literature most pertinent to your project. We consider the following key strategies in turn: using Boolean logic; using phrase searching and proximity operators; using truncators and wildcards; determining which fields are relevant to search; and limiting searches.

Boolean logic

Boolean logic is useful when your search involves more than one search term and you need to be more specific about how the terms relate to each other. The three Boolean operators, AND, OR and NOT, are explained in Table 7.3[4] and Figure 7.1.

Table 7.3   The use of Boolean operators to refine a literature search.

Operator	Process	Result
OR	Requires either or both terms to be present in the document, e.g. women OR woman	Increases the number of documents retrieved
AND	Requires both terms to be present, e.g. women AND self-perception	Reduces the number of documents
NOT	Requires the term to be absent, e.g. career NOT vocation	Reduces the number of documents, but runs the risk of eliminating a relevant document

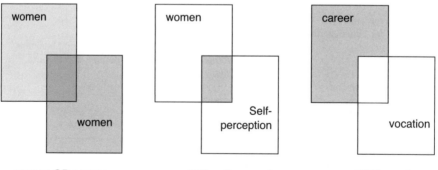

women OR woman   women AND self-perception   career NOT vocation

Figure 7.1   The Boolean operational concepts of OR, AND & NOT

Boolean logic is used to enlarge or restrict your search results.

Phrase searching and proximity operators

Phrase searching and proximity operators enable you to establish a connection between your search terms, allowing you to be more specific about how and where the terms might most productively combine. This is particularly important when you are searching full-text articles. Phrase searching involves searching for words that are in a set order and adjacent to one another, placing the phrase in inverted commas, as indicated in Table 7.4.

Table 7.4 Comparison of results with and without phrase searching.

Search statement	Potential result
"glass ceiling" [as a phrase]	Many women pursuing careers in management find themselves encountering a **glass ceiling**
Glass ceiling [as a normal search without phrase or proximity syntax]	A sign of prestige for managers was to be located in an executive office with a high **ceiling** and large expanses of **glass** windows with a view

Some literature search tools also provide proximity searching capabilities. For instance, they might use terms such as NEAR or ADJ (short for "adjacent") or SAME or WITH (to say that the words must appear in the same sentence). Table 7.5 demonstrates how proximity operators can impact on search results.

Table 7.5 Impact on search results of using proximity operators.

Search statement	Potential result
self (ADJ) esteem	The importance of **self esteem** for women seeking to advance their careers
self (NEAR) esteem	The process by which a woman comes to terms with **self** and career can influence the **esteem** in which she is held by others

Using truncators or "wildcards"

Truncators allow you to use a special symbol (frequently *) in the place of a particular letter or letters to broaden or restrict your search results. For example, fish* would retrieve fish, fisher, fishermen, fisherwomen, fishers and fishing. When used as a wildcard, the * replaces a single letter, and is useful for words with different spelling variations e.g. organi*ation would produce results for both organization and organisation.

Determining which fields to search

When you use a literature database, you can specify in which field you wish to search for a particular term. For example, you might choose to specifically search by author, title, subject (general conceptual area covered), keywords (identified by the writer or indexer as key concepts covered in the paper), or full text (the whole document). Your search results can be significantly affected by the field you nominate to search. Let's take an example from the discipline of civil engineering. You might be researching the optimal design for single-lane roundabouts. If you searched for the term "roundabout" in the title field you would get very different results than if you searched for the same term in the subject or full-text field. For instance, you might get all the articles that had "roundabout" as a word in the text, but had nothing to do with engineering. For instance, "..in a roundabout way" …

Limiting searches

Many databases also allow you to limit your searches, for example, by: date (to retrieve references written after or before a particular year); material type (to retrieve only conference papers, refereed versus non-refereed journal articles, or newspaper articles); language; or country of publication.

Tips for learning more about search syntax

Symbols and syntax to specify Boolean logic, proximity operators, search specific fields, apply truncators or wildcards or limit your search are not standardized. It therefore pays to become familiar with the syntax used in your commonly accessed search tools. Each will have a "help," "tips" or "advanced search" section where these are outlined. We recommend printing these out and referring to them while planning and conducting your searches.

Keeping a record of your searches

Methodically maintaining a record of your searches enables you to:

- evaluate which databases or search terms are most effective in your area of research;
- keep a record of what you have and haven't done in your searching, which can be important if you are interrupted or only have small blocks of time in which to conduct your searches;
- repeat successful searches at a later time to update your literature;
- stay focused and complete your searches if you are led off track.

A record of your searches might include such details as key words, date searched, time spent, search tools consulted, and the number of "hits" or relevant references, as exemplified in Table 7.6.

Table 7.6   Hypothetical sample record of literature search history.

Key Words	Current contents		Emerald		Expanded Academic ASAP		Google Scholar	
	DATE	HITS	DATE	HITS	DATE	HITS	DATE	HITS
{women OR woman} AND organi*ation*	7 May 06	576	1 June 06	230				
{women OR woman} AND career	7 May 06	234	1 June 06	129				
{Self-perception OR self-confidence} AND {women OR woman}	7 May 06	56	1 June 06	26!!				
"glass ceiling" [phrase]	12 Jan 07	38	12 Jan 07	80				
women AND "glass ceiling"	12 Oct 06	10!!	12 Jan 07	60				
women AND "glass ceiling" AND {Self-perception OR self-confidence}			12 Jan 07	13 !!				

Note that a symbol has been used (!!) to indicate results which are of particular value and relevance.

See the **Organizing and Managing Your Research Website**

for templates for recording search results.
http://www.sagepub.co.uk/phelps

Tools for locating literature

Knowing what type of source to search, and how to get the most from each, is an important research skill. In this section we consider in turn: electronic literature databases, including citation indexes; library catalogues; locating books in and out of print; e-book sources; periodical directories; search tools for specific types of resources; and harnessing the skills of librarians. We discuss searching the Web in Chapter 8.

Electronic literature databases

Literature databases generally provide access to journal articles, conference papers, reports or other occasional papers, although some include electronic versions of books. Of the huge number of literature databases available, some have a general focus while others are much more specialized. Your university library will subscribe to a wide range of databases and we suggest you familiarize yourself with the ones commonly used in your discipline area, examples of which are provided in Table 7.7.

Table 7.7　Examples of commonly used literature databases by discipline.

Discipline	Databases
Natural sciences	ScienceResearch, Wiley Interscience
Engineering	Engineering and Applied Science Online
Health sciences	Medline; PubMed; SPORTDiscus
Education	Expanded Academic; ERIC
Business & Management	Emerald Intelligence; LexisNexis International
Social sciences & Humanities	Expanded Academic
Law	LexisNexis International; Lawbook Online
Arts	Art Abstracts; Music Index
General coverage	Current Contents, Proquest

Each database will have an "about" or "information" section that explains its coverage. Don't overlook the many general coverage databases and think a little laterally about whether your topic might be covered in journals outside your specific discipline area.

Databases also vary in terms of the nationality of their coverage (e.g. some only include material from the USA) and whether they are full text or only provide bibliographic details and abstracts. Some will index only scholarly papers while others will include newspaper and magazine articles. Some will contain diverse resources such as conference papers, reports and theses while others will not. We suggest you develop your own list of relevant and available databases and annotate the specific characteristics that are relevant to your own research, as the example in Table 7.8 illustrates.

Each database will have its own look and feel, and the interface and screen designs will differ between companies and even between databases. While this may initially be a little confusing, all will have common key features. Being aware of the fundamental searching skills and strategies outlined in the previous section will enable you to move between them fairly seamlessly.

Understanding and saving your search results

In Chapter 2 we discussed the general nature of databases and defined records and fields. To understand the format of your search results these concepts

Table 7.8 Creating a summary of relevant literature databases.

This example relates to research into women's careers in management.

Database	Fulltext	Nationality	Notes regarding relevance
Current Contents	No	International	General coverage but can search sub-collections: Social & Behavioral Sciences (SBS); Business Collection (BC); Arts & Humanities (AH)
Emerald Insight	Yes	International (Emerald publications only)	Management literature in niche areas including change management. Includes *Women in Management Review*
Expanded Academic ASAP	No but enhanced access to fulltext	Predominantly U.S.	Humanities and social sciences. Both peer reviewed and non-peer reviewed. Includes journals, magazines and the *New York Times*
LexisNexis International	Yes	Predominantly U.S. and U.K.	Case law and related documents
AIM (Australian Institute of Management) Management & Training Database	No	Australian plus some New Zealand and South-East Asian	Journal articles from management, training, human resources, communication and marketing
Australian & NZ Equal Opportunity Law Library	Yes	Australian and New Zealand	Law focus. Provides access to: Federal and state Equal Opportunity Legislation, Australian & NZ Equal Opportunity Commentary and Equal Opportunity Cases

become important. Each database will vary in its display of records and will provide different options for saving and/or exporting the results of your search to another program. Many provide other features such as allowing you to link to related citations (see also the section on citation indexes below) or to subscribe to updates or tables of contents. The image in Figure 7.2 is drawn from one example database. This figure also indicates how, by locating one relevant paper, you can follow links from the allocated subject headings to locate other articles which have been allocated the same subject heading. This is useful when you are performing a reconnaissance search or browsing.

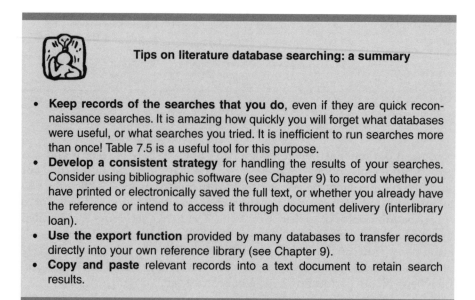

Figure 7.2   Display format of results from a search in a literature database

Note the ability to mark records for batch processing and to link from this record to articles with the same subject. Example is from ProQuest.

 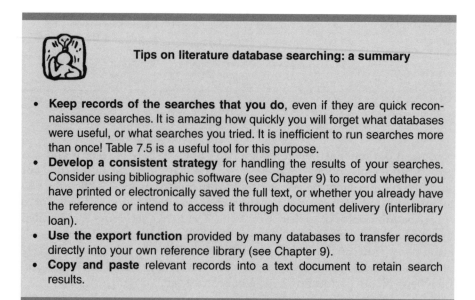

Tips on literature database searching: a summary

- **Keep records of the searches that you do**, even if they are quick reconnaissance searches. It is amazing how quickly you will forget what databases were useful, or what searches you tried. It is inefficient to run searches more than once! Table 7.5 is a useful tool for this purpose.
- **Develop a consistent strategy** for handling the results of your searches. Consider using bibliographic software (see Chapter 9) to record whether you have printed or electronically saved the full text, or whether you already have the reference or intend to access it through document delivery (interlibrary loan).
- **Use the export function** provided by many databases to transfer records directly into your own reference library (see Chapter 9).
- **Copy and paste** relevant records into a text document to retain search results.

Citation indexes

Citation indexes are particularly useful when there are a number of known papers that are key to your research and you want to locate other relevant or related publications. The most common approach to tracking down citations is "backward chaining," following up references provided in the reference list of a known source. "Forward chaining" involves identifying articles which have subsequently made reference to a known article.

Sometimes, citation indexes are used to ascertain a work's credibility. If a paper has been widely cited it is considered to have had a strong impact on that discipline. In universities, this sometimes translates into a means of evaluating the quality of research output, and a numerical score known as an "impact factor" is derived from citation indexes. Ironically, highly controversial and perhaps not-so-credible papers can also produce high impact factors as they may be widely referred to in a less-than-positive light.

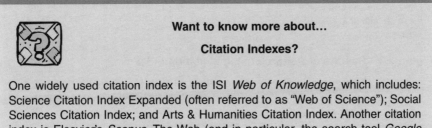

Want to know more about...

Citation Indexes?

One widely used citation index is the ISI *Web of Knowledge*, which includes: Science Citation Index Expanded (often referred to as "Web of Science"); Social Sciences Citation Index; and Arts & Humanities Citation Index. Another citation index is Elsevier's *Scopus*. The Web (and in particular, the search tool *Google Scholar*) can also be used as a tool for citation linking and we suggest some strategies for this in Chapter 8.

Citation indexes generally allow you to search for references in the same way as other databases do (e.g. by subject or keyword). However their real strength is when you already have a specific reference for which you want to locate related citations. In this case you are most likely to search by author or title, as shown in Figure 7.3.

Tips on using Citation Indexes

- Try the online tutorials found in many citation databases.
- Try a citation search with 1–2 of the key papers (or authors) in your topic area. Are the results useful?
- Try searching a citation index if you have published any journal articles, books or book chapters yourself, to see whether any writers have subsequently referenced your work.

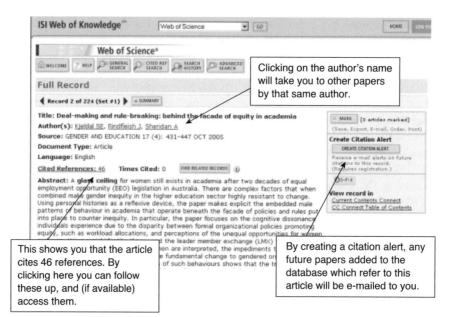

Figure 7.3 Results of a search using a citation index

This indicates how you can link to related references or be notified in future as such articles become available. Example is from ISI Web of Science.

Enhanced access to full text

Your ability to access the full-text article found in a database will depend upon whether your library has subscribed to the particular journal. If the library subscribes to the journal in electronic format, you may be able to access full text through a service known as SFX. If the full text of the article is available through your library, the SFX software will tell you where it can be located. Your library will tell you whether they provide such a service, or alternatively, you may just see the SFX button **⑤s·f·x** when you are searching. Note that SFX also provides a Citation Linker (citation index) facility.

Library catalogues

Library catalogues are an essential companion to database searching, in that when you locate a non full-text article in a database, you may then need to search for libraries that hold the physical copy. For example, suppose in conducting your search you locate the article by Kjeldal cited in Figure 7.3. You note that the article is not provided in full text. You would then turn to a library catalogue to determine where you can access the journal *Gender in Education*. You would also need to remember to check that the library holds volume 17 and issue number 4. If the journal is not held by your institution's library, then you may need to arrange for document delivery (interlibrary loan) as described below.

Searching library catalogues

Searching a library catalogue is similar to searching a database (remember that the catalogue is just another type of database). The example below in Figure 7.4 illustrates what a library catalogue might look like.

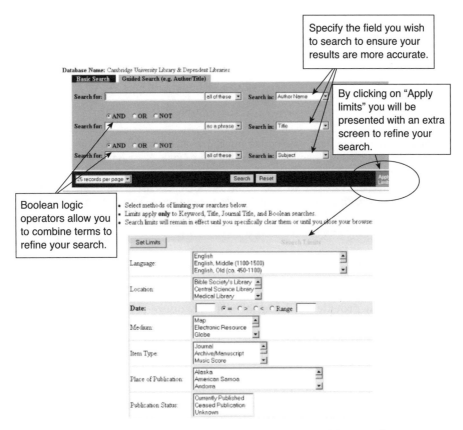

Figure 7.4   Guided (advanced) search indicating the ability to refine your search results

Boolean logic and applying limits on searches will enhance the relevance of your search results. Example is from the University of Cambridge library catalogue.

Locating and consulting a range of library catalogues

There may be times when it would be useful to consult library catalogues other than that of your own institution. While locating an item in a library on the other side of the globe may seem of limited use, such a search allows you to:

- be confident that you are aware of a wide range of literature in your field (even if you don't necessarily access the full-text item);
- become aware of new publications that you can either purchase or order into your local library (see also the section below on online bookshops);
- obtain full bibliographic information for incomplete references (for instance, where you have missed recording publication or ISBN details of a source no longer held, or when you wish to purchase an item);
- pursue interlibrary loans;
- do a search before visiting a library in person, making your visit more time efficient and productive.

Feature Website: LibDesk

http://www.libdex.com

Many libraries have their catalogues publicly available on the Web and a very useful tool for locating them internationally is LibDesk. Consider, for instance, a project where you become aware of a legal precedent established in Alberta, Canada which is relevant to your own research. By using LibDesk you can browse library catalogues by country, which can then lead you to a link to the catalogue of the Law Society of Alberta.

Books in- and out-of-print

BooksInPrint.com (http://booksinprint.com) is an authoritative bibliographic resource which provides a listing of in-print, out-of-print and forthcoming books. It also lists audio and video titles. This is particularly helpful for finding or checking full bibliographic details of resources and locating a reasonably definitive list of publications, ensuring that you can be confident about knowing what books have been published in your field. If your institution has a subscription, you can also read the first chapter of many print-based publications.

Other valuable sources of information are online bookstores or book dealers. Some specialize in out-of-print material, including books, maps, prints, manuscripts and photographs, particularly useful if you are doing historical research.

Want to know more about....

Books in and out-of-print?

Books In-Print

Amazon.com   http://www.amazon.com
BookBrain.co.uk   http://www.bookbrain.co.uk
Co-op Bookshop   http://www.coop-bookshop.com.au

(Continued)

Books Out-of-Print

Alibris	http://www.alibris.com
Bibliopoly	http://www.bibliopoly.com
BookFinder	http://www.bookfinder.com
See also BUBL's list of bookshops	http://bubl.ac.uk/link/types/bookshops.htm

Electronic books (e-books)

A number of sources now exist for electronic access to the full text of books. Some are provided by libraries, others by publishers, while community groups and other networks also digitize copyright-free or out-of-print publications and distribute these to others online. Table 7.9 gives a sample

Table 7.9 A sample of sources of e-books and other digital resources.

University of Virginia e-books	http://etext.lib.virginia.edu/ebooks	Classic British and American fiction, major authors, children's literature, American history, Shakespeare, African-American documents, the Bible. Provided in either Web (HTML) format or for use with Microsoft Reader or Palm Reader
Project Gutenberg	http://www.gutenberg.org	Thousands of free electronic books which are produced by volunteers
Academic Materials from e-bookopolis	http://e-bookopolis.com	Commercial distributor of e-books to subscribers
Netlibrary	http://www.netlibrary.com	Commercial distributor of e-books to subscribers
eBooks.com	http://edrs.com	Commercial distributor which allows purchase of whole or part of e-books
Amazon.com	http://amazon.com	Well-known online book seller. Some publications can be purchased in electronic format
Online Books	http://www.cs.cmu.edu/books.html	Produced by John Mark Ockerbloom from the University of Pennsylvania. Free access
NetLibrary	http://www.netlibrary.com	Commercial distributor of e-books to subscribers

(not exhaustive) of sites that distribute e-books and other digital resources. See also Chapter 10 for other sites specializing in electronic access to primary documents and data. Check whether your library subscribes to services that provide access to scholarly texts in digital format.

Some e-books are designed to use specific software such as ebrary (http://www.ebrary.com/corp), Microsoft Reader (http://www.microsoft.com/reader) or eReader (http://www.ereader.com) while others use formats such as PDF (see Chapter 2). Most are able to be read on any standard computer with the appropriate software installed, but some formats also can be read using a Palm or Pocket PC or other handheld device. Most e-book reading software allows you to take notes while reading, make annotations related to specific parts of your text, search for occurrences of particular words, mark or highlight segments of text and then index these notes.

Periodical directories

Although literature databases are an important way of identifying key journals in your field, there are nevertheless many journals that are not indexed in commonly accessible databases. For example, as the majority of databases are biased toward literature from western countries, other internationally important journals may not be represented. To feel confident that you are well informed about publications in your discipline, you may be wise to look beyond standard databases.

Ulrich's Periodicals Directory (http://www.ulrichsweb.com) provides comprehensive information on journals (or serials) published throughout the world on all subjects, including those published irregularly, those that are circulated free of charge and those that are accessible only through paid subscription. Most producers of journals register their publication with Ulrich's as it is considered the most comprehensive and authoritative source (see Figure 7.5).

Tools for locating specific resources

You will find a range of other search tools available online which can assist you to locate specific types of resources other than books and journals, a sample of which is summarized in Table 7.10.

Interlibrary loan and document delivery services

With the exponential growth in available publications, you cannot expect your local library to hold all resources necessary for your research. However, almost all university libraries offer interlibrary loan and document delivery services which enable them to access literature held in other libraries.

As with most search tools, an advanced search option is also available to refine your results.

Symbols are used to indicate whether journals have a (paid) review available, are refereed, are available in electronic format or are available with open access, as indicated in the legend.

U L R I C H ' S
PERIODICALS DIRECTORY™

The global source for periodicals information since 1932

HOME | USER
Advanced Search Browse

Quick Search Keyword ▾

Search Results: Displaying 251-275 of **1,517** results
Keyword: forestry

LEGEND	
★ Reviews	**TITLE**
ℳ Refereed	Click again to sort ascending.
E Electronic	
✛ Open Access	

REVISE SEARCH ▶   NEW SEARCH ▶

View Selected, View All - This Page, or Add to List

⟡ TITLE ◇	PUBLISHER	COUNTRY	ISSN	START YEAR	STATUS	PRICE
☐	Central America Forestry Journal	CATIE	Costa Rica	Not Supplied	1992	Active	USD 25.0
☐ E	Central Atlantic Environmental Directory	Harbinger Communications	United States	1087-8491	1996	Active	USD 18.5
☐ ℳ	Centralblatt fuer das Gesamte Forstwesen	Bundesamt und Forschungszentrum fuer Wald	Austria	0008-9583	1875	Active	Contact Publishe
☐	Centre d'Ecologie Forestiere et Rurale. Communications	Centre d'Ecologie Forestiere et Rurale	Belgium	Not Supplied	1943	Ceased	See Full Record
☐	Centre de Recherche et de Promotion Forestieres. Documents	Centre de Recherche et de Promotion Forestieres	Belgium	0775-3446	1968	Ceased	See Full Record

Figure 7.5   Sample results screen from Ulrich's Periodicals Directory

The example search used the subject "forestry". The results indicate the international coverage of the database.

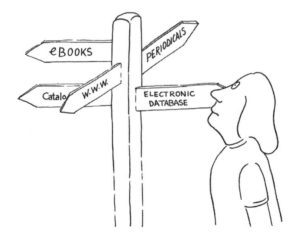

Many publishers, database providers and other private companies also provide document delivery services, which can be accessed by either institutions or individuals. Users usually either subscribe to the service (with monthly or annual fees) or pay per article requested using a credit card.

Table 7.10 A sample of the range of search tools available online.

Newspapers	
Onlinenewspapers.com	http://www.onlinenewspapers.com
Newslink	http://newslink.org
Nettizen.com	http://www.nettizen.com/newspaper
Australian Newspapers Online	http://www.nla.gov.au/npapers
Dissertations and Theses	
ProQuest Dissertation Abstracts on the Web	http://wwwlib.umi.com/dissertations
Australian Digital Thesis Program	http://adt.caul.edu.au
UMI's Dissertation Publishing	http://www.umi.com/products_umi/dissertations
Conference Proceedings	
ProceedingsFirst (FirstSearch)	Check with your librarian to see whether your institution has access
Maps and images	
Alexandria Digital Library	http://www.alexandria.ucsb.edu
See also Chapter 10 in relation to digital repositories	

Where these delivery services operate via fax or electronic transmission, you may receive an electronic or hard copy of that important article within a day or two. Examples include Ingenta Connect (http://www.ingenta.com) and Infotrieve (http://www4.infotrieve.com).

Your most valuable resource – the reference librarian

Perhaps the most important literature searching tool of all is the reference librarian. Getting to know your librarian could be the one of the best investments of time you make. Librarians keep up-to-date with technological developments and are trained in advanced searching strategies, so they will be able to advise you on the best place to begin your literature searches and how to make the most of the range of search tools available.

Monitoring literature

Although you may conduct quite a comprehensive literature review early in your project, you will need to keep monitoring the literature throughout your research, right up to the point of finalizing your dissertation or report.

While this may feel like a daunting prospect, there are techniques you can utilize to streamline the process.

As you continue your research, you will progressively identify core sources of relevant information that are regularly updated, such as:

- **key journals** that you need to monitor as new issues become available;
- **government or organizational websites** that regularly put out new reports or announcements related to your research;
- **professional groups or conference websites**, where papers are regularly published or promoted.

You are likely to discover such key sources early in your research process, but how will you remember to keep returning to them as your work progresses? While it may seem an unforgettably high priority at the time, in another 6 months this urgency may have completely slipped your mind. A number of strategies can keep you up-to-date without having to rely solely on your overworked memory. Such strategies include:

- subscribing to table of contents services;
- setting up journal monitoring lists;
- accessing research-in-progress databases;
- using RSS technology to be notified when websites are updated (see Chapter 8).

Table of contents services

Many publishers of journals offer alerting services that allow you to sign up to receive an e-mail each time a new issue of the journal is published, usually containing the table of contents. In most cases you can link directly to a webpage containing the abstract and, in some instances, the full text (although you may need to pay for this latter service).

Journal monitoring lists

As table of contents services are not provided by every journal, we suggest putting in place supplementary systems for methodically monitoring key journals in your field. A journal monitoring list can record:

- all your frequently consulted journal titles;
- the topic area covered by the journal;
- key details such as where you can access tables of contents, abstracts etc.;
- where you can locate the full text of articles;
- the date you last accessed the journal;
- any other notes, such as the back issues that you have browsed through, or your intention to come back to the journal, say every 6 months.

Of course the same document might equally include links to other types of information resources that you need to return to regularly, such as conference websites. In this case you can annotate what time of the year the conference occurs, and thus know when to return to the site each year. You can use a spreadsheet or a table created in a text document for this type of monitoring (see Figure 7.6). You can also include website addresses as hyperlinks, providing ready access to further current details. Once you have created such a list, of course, you need to revisit it as part of a regular routine (see Chapter 3 in relation to notes and reminders).

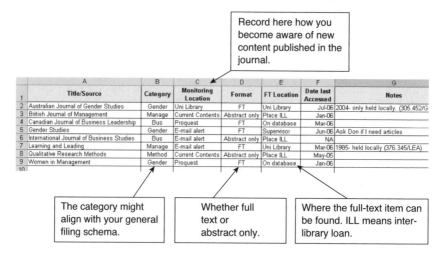

Figure 7.6   A journal monitoring list, set up using a spreadsheet

See the **Organizing and Managing Your Research Website**

for templates for recording search results.

http://www.sagepub.co.uk/phelps

Research-in-progress databases

It is very helpful to have access to papers before they are actually published, particularly in fast-moving fields of research such as medicine, political science or environmental science. While your informal networks can be a good source of such papers, a number of databases exist that allow you to access such information. Generally these are country or sector specific. Examples are provided in Table 7.11.

Table 7.11 Examples of research-in-progress databases.

The (U.S.) Federal Research In Progress Database	http://grc.ntis.gov/fedrip.htm	Information about ongoing federally funded projects in the fields of the physical sciences, engineering and life sciences
Research in Progress Catalogue (Canada)	http://www.nonprofitscan.ca/ progress.asp	Information about ongoing and recently published work on the Canadian non-profit sector
Australian Research Council Research Outcomes: Grants	http://www.arc.gov.au/grant_ programs	Information about grants allocated by the Australian Research Council

Over to you...

1. What literature-searching strategies do you use most frequently? Which of the strategies we discuss in this chapter might you usefully add to your repertoire?
2. What are the key terms and/or phrases you would use to search for literature relevant to your research? How could you limit your searches to take account of the specifics of your research project?
3. What databases, accessible through your institution, are relevant to your research topic?
4. How could searching a citation index be useful for your research?
5. Subscribe to table of contents alerts for key journals in your discipline area.
6. Develop a journal monitoring list.

Notes

1 Phelps *et al.* 2006.
2 For example, Hart 2000; O'Leary 2004; Oliver 2004.
3 Adapted from Ellis 1989.
4 Derived from Henninger 1999.

Chapter 8

Strategic Web Searching

While searching literature databases is a very important strategy for finding material for your research, the Web also offers a vast repository of valuable information (and lots of garbage too!). Members of the "Google generation" consider themselves fairly adept Web searchers. Given the apparent ease of obtaining a long list of search results, this level of confidence is not surprising. However, in our experience few students employ more than one or perhaps two online search tools and rarely have considered whether the tools they use are the most effective and efficient for the job. Many express frustration about the quality, relevance and sheer quantity of the information they locate. Some are quite ineffective in how they deal with the results of their searches, even writing down long website addresses to maintain a permanent record.

As the Internet is a largely unregulated environment, learning how to be strategic in the way you search, locate and critique the quality of information available has become an essential research skill. In this chapter we assume you are familiar with the basics of accessing the Web (see Chapter 2) and focus on:

- Web searching tools, in particular search engines, search directories and search visualization tools;
- improving your search results;
- managing your frequently used websites;
- evaluating Web-based information.

Web-searching tools

If you are like many people who use the Web, you probably rely on one search tool to the exclusion of all others. However, there are many types of search tools available, each with different strengths and relevance for different contexts. It is common, for instance, to confuse search engines and search directories, which represent very different ways of accessing information and can produce quite different results.

Search engines and meta-search engines

Search engines are online tools that allow you to find information on the Web on topics that you specify. They use automated techniques (referred to informally as "robots" or "spiders") to trawl through websites, indexing them according to words that appear on their pages, or alternatively words embedded within the html code to assist search engines to find their site (known as "metadata"). **Meta-search engines** search several search engines at the same time and combine the results. This is useful when you want a more comprehensive search.

Want to know more about....

Search engines and meta-search engines?

Search engines

Google	http://www.google.com
Altavista	http://www.altavistsa.com
Excite	http://www.excite.com

Meta-search engines

Metacrawler	http://www.metacrawler.com
AllOneSearch	http://www.allonesearch.com
Dogpile	http://www.dogpile.com

If you do the same search using different search engines, you can get quite different results, not only in terms of what is retrieved, but also in the way results are displayed. For example, some search engines rank the relevance of the results. The criteria used to produce these ratings vary among search engines, but they are generally based on the presence, placement and frequency of searched terms on the site. An exception occurs with "sponsored links" where a website creator has paid for their site to rank higher or appear more frequently than other sites. Such paid advertising is one way the search engine companies can keep their service free. Some search engines make this sponsoring explicit, while others do not.

Search directories

Search directories (also known as subject directories or guides) are quite different from search engines as they are organized by a hierarchical scheme or structure. Some, for instance, are arranged according to the Dewey Decimal or Library of Congress system (traditionally used for arranging resources in libraries). Search directories differ significantly from search engines as they are generally indexed by people rather than by computers. The resulting information is therefore of higher quality and the categorization is more selective, logical and consistent. Examples of search directories are provided in Table 8.1.

Table 8.1 Examples of search directories.

Directory	URI	Details
WWW Virtual Library	http://www.vlib.org	The oldest Web directory is run by independent volunteers including experts from academia, industry and the volunteer sector
BUBL	http://www.bubl.ac.uk	Uses the Dewey Decimal system to present research and academic materials. Indexed by UK volunteer subject specialists who also provide annotations about the sites
OMNI	http://omni.ac.uk	Hand-selected and evaluated Internet resources aimed at students, researchers, academics and practitioners in the health and medical sciences. Materials are selected on scope, accuracy, currency and uniqueness
INFOMINE	http://infomine.ucr.edu	Relevant to staff and students at the university level. Built by librarians, the directory contains resources such as electronic journals, electronic books, bulletin boards, mailing lists, online library catalogues and directories of researchers
AllLearn	http://www.alllearn.org	Produced by academic specialists at Oxford, Stanford and Yale universities

Feature Web Resource: Google Scholar

http://scholar.google.com

One popular and valuable tool for locating high quality resources on the Web is Google Scholar. This hybrid search engine and search directory provides access to details of scholarly literature such as peer-reviewed papers, theses, books, abstracts and articles across all disciplines. Materials are drawn directly from academic publishers, professional societies, preprint repositories, universities

(*Continued*)

and other scholarly organizations. Google Scholar ranks your search results based on the full text of each article (if available online), the author, the publication in which the article appeared, and how often the paper has been cited in other scholarly literature. If only the abstract or citation is available, Google Scholar can determine whether your library has access to the full-text article. Note that you need to be searching Google Scholar from an on-campus location of a participating organization.

Google Scholar can be used as an effective **citation index** (see Chapter 7) in that it facilitates identification of articles that have cited each listed reference. As with other citation indexes you need to follow the guidelines in relation to the format for entering authors' names and be aware that the more common the name you are searching for, the more specific your author format should be, for example you can enter:

author:"jones" or
author:"p jones" or
author:"peter r jones"

An advanced search page also allows you to refine your search results. In particular, you can limit results to specific discipline areas.

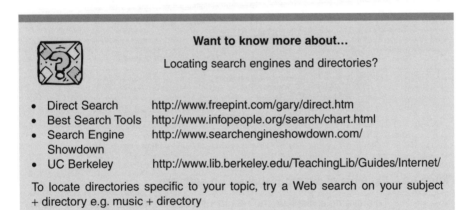

Want to know more about…

Locating search engines and directories?

- Direct Search   http://www.freepint.com/gary/direct.htm
- Best Search Tools   http://www.infopeople.org/search/chart.html
- Search Engine   http://www.searchengineshowdown.com/
  Showdown
- UC Berkeley   http://www.lib.berkeley.edu/TeachingLib/Guides/Internet/

To locate directories specific to your topic, try a Web search on your subject + directory e.g. music + directory

Search visualization tools

Search visualization tools group and display results visually. When you move your mouse over parts of the display, summarized details of the located resources are highlighted. You can also zoom in on the map to explore particular subcategories in more detail, as indicated in Figure 8.1. Examples of search visualization tools include Kartoo (http://www.kartoo.com) and Grokker (http://www.grokker.com).

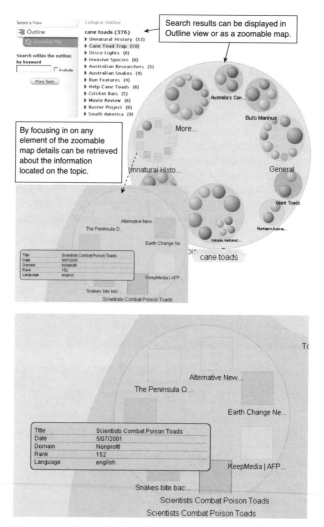

Figure 8.1 Example of search visualisation software

This example displays the results of a search for information on cane toads. Example is from the demonstration version of Grokker (http://www.grokker.com).

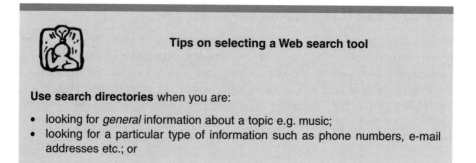

Tips on selecting a Web search tool

Use search directories when you are:

- looking for *general* information about a topic e.g. music;
- looking for a particular type of information such as phone numbers, e-mail addresses etc.; or

(Continued)

- wanting higher quality information, accurately allocated by humans to a particular category.

Use search engines when you are looking for *specific* information about a topic, for instance a very particular fact or the source of a quote. Search engines are most appropriate for very current facts and information that changes rapidly.

Use meta-search engines when you want the highest recall on specific information, i.e. an exhaustive search.

Use search visualization tools when you want to explore large sets of disparate results and understand the relationships between them.

Beyond text searches

A range of search engines, directories and other search tools allow you to locate resources other than the usual academic papers, including images, movies and audio. For instance, you might want an image to bring to life a presentation or to depict a concept more clearly in a survey.

Many of the major search engines offer specialist media-type search tools. An example of an image search is displayed in Figure 8.2, however similar search tools exist for audio and video.

Remember, locating images in this way does not mean that you have permission to use them. There are, however, ways of locating copyright-free resources. Try using a *text* search using the search terms + free and + graphic (or + image) e.g. trebuchet + free + image.

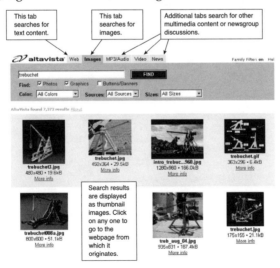

Figure 8.2   Results of an image search

The search results show thumbnail representations of the images located. Click on each image to go to its source website. Example is from Altavista's image search engine.

Feature Website: Search the Sky Skyview

http://skyview.gsfc.nasa.gov

Developed and maintained with support from NASA, this site provides a virtual observatory on the Web. You can search the sky not just as your eyes see it, in visible light band, but in all wavelengths from radio to gamma-ray. Instead of using keywords you enter coordinates (as explained on the site). Type in 5 234 34.94 + 22 00 37.60 and you will be shown a view of the sky at those coordinates: the Crab Nebula (Figure 8.3).

Figure 8.3 Results from a search on Search the Sky Skyview

Image shows visible light from the centre of the Crab Nebula.

Want to know more about...

Locating multimedia resources?

- Google image search — http://images.google.com.au
- Altavista image search — http://www.altavista.com/image
- Altavista audio search — http://www.altavista.com/audio
- Pics4Learning — http://www.freeimages.com
- FreeImages.com — http://www.freeimages.com
- Findsound.com — http://www.findsounds.com
- NASA's Photo Gallery — http://nssdc.gsfc.nasa.gov/photo_gallery

Other search tools

Other specific Web-based search tools are mentioned elsewhere in this book, for example those designed to:

- review and provide downloads of software (Chapter 2);
- identify sources of funding such as grants and scholarships (Chapter 5);
- locate e-mail addresses or phone numbers (Chapter 6);
- identify mailing lists and discussion groups relevant to your interests (Chapter 6);
- gain access to international library catalogues (Chapter 7);
- source statistics (Chapter 10).

Improving your search results

All search engines and directories use the type of search syntax we outlined in Chapter 7, including Boolean logic; phrase searching and proximity operators; truncators and wild-cards; and the ability to limit searches. If you haven't already read Chapter 7, now is the time to do so. However, be aware that the symbols required to improve your search may differ between search tools. For example, instead of using "AND" you might have to use a + sign; "NOT" may require a – sign. Consult the help section of each search tool you use.

Many search engines also provide an advanced search facility that guides you through the process. As the example in Figure 8.4 indicates, searching "all of the words" equates to AND; searching "at least one of the words" equates to OR; searching "without the words" equates to NOT and the "exact phrase" search provides a phrase search. There is also the ability to specify limits on language, file format, date etc.

Table 8.2 illustrates how combining search terms appropriately using search syntax can significantly refine your search. Note the variation in results obtained from using different search tools.

Reading and navigating web addresses

A Universal Resource Identifier (URI otherwise referred to as URL)[1] is the unique address allocated to each webpage. Behind the scenes, each website address starts with a numerical string (for example http://324.132.34.23), however most websites obtain a domain name, which enables them to replace

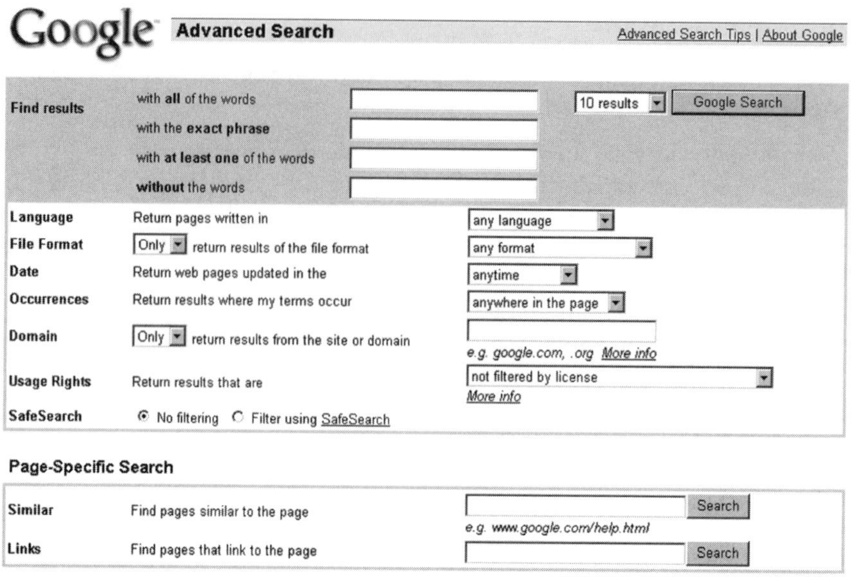

Figure 8.4   The advance search options available when performing a Web search

Example is from Google.

Table 8.2   Comparison of search results using refined searches across three search engines.

Search request	Results using Google	Results using Altavista	Results using Yahoo
Tectonic	3,980,000	3,600,000	3,610,000
Tectonic plate	1,340,000	981,000	1,030,000
"tectonic plate"	205,000	836,000	219,000
Tectonic plates	792,000	557,000	834,000
"tectonic plates"	435,000	557,000	557,000
"tectonic plates" OR "tectonic plate"	35,000	43,500	44,700
"tectonic plates" OR "tectonic plate" +India	995	1,670	1,640
"tectonic plates" OR "tectonic plate" +India +proterozoic	295	25	27
"tectonic plate" +India +proterozoic	350	1	26
"tectonic plate" +Nepal +proterozoic	41	0	6
"tectonic plate" +Nepal + "early proterozoic"	0	0	0

their number with a more friendly address in the following format: http://www.yourorganization.organizationtype.country, for example http://www.greenpeace.org.uk.

Knowing how to read and interpret URIs can assist you in critiquing the nature, origin and quality of websites. The URI for a site can indicate what country the information is from and whether the website is produced by a commercial, government or educational organization such as a university. Examples of URI components are provided in Table 8.3.

Table 8.3 Examples of URI components.

Country codes		Organization types (Australian and U.S. codes)	
.au	Australia	.com	Commercial
.ca	Canada	.edu	Educational
.fr	France	.gov	Government
.nz	New Zealand	.mil	Military
.uk	United Kingdom	.net	Network
.us	United States*	.org	Non-government organization

*The United States, the country in which the Internet originated, does not usually use its country code.

Thus, a site whose URI begins with http://www.health.nsw.gov.au can be identified as belonging to an Australian government organization. An educated guess would be that it is a department concerned with health, based in the state of New South Wales (NSW).

Understanding how URIs function can also assist in navigating from a particular webpage to the home page or parent page, even when no link is provided. For instance, if you conduct a Web search you may find a particularly relevant paper, but the webpage does not include the full bibliographic details. Deleting the end parts of the URI will take you progressively to the parent directory of the page, thus (generally) enabling you to find the home page.

For example, say you did a Web search and arrived at an article with the URI: http://www.ascilite.org.au/conferences/auckland02/proceedings/papers/ellen_sims_et_al.pdf. This paper, titled "Visual literacy: What is it and do we need it to use learning technologies effectively?" is evidently a conference paper but with no full bibliographic details provided and no link back to the conference home page. By deleting "ellen_sims_et_al.pdf" from the URI, you are taken to a page which allows you to navigate back to the parent directory, and find the referencing details.

Managing important websites

An important part of organizing and managing your research is knowing how best to deal with websites, particularly those you need to visit frequently. We consider some useful strategies in this section.

Managing bookmarks/favorites

Bookmarks or favorites (the terms vary depending on your browser) are permanent records of the website addresses (URIs), enabling you to return quickly and easily to the marked site. Adding a bookmark is as simple as selecting this option from a menu while viewing a website. However, continuing to add bookmarks will mean you end up with a long, unmanageable list. Learn to create folders and organize your bookmarks in them. When creating a structure of folders for filing your bookmarks use your filing schema (see Chapter 4). Your folder structure might also include:

- search engines;
- online journals, with subfolders for different subtopics or disciplines;
- professional groups and conferences;
- library catalogues and databases;
- personal interests.

Saving webpages as offline content

Some browsers provide you with the ability to make a bookmarked website available off-line by saving the content (text and images) of the page to your computer's hard drive. You can also set the options to download sub-pages of the page being added, however be aware that this can take time and a considerable amount of hard disk space if you save the images as well.

If you have limitations on your Internet access, saving webpages in this way can minimize the time you spend online and provide backups of Web-based information that may be transient in nature. However, there may be legal issues associated with this activity in particular countries. There are also programs available that perform this function in more sophisticated ways, for example WebWhacker (http://www.bluesquirrel.com/products/Web whacker) or SurfSaver (featured below).

Feature Software: SurfSaver

http://www.askSam.com

SurfSaver is an ideal tool for anyone doing online research. It is a browser add-on, which allows you to download and store webpages into allocated folders on your own computer. You can save multiple linked pages at once, by designating the number of levels you wish to save, and whether you want to limit to pages in the same root directory. You can also state whether you want to save images or not and can modify the page title, add keywords or notes. SurfSaver then allows you to search saved sites by word or phrase. Adding terms such as "to do" or "to follow up" can be a useful way of managing your Web-searching activities.

Creating a personal links page

While you may be happy to stick with the home page that automatically comes up when you open your browser, you can, of course, change your home page to any site you visit frequently, such as your preferred search engine. You generally do this in the preferences or options area of your program. However, creating your own links page and setting it as your home page can give you immediate access at a single click to your most visited websites. To set up your own links home page, follow these steps:

- Create a simple website (see Chapter 6) or a word-processed document saved in HTML format.
- Include a list of links to your most frequently accessed sites, perhaps arranged in a table so you can group related resources.
- Save this page to your hard disk.
- Right click on the file to view its properties and copy and paste the file location (e.g. C:\MyDocuments\MiscelResources\MyLinks.html) into the preferences/options area of your Web browser, as shown in Figure 8.5.

Now each time you open your Web browser you will see your list of links as a visible reminder to keep returning to your preferred sites.

Figure 8.5   **Updating your home page to be set to your personal links page**

After creating your file you can find out its file address by looking at the file properties. This address can then be copied and pasted into your browser properties. Example is from Internet Explorer.

Websites that change frequently, such as news sites or blogs (see Chapter 6) will sometimes use a technology called RSS (Really Simple Syndication) that is designed to notify subscribers when their website has been updated. Sites providing RSS usually have a button or link that says XML, RSS, or Syndicate this site. It also may be displayed with one of the following orange symbols: ⧉, XML or RSS .

To subscribe to RSS you need to install a freely available small program known variously as a "feed reader," "news aggregator" or "RSS Reader" (see examples below). Once installed, you can simply click on one of the RSS buttons or links. The software will add the link to your RSS reader and you will be notified when changes are made to that site.

Want to know more about...

RSS Feeds?

Further information about RSS

Wikipedia	http://en.wikipedia.org/wiki/RSS_%28file_format%29
Commoncraft	http://www.commoncraft.com/archives/000528.html

Examples of RSS readers

NewsGator	http://www.newsgator.com
Bloglines	http://www.bloglines.com

Ready references on the Web

Reference material of all kinds, dictionaries, thesauri, atlases, news, time-zones or currency converters, can be found on the Web in a variety of formats. Some are available free of charge, while others require a subscription. We provide a sample of general interest sites in Table 8.4 (see also Wikipedia and Translation tools featured in Chapter 6).

Evaluating Web-based information

When we all relied on print-based publishing there were more checks and balances available to assist us to determine whether the information we found was reputable. With the advent of the Web, where anyone can be a publisher, information is more difficult to assess for quality on appearances alone. Furthermore, few people fully appreciate how individual search engines work, or realize that they may filter, rank or block certain websites. For these reasons in particular, it is important to evaluate not only what you locate, but also to be wary of what your search tool might have excluded.

It is beyond the scope of this book to advise you on the essential tasks of critically reviewing, analyzing and synthesizing information. However, we recommend you adopt the framework suggested in Table 8.5 for evaluating information you retrieve from the Web, to ensure it is of an acceptable standard for scholarly work. If you are at all unsure about the validity of a resource you have found on the Web, then you would be advised to talk to your supervisor or other researchers in your disciplinary area.

Table 8.4   A sample of reference sites available on the Web.

Encyclopedias

Encyclopaedia Britannica Online	http://www.britannica.com
MSN Encarta	http://encarta.msn.com
Encyclopaedia.com (Columbia Encyclopaedia)	http://www.encyclopedia.com

Dictionaries (The more authoritative sources generally require subscription for full access)

YourDictionary.Com	http://www.yourdictionary.com
Merriam-Webster Online	http://www.m-w.com
Macquarie Dictionary Online	http://www.macquariedictionary.com.au
Oxford English Dictionary Online	http://www.oed.com

Atlases, maps and travel sites (Many provide access to a range of additional resources such as currency conversion, flags, time zones, population and climate)

Embassy World	http://www.embassyworld.com
World Atlas.com	http://www.graphicmaps.com/aatlas/world.htm
National Geographic Map Machine	http://plasma.nationalgeographic.com/mapmachine
Go Currency.com	http://www.gocurrency.com

Quotation sites (Useful when you are looking for a well-known quote for a thesis or presentation. Most provide free access and are compiled by users for users)

Bartleby.com	http://www.bartleby.com/quotations
ThinkExist.com Quotations	http://www.thinkexist.com
Wikiquotes	http://en.wikiquote.org

Weather (Important sources when planning fieldwork, or just to pack the right clothes when going to that conference!)

BBC Weather	http://www.bbc.co.uk/weather
CNN.com Weather	http://www.cnn.com/weather

Research jobs (Of course you will also find sites relevant to your preferred geographical destination or discipline)

Academic Jobs EU.com	http://www.academicjobseu.com
Research Jobs Australia	http://www.researchjobs.net.au
Jobs.as.uk	http://www.jobs.ac.uk

Calculators (basic, scientific, graphers, converters, equation solvers)

Math.com	http://www.math.com/students/calculators/calculators.html

Table 8.5   Framework for evaluating information sourced from the Web.

Evaluation criteria	Questions to ask yourself
Author	Is the author clearly identified? Does the site indicate the author's institutional affiliation (such as a university)? Is this verifiable – for instance, does the institution's website link to that individual's site? Does the site provide an indication of the author's training and/or qualifications and are these relevant to the content?
Authority/accuracy	Is there any indication that the work has been peer reviewed or refereed? Is this able to be independently verified? Has the author and their work been widely cited within the research or professional community?
Currency	Is the date of original writing or updating displayed? Is it important that the information is current? Is it information that becomes out-of-date quickly?
Hosting	Is the website mounted on a reputable and relevant organization's Web server? (Note that you can often determine this by navigating up the website directory structure, as explained earlier in the chapter) Is there some indication that the webpage has been established for some time?
Purpose	Is the information intended to persuade or sell a product or service? Is the information controversial? Might the author bring a particular agenda to the topic? How appropriate is the scope and depth of content coverage for your own needs?

Over to you...

1. What search engine do you favor for your Web searches? Try comparing another two or three search engines on your next Web search.
2. What search directories might be relevant for your research? Ask your university librarian to recommend any appropriate directories for your research area.
3. Compile a list of the sites you visit regularly as part of your research (and other activities as well if you wish). Create a links page as your home page and trial it for a month.
4. What is the quality of information like that you usually retrieve from the Web? Use the checklist template in Table 8.5 to evaluate the results of your next search.

Note

1   While URL was the term originally applied to a Web address, and has tended to remain the preferred term, since 1994 the term Universal Resource Identifier (URI) has officially subsumed URL.

Chapter 9

Managing and Organizing Your Literature

We have encountered many a researcher who has no methodical system for managing and organizing their literature. A dead giveaway is their large piles of literature on the floor of their office and their inability to find you that key article they mentioned to you last week. These are the researchers who are constantly frustrated by not being able to find the source or page number for that quote in the final stages of their write-up and spend days compiling their reference list in the final throes of their thesis preparation.

With the ease of accessing literature through electronic databases and the Web, your collection of literature that you then need to read, absorb, summarize and file for future reference can mount quickly and present quite a management headache. In Chapter 4 we offered strategies for good filing and storing of both your hard copy and electronic resources. Here, however, we focus specifically on managing and organizing your literature. Our aims in this chapter are to:

- focus on the key role that bibliographic software (such as EndNote) can play in not only keeping you on top of your research literature, but also assisting you in your research writing;
- suggest a strategic process to work through when engaging with and handling your literature;
- provide guidance on how to read and take notes efficiently.

Bibliographic software

In the past, organized researchers used boxes of cards upon which they painstakingly recorded the bibliographic details of their literature, sometimes even creating multiple cards for each reference in order to file them by author, title and subject. With the advent of bibliographic software, the tedium has been taken out of this essential research activity, enabling effective management of your literature.

The three key research functions that bibliographic programs perform are:

- **recording bibliographic information** (e.g. author, title, publisher), about papers, books and other literature as well as additional information such as keywords, categories, abstracts or notes;
- **facilitating searching for specific references** or groups of references, enabling you to find and manage your literature and providing an index for your filing system;
- **creating reference lists automatically from inserted citations**, using your preferred reference style (for example, APA, Harvard, Chicago, Numbered).

In addition to these basic functions, the software has the potential to enhance considerably your literature management since it can also be used to:

- support physical filing of hard copies of journal articles and retrieve references from your filing system;
- manage and process interlibrary loans;
- organize literature summaries and notes;
- import references directly from databases;
- shape your writing process.

The great advantage of bibliographic software is its time-saving capacities. You only enter the bibliographic information *once* in the database and never again have to retype it when you need to format references for papers or create lists of references. You will get the most from your bibliographic software if you adopt it in the early stages of your research process, however it is (almost) never too late to start.

How does it work?

Bibliographic software is just like any other database program (see Chapter 2) in that it comprises records and fields. The overall database is usually referred to as a "library." Each piece of literature entered in the database becomes one "record" and each record consists of a range of fields containing information specific to the bibliographic references (title, author, publisher etc.), as illustrated in Figure 9.1.

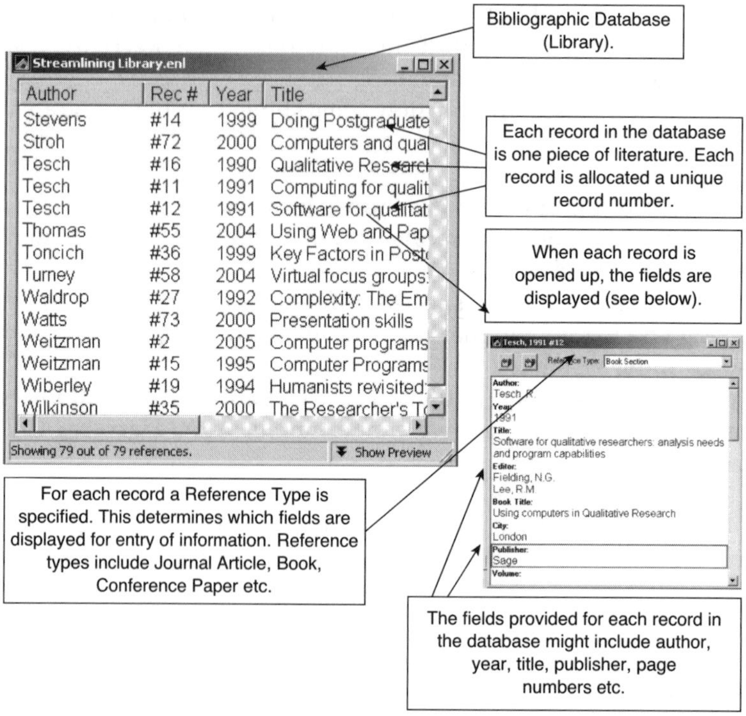

Figure 9.1 **The structure and appearance of a bibliographic database**

The overall database acts as a 'library', with each paper being a record in the database. Each record consists of a number of fields. Depending on the reference type selected, the names of the fields will vary. Example is from EndNote.

Entering references into the library is generally as simple as creating a new reference, selecting the appropriate material or reference type (for instance, book, journal article, report, thesis etc.) then filling in the appropriate details in the required fields (as illustrated in Figure 9.1). Once you have finished entering the details and close the reference, it will be saved. Often the program will, at this stage, allocate each record a unique identifying record number.

We have worked for many years observing and assisting researchers use bibliographic software. We have seen things go smoothly, without a hitch. However we have also seen many students come to grief, not because of the limitations of the software, but because they haven't understood properly how to use it, and rather than seeking assistance when things don't seem to be going as planned, they give up and start to format their references manually.

It is important to adhere to the program's guidelines for the format in which certain data are entered. Generally punctuation is kept to a minimum, for example, when recording page numbers for an article you would enter, say, 5–18 not pp. 5–18. The software will determine the way these page numbers appear in your reference list depending on the rules of your chosen referencing style. When recording multiple authors, each author usually is listed on a separate line and the program will vary the author format and add punctuation when it displays the reference.

When writing your research papers, use the bibliographic program to insert selected references into your paper as citations. It is also important to use the software to make any changes to automatically inserted citations, rather than doing this yourself in the text. For example, if you insert a citation, it may display as (Jones, 2003) in your paper. If your writing requires you either to exclude the author from the brackets or add a page number or comment within the brackets, use the program to do this, as Figure 9.2 demonstrates.

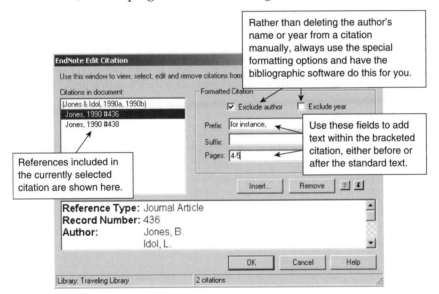

Figure 9.2　**Making changes to citations using bibliographic software**

In this example, the citation will no longer read "(Jones & Idol, 1990a, 1990b)" but rather might appear in text as "Jones & Idol have speculated (for instance, 1990a, p. 4–5, 1990b, p. 20)". Example is from EndNote.

To reiterate, **make sure that you familiarize yourself with the data entry requirements**, and be consistent with how you enter your data, particularly in relation to names and capitalization of titles, for example learn the difference between maximal and minimal capitalization.[1] If you use the wrong data entry format then the software will not be able to format your references consistently and according to the style guidelines.

Selecting bibliographic software

Consider the following features and capabilities when selecting and using bibliographic software.

- Customize reference types (i.e. change the available fields for each material type and the types of material types available).
- Customize output styles – although many programs come with a wide range (even hundreds) of referencing styles (APA, Harvard, etc.), it is useful to be able to modify or create styles yourself in whatever format you need.
- Handle footnote referencing, including use of *"ibid."*
- Exclude authors or years easily from in-text citations.
- Sort the library in whatever order you wish.
- Search, including the use of Boolean operators (see Chapter 7).
- Allocate each reference a unique number that can be used for filing – some programs support multiple series of such numbers within the same database.
- Establish term lists or authority lists (see below) on any field – some programs automatically generate term lists from entries while others come with a journal name term list including ISSN codes and standard abbreviations.
- Do spell checks.
- Plug-in (operate from within) your word processing program.
- Import data from online literature databases or the Web. Check with your librarian to see whether your software provides the necessary z39.50 connection. If you use this strategy, employ a consistent note in one of the fields to distinguish between those articles for which you only have bibliographic details and those that you have actually accessed.
- Link directly to files stored on your computer such as electronic versions of a paper, word processed notes or summaries.
- Store images or other objects.
- Post bibliographic databases to the Web or share libraries across a network.
- Operate compatibly with palmtop computers.
- Perform global editing, for instance, to find a group of references and change the text or a field for all references in that group – this is useful if you want to label a group of references or fix common spelling issues.
- Share papers written with others using the bibliographic software.

Examples of bibliographic software are provided in the software table at the end of the chapter.

Making the most of your bibliographic software

Many people are taught the "technical" process of using the software but don't realize or come to use its full potential. Bibliographic software is more than just a place to store your references. The following strategies will enhance your overall organization.

- **Have just one bibliographic database** (or library), rather than maintaining different libraries for different purposes. If you need separate subsets at any stage you can always search on a criterion and copy and paste the smaller set across to a temporary library.
- **Maintain a common library** if you work within a team of researchers, and develop a common filing system for sharing literature. Some programs facilitate networking of databases or are Web-based. Alternatively, if you want to maintain individual databases using the same software, you can reduce duplicated effort by copying individual records into a temporary library, and sending it to your colleague who can copy and paste those records into their own collection. This is particularly useful where records are "value-added," i.e. they include additional notes or summaries.
- **Use the term list feature** to save time and enhance consistency, for example, use it for:

  - keywords – if you want to use these to search and relocate articles you need to ensure consistency, e.g. "help seeking" versus "help-seeking" or "organizational behaviour" versus "organizational behavior";
  - publishers – consistency is important e.g. check for "Sage" versus "Sage Publications";
  - filing categories (see later in this chapter).

- **Use the link function** within your library to hyperlink directly to electronic files.
- **Copy a reference from the library in its formatted style**, when e-mailing references to colleagues (EndNote, for example, uses Control-K for this action).
- **Consider modifying styles** so that they display/print the extra customized fields in your database. For example, output of a record in APA style might look like this:

Triantafillou, E., Pomportsis, A., Demetriadis, S., & Georgiadou, E. (2004). The value of adaptivity based on cognitive style: An empirical study. *British Journal of Educational Technology*, 36(1), 95–106.

Modifying this style as "APA full details" might output the record like this:

> **Record #**: 1139
> Triantafillou, E., Pomportsis, A., Demetriadis, S., & Georgiadou, E. (2004). The value of adaptivity based on cognitive style: An empirical study. *British Journal of Educational Technology*, 36(1), 95–106.
> **Label**: ID – Instructional Design
> **Keywords**: Online Learning; Learning Styles
> **Notes**: Examines the influence of cognitive style, specifically field dependence/ independence on students' interaction in online learning. Relevant to metacognitive approach to learning.
> **Notes**: Copy on File

This is useful for constructing summary pages, sending references to your colleagues or transferring notes directly to your word-processed document.

- **Customize additional fields** to your own needs, for example:

    - **broad research category** – this might correspond with your overall filing schema and hence with the way you organize your filing cabinet (see Chapter 4 as well as further notes on filing provided below);
    - **keywords** (see also the note above regarding Terms List to ensure consistency);
    - **location of the copy or original**, for instance, whether you have an electronic or a hard copy of the paper, whether you borrowed a copy from a friend, whether it is held by the local library (and perhaps even with the shelf location in case you need to find it again);
    - **details of articles not yet held**, or in the process of being located – for instance, the date you requested a copy from your library's document delivery service or the date you ordered a copy from your bookshop to track any non-received items and to guard against double-ordering;
    - **a rating scale or other marker** indicating relevance of the reference to your work;
    - **notes, summaries or extracted quotes** can be centrally recorded in your database, keeping these notes with their full bibliographic details and enhancing the searchability of your database (don't forget to record page numbers next to direct quotes).

- **Add a single bibliography to multiple, linked documents such as a thesis** in EndNote. For example, disable the automatic formatting feature ("cite-while-you-write") and "unformat" the citations, so that no reference list appears at the end of each chapter file. Then create a Master Document (as described in Chapter 12) and format the bibliography from within the Master Document.

Feature Software: BiblioWeb

http://www.biblioscape.com/biblioweb.htm

BiblioWeb is a bit different from the more familiar stand-alone bibliographic programs in that it is used entirely through your Web browser, making it ideal for use by research teams and groups.

Registered users can be assigned different rights to a particular bibliographic library, and can be identified as either "writers" (those who can add, delete and change records) or "readers" (those who can only access the data). Formatting of documents happens by transferring your document (in RTF format) to the server, which then formats it according to your selected style and sends it back to you. BiblioWeb can also be used to run a Web-based forum.

Strategic handling of your literature

Making the most of bibliographic software is only part of the solution to the problem of how to manage your literature effectively. You also need to be very strategic and methodical throughout the whole process of handling your literature, from the moment you identify an article of interest, through reading and summarizing it, to incorporating it into your research argument, and ultimately storing it in your filing system.

- Make an entry in your bibliographic database as soon as you realize a reference is relevant and of interest, whether you have the full article or not.
- Use your bibliographic software to record all relevant information such as whether you have the full text of the article, whether you need to send away for it on interlibrary loan, whether you need to follow up the authors etc.
- Make sound decisions as to whether you need to print or photocopy articles, or whether it is preferable to retain a copy in electronic format (see discussion of these issues in Chapter 4).
- Determine where you will place your articles while you are in the process of reading and taking notes from them (see Chapter 4).
- Establish a good system for filing of both print and electronic copies (see next section).
- Engage in good reading and note-taking processes (see later in chapter).

Filing print and electronic copies of literature

In Chapter 4 we considered a range of good filing practices for the management of both print and electronic documents. We also suggest here these more specific strategies for filing your research literature.

- **Draw on your filing schema** (see Chapter 4) to develop broad categories for filing your literature. We'd also suggest you give each category a code, for example:

GT = General Theory
ME = Methodology
AA = Broad research topic A
BB = Broad research topic B
TT = Teaching focus A
ZZ = Teaching focus B

Each of these categories becomes a section in your filing cabinet.

- **Give each reference a unique identifier.** You could use the category code (as above) followed by the unique number allocated by your bibliographic software. This will mean that you can easily label each article and cross reference it to your electronic library. Since each number is unique, the sequence of articles in each section of your cabinet won't be complete, but it doesn't need to be. For example, the order of articles in your filing drawers might run:

GT1, GT4, GT8, GT16….
ME3, ME9, ME10, ME11..
AA2, AA7, AA12, AA13…
TT5, TT6, TT14, TT15….

- **Methodically label each hard copy article before you file it** – e.g. attach to each paper a brightly colored slip which allows you not only to identify the article as your own, but also to monitor where you are up to with processing it. For instance, you might record the filing location and the date you added the reference to your library, tick off when you have summarized and made notes or when you added it to your thesis or report or even give it a relevance rating (see Figure 9.3).
- **Save electronic copies of archived literature in a single folder** on your computer. Within this folder you may have subfolders which represent the relevant categories in your filing schema (above). Name each file consistently e.g. using the unique identifier above (e.g. GT45). This will remain unique and is preferable to file names such as smith.pdf or jones.doc.

 See the **Organizing and Managing Your Research Website**

for templates for labeling hard copies of your literature.
http://www.sagepub.co.uk/phelps

Category		Category	
Number		Number	
Author _____		Author _____	
Added to Endnote ☐ Keywords Added:☐		Added to Endnote ☐ Keywords Added:☐	
Related to: _____		Related to: _____	
Rating: High:☐ Medium☐ Low:☐		Rating: High:☐ Medium☐ Low:☐	
Notes taken:☐ Date Added: _____		Notes taken:☐ Date Added: _____	

Figure 9.3   Example of slip for labeling hardcopies of your literature

Reading and note taking

You might know some researchers who get by with reading an article, assigning at least some concepts to memory, and then adding the paper to a growing pile on their floor. We would encourage you to get into good reading and note-taking habits as early in your research process as possible. Try the following strategies:

- **Minimize double handling.** Never pick up and put down an article without doing something with it and try to deal with most of your papers only once.
- **Highlight key points and write notes in margins**, whether you do your reading on print or on screen (see Chapter 4 for the pros and cons of both). For each article decide whether you are likely to just pick up general ideas or quote directly from it.
- **Leave the article for 24 hours** to allow some time to reflect on the relevance of ideas to your research, particularly if it is a significant work. Try not to leave too long before returning to consolidate your notes.
- **Summarize key points and type or scan quotes** so that you can file the original and decrease the quantity of literature you need to return to. It is also much easier to then locate the original if needed. We suggest you do this in your bibliographic database.
- **Be consistent about the location and format for your notes** (see recommendations above for using bibliographic software for this purpose).
- **Consider transferring summaries and notes to the most logical and useful end locations,** for example, directly into your report or thesis document. They don't always stay in exactly that place, but this strategy helps to locate literature within your thesis structure and argument, and also allows you to connect content of a similar nature.

- **Ensure that each note you take will stand alone** without you needing to go back to the original. For example, always include the citation after every quote or paraphrased set of notes so that you will not lose the original reference. If you take notes within bibliographic software this is not necessary, however you do need to record specific page numbers for quotes.
- **Know when enough is enough.** Literature searching is an endless process. Your time limits and overall project management (see Chapter 5) will force you to call a halt at some stage.

Reading and note taking is the start of the writing process, which we deal with further in Chapter 12.

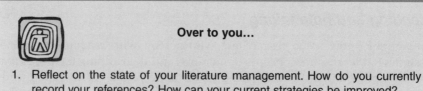

Over to you...

1. Reflect on the state of your literature management. How do you currently record your references? How can your current strategies be improved?
2. If you have been using bibliographic software for a while, are you making the most of it? What particular tips might you now adopt?
3. How might you improve your literature-filing processes?
4. How might you change your current reading and note-taking strategies to increase your efficiency and effectiveness?

Note

1 Maximal capitalization (title case) uses capitals for all the main words in the sentence whilst minimal capitalization (sentence case) only uses a capital at the beginning of the phrase or sentence. Many styles use maximal for book titles and journal names and minimal for chapter and journal article titles.

Examples of bibliographic software.

Software	Manufacturer/ developer	Platform	Website	Licensing	Demo on Website?	Special features
BiblioExpress	SG Software	Windows	http://www.biblioscape.com	Freeware	✓	Free edition of Biblioscape. Produces small, easily shared files
Bibliographix	Bibliographix	Windows	http://www.bibliographix.com	Freeware & commercial	✓	Combines reference management, information retrieval and Idea Manager. Basic version free but limited
Biblioscape	SG Software	Windows	http://www.biblioscape.com	Commercial	Tour only	Lite, Standard, Professional, Librarian and Palmtop versions
BiblioWeb	SG Software	Web-enabled	http://www.biblioscape.com/biblioweb.htm	Commercial	Example on site	Users are assigned "read" or "write" privileges. Allows groups to share a common database. Supports a threaded discussion
Bookends	Sonny Software	Mac	http://www.sonnysoftware.com	Commercial	✓	Used with Reference Miner (free) to import from Amazon, PubMed and Library of Congress
Citation	The Write Direction	Windows	http://www.citationonline.net	Commercial	✓	Online searchable style guide. A variation called Legal Citation supports legal research and writing (e.g. statutes, cases)
EndNote	ISI Research soft	Windows, Mac	http://www.endnote.com	Commercial	✓	Can store images and operate on a network. Highly customizable. Unlimited library size
Getaref	DatAid AB	Windows	http://www.getaref.com	Commercial	✓	Journal name database includes ISSN codes and abbreviations. Supports multiple series of unique identifying numbers

(Continued)

Software	Manufacturer/developer	Platform	Website	Licensing	Demo on Website?	Special features
Ibidem	Nota Bene	Windows	http://www.notabene.com	Commercial	✓	Works with BookWhere for Internet searching
Library Master	Balboa	Windows	http://www.balboa-software.com	Commercial	✓	Bibliographic and data manager (see Chapter 4)
Papyrus	Research Software	Windows, Mac	http://www.ResearchSoftware Design.com	Freeware	✓	Stores and cross-links your references, notes and graphic images. Links your references to the Internet
ProCite	ISI Researchsoft	Windows, Mac	http://www.procite.com	Commercial	✓	Searches the Internet and imports from databases. Available as a network program
Reference Manager	ISI Researchsoft	Windows	http://www.refman.com	Commercial	✓	Makes references collections available on the Web. Shares databases on a network
RefViz	ISI Researchsoft	Windows, Mac	http://www.refviz.com	Commercial	✓	Used with Endnote, ProCite and Reference Manager as a search visualization tool (see Chapter 8)
RefWorks	RefWorks	Web-based	http://www.refworks.com	Commercial	✓	Used through your Web browser. Enables sharing of bibliographic databases
Scholar's Aid	Scholar's Aid	Windows	http://scholarsaid.com	Freeware Lite version	✓	Automates transferal of notes into the paper being written, including page numbers. Automated backup feature
WriteNote	ISI Researchsoft	Web-based	http://www.writenote.com	Commercial	Interactive tutorial	Allows RTF documents to be uploaded and formatted; paper can then be downloaded. Annual subscription required

Chapter 10

Designing Data Collection Systems

Collecting data lies at the heart of the research process. Our aim in this chapter is not to reproduce information in other texts about research design. Nor do we focus on discipline-specific forms of data collection. Rather, we introduce some general organizational aspects of data collection and consider a range of generic tools and strategies that can assist you to collect and store different types of data. This chapter should be read in conjunction with Chapter 11 on managing data analysis.

Specifically, the chapter covers:

- tips on planning and managing the process of data collection;
- tips on using multimedia forms of data, including video and audio;
- strategies for using computer-based data input systems, including behavior observation and repertory grid software;
- the range of uses for simulation software;
- how to collect data online, including surveys, interviews and focus groups;
- a selection of data that can be sourced via the Web.

Planning and managing data collection

Whether you are conducting qualitative, quantitative or mixed method research, time invested at the planning stages can make data analysis much more efficient, easy and potentially more accurate and reliable.

- **Decide how you will analyze your data when you are designing your data collection approach**. This is equally so for both quantitative and qualitative research. "The most intricate statistical analysis will not fix or improve a poor design."[1]
- **Make sure you consider issues such as theoretical and methodological appropriateness, sampling and research instrument design**, information that is available in a range of excellent texts, but not covered here. The software we showcase in Chapter 4 (Methodologist's Toolchest) can be a valuable aid for planning data collection.
- **Organize your data in a form that will facilitate its analysis**. If you intend doing statistical analysis, it is advisable to record your data in a spreadsheet or database in a format that can be exported easily into a statistical software package (see Chapter 11). Qualitative data, whether audio, video or transcribed text files, should also be organized using consistent systems.
- **Don't collect more data than you need**. It may be tempting to keep collecting and collecting, but this is frequently a major obstacle to completing research. While you may just love being out in the field catching and tagging rats, at some point you have to come inside and do something with all that data!
- **Avoid the temptation to collect data that is not central to your research questions**. If you are designing a survey, for instance, don't include questions that are superfluous to your needs, just because they might be useful or seem interesting. Again, this emphasizes the need for a clear design and rationale before you start collecting data.
- **Be clear about your population and the appropriateness of your sample** (see Chapter 11).
- **Have a look at how others have designed data collection instruments** (such as surveys or interview schedules) but be cautious about simply applying these uncritically to your context.
- **Make sure that the instrument you plan to use is going to measure what you want it to measure**. This may sound obvious, but it is a problem that arises time and time again. The name of an instrument is not necessarily a good indicator in all situations, for instance a "quality of life" measure may not be appropriate for a sample of people with disabilities if it asks questions designed for a different population.
- **Consider cultural issues in planning your data collection** processes and instruments, such as language, terminology, interpersonal protocols, and so on. For instance, taking a survey instrument originally used in Britain and using it unchanged in Thailand may lead to issues in the validity of the data you collected.

Multimedia data collection

Here we consider strategies for collecting audio, video and still image forms of data.

Audio data collection

There are many circumstances that arise during the course of your research when you could make use of information gathered through audio recording, for instance:

- when you need to conduct interviews with individuals or groups;
- when you meet with your supervisors or supervisory panels;
- when you want to record reflections and observations.

"As a hammer is essential to fine carpentry, a good tape recorder is indispensable to fine fieldwork."[2] While you will no doubt be familiar with analogue (tape) cassette recorders, digital recording equipment is readily available to researchers. In this section we consider these formats and the factors you should consider in both selecting audio recording equipment and using it as a means of data collection.

Analogue or digital recording?
The advantages of conventional **analogue (tape) recorders** include:

- the equipment is inexpensive and readily available;
- the equipment is straightforward to use and requires minimal training;
- you can listen to analogue cassettes in the car or on other standard tape recorders;
- recordings made using an analogue recorder can be digitized by re-recording the cassette tape to a computer. This is best done by connecting the tape recorder (line out) directly to the computer (line or mic in), and preferably using audio software (see below) to record. Transferal usually takes place in real-time, however, so it is a case of setting up the process and going off for a long lunch.

Digital recording devices offer a number of advantages over analogue recorders, including:

- improved sound quality, since there is no inherent tape hiss (although quality will still depend on microphone quality and ambient noise);
- the ability to transfer sound files directly to your computer or network for ease of storage, backup and transfer to colleagues (e.g. via e-mail);
- the ability to edit sound files digitally since you can instantly access any point on the recording, break longer recordings into smaller segments, delete extraneous content, adjust recording levels or improve sound quality;
- the ability to keep track of data about the audio data file (known as "metadata") such as the date and time of recording, author's details, subject matter, recording duration, priority, typist details, transcription time and so on.

Choosing a digital recorder and software

Digital audio recorders vary considerably in price, quality and complexity and it is a false economy to purchase a cheap recorder if the poor audio quality increases the cost and time of transcription.[3] Some recorders are designed specifically for audio recording while others designed for playback of digital music can also be used for recording. The range includes:[4]

- **Handheld computers** (such as Palm PCs or PDAs) can be used to record sound and have the advantage of wider application. They are, however, relatively expensive and many do not support external microphones.
- **Desktop and laptop computers** are already available to most researchers and may be a cost-efficient approach for phone or office-based interviews, although they are more cumbersome for field research.
- **Music players such as MP3 Players or iPods** are specially designed for listening to music and have the key advantage of portability and (bonus) recreational use. They range considerably in price relative to the amount of storage space and quality. While many have an internal microphone, most lack a microphone input jack to enhance recording quality. Some do not facilitate transfer of files to a hard drive, which is essential for backup and analysis. Even the most basic can, however, serve as a good means for recording researcher reflections.
- **MiniDiscs** generally provide high quality sound recording, are very portable and allow long recording time. They usually fall in the mid-price bracket and vary considerably in their ease of file transfer and whether you can use an external microphone. They do, however, provide other functionality such as data storage.
- **Voice recorders** are specially designed devices for recording memos, dictated letters and interviews. Prices vary considerably and the more expensive ones have microphone jacks and interface with computers using USB or memory cards. Most store audio in highly compressed formats and come with software to manage audio files on the computer. Again, the quality, functionality and usability of this software can vary considerably.
- **Professional solid-state recorders** are used by professional broadcast journalists and are rugged and reliable but very expensive and unlikely to be useful for the average researcher.
- **Portable CD or DVD recorders** are expensive but produce excellent quality, enabling you to record large quantities of data directly to a disk.

Issues to consider with digital recording

When choosing a digital recorder and compatible software, consider these key issues:

- **Amount of storage space** of the media and associated recording times. Make sure the recording times available match the demands of your particular research project.

- **Ability to use an external microphone**. Internal microphones are usually of low quality and can be difficult to position close to interviewees, particularly in group contexts. Some recorders provide only a line-in rather than mic-in jack, and you may need a microphone with a booster if only line-in is available.
- **Size, portability and intrusiveness in an interview**.
- **Display functions on the recorder itself**, for instance, indicating remaining battery life, recording time, length of interview etc.
- **Ease of transferring files** from your audio device to your computer (e.g. via a USB cable or media cards) and whether transfer occurs in real time (i.e. a 1-hour interview takes 1 hour to transfer) or is instantly transferred as a whole file.
- **File format that the audio is stored in**, including the compression rate (and hence the amount of hard-disk space required on your computer) and its compatibility with other software. This is particularly important if you are sharing files with others.
- **The interface for organizing files** on both the hardware and software, including the ability to create folders and move files between folders, rename files, delete files and duplicate files.
- **Features to enhance the sound quality.** These are most commonly used following conversion of audio from analogue to digital format but are only recommended if audio is required for presentation purposes or if sound quality is too poor for transcription.
- **Ability to apply erase protection** on files.
- **Voice activation** features.
- **Battery life and ease of replacing and/or recharging batteries.** Some models provide a docking station which recharges the recorder.
- **Shortcuts and easy key strokes** to play, stop, cue, skip forward and skip backward, replay, mark (bookmark) or break files, facilitating checking, correcting and transcribing (see below).
- **Ability to use a foot-operated switch** for hands-free transcription.
- **Ability to "attach" or associate text, pictures and other file formats** to the sound file, providing the ability to link text and images to the audio. Note that some data analysis software (see Chapter 11) allows direct coding of digital audio files.

A selection of shareware, freeware and commercial software products that perform some or all of these functions (and more) are listed at the end of this chapter.

Transcribing audio to text

There are data analysis programs that facilitate analysis of untranscribed video and audio data (see Chapter 11). However, if you are like most qualitative researchers who collect audio data, you will want to transcribe that data into text format. Some researchers view transcription as something that can be done with administrative/clerical assistance, i.e. they are primarily interested in the actual words spoken. Others see transcription as a critical part of their research process and prefer to do it themselves, noting aspects such as changes in tone of voice and silences. This also provides feedback on the effectiveness of the type of questions they asked and the resulting quality of the data. This "immersion in the data" brings with it insights, ideas, interpretations and re-interpretations and for some types of research it is often just as relevant to note what is *not* said, or *how* something is said than it is to simply transcribe *what* is said.[5]

If you are hoping that software will transcribe your recordings at the touch of a button then you will probably be disappointed. As discussed in Chapter 2, there are limitations in using voice recognition software, and these problems are compounded when transcribing research data. In particular, the difficulty of training software to recognize multiple voices (as in the case of interviews) remains a barrier. Most normal conversations (such as from interviews) will be too fast and lack the kind of clarity required for voice recognition software to transcribe. If you have already trained a voice recognition program to recognize your voice, an option is to listen to the audio and then dictate it into your transcription document.

More commonly, researchers still rely on listening to their recordings and typing up the text. The average speed of transcription ranges from 1:5 to 1:10 although a really fast transcriber might reach 1:3. In other words, for each hour of interview you will need to allow 5–10 hours for transcription.

To improve transcription:

- **use foot or knee-operated mechanisms** to play, pause, rewind and stop the sound to leave your hands free for typing and note making;
- **use keyboard shortcuts** to play, pause, rewind if you are using digital audio software;
- **devise a set of symbols for non-verbal aspects of conversation**, e.g. you might use „„ for a pause, or ☺ or [laugh] for laughter, remembering, of course, to be consistent;
- **take frequent breaks** – it's a tiring and potentially harmful activity (see Chapter 3 on health and safety).

Telephone interviewing and recording

Technically there are many ways of recording phone conversations. Legally, the issue is a little more blurred. Many countries have in place legislation which regulates the recording of telephone calls. In some instances, recording is allowable providing the interviewee is told at the beginning of the conversation and given the choice to either end the call, or not to be recorded. It is important to check privacy regulations in your own country and to ensure you have ethical clearance. Telephone recording options include:

- **Telephone conferencing** facilities provided by many phone service providers mean that they will manage the recording process for you after making the connections with all participants.

- **A good quality speaker telephone** means you can record what is said using either analogue or digital recording equipment.
- **A telephone coupler** is a relatively inexpensive device that can be inserted in the line between your telephone and handset and then connected to your audio recording equipment. Unfortunately your voice will usually sound much louder than the person's you are interviewing. There are much more expensive alternatives (known as digital hybrids), but these are unlikely to be practical for most small research projects.
- **Internet telephony** (discussed in Chapter 6) allows you to bypass your telephone and use your computer. You could use one of the programs listed at the end of this chapter to record all audio going through your computer to achieve a digital recording of your phone interview.

Computer-assisted telephone interviewing

Computer-assisted telephone interviewing (CATI) is a telephone surveying technique which uses a computer-based questionnaire instead of a paper-based one to provide a script for the interviewer. The software customizes the questionnaire automatically depending on the answers provided, or information already known about the participant. CATI software usually includes question scripting, question sequencing, assisted data entry, data validation and interview scheduling. Computer-assisted personal interviewing (CAPI) uses similar software to CATI, except that the interview is done face-to-face.

 More tips on audio data collection

- **Be conscious of the quality of sound** as it will make a significant difference to the time and effort required to transcribe or listen to the recording and thus the overall value of the data. Placing a recorder in the middle of a table during a group discussion, for instance, can lead to bad quality audio. Wherever possible use a high quality microphone.
- **Be conscious of the length of the recording medium**. If the recording device reaches the end of its recording time you can lose valuable data.
- **Be conscious of the ethical aspects of audio data collection**. Interviewees must provide informed consent and be aware when recording starts and finishes. They should also have the right to turn the recorder off at any time during an interview, so keep the recorder within easy reach and tell them how they can stop recording if they wish.
- **Be prepared to keep manual notes** before and after the recorder is turned on.

Video data collection

The use of video as a data collection tool has become much more feasible since the advent of small, high quality, affordable digital video recorders and easy-to-use video editing software. Moving images provide a form of data that offer insight into contexts and subject matter that simply can't be gained through other means. In this section we consider the benefits and issues to consider when using video and provide some tips for making the most of video as a data collection strategy.[6]

Benefits of video for data collection
Video can:

- **allow you to make observations without being present**, thus support-ing more naturalistic fieldwork;
- **document actual versus espoused behavior**, overcoming issues of lack of reliability in self-reporting;
- **provide insights into interactions** such as gesture, eye movement, manipulation of materials or use of computers;
- **enable you to watch an action sequence repeatedly**, allowing micro-analysis of interactions;
- **permit more than one researcher to watch and make judgments about the data**, thus checking or confirming observations and conclusions;
- **reveal and record unforeseen factors** that might not otherwise be recog-nized, such as non-verbal signs;
- **be shared with participants**, enabling them to express their own inter-pretation of their behavior;
- **enable you to return to the video data later in time** when the signifi-cance of an event may have emerged or patterns, regularities and trends have started to become apparent;
- **enable still images to be extracted for separate analysis or reporting**;
- **enable data collection over the Internet using a webcam**, for example, for conducting an online interview, where the interviewer asks questions in real time. Recording the video provides a permanent record of the interview.

Issues associated with video as a data source

- **Video is not more objective** than other forms of observation. Your per-sonal interests and theoretical orientation will inevitably determine which parts of the action you perceive to be relevant, reliable or usable. "Every time a video camera focuses on one thing, it tends to deempha-sise or ignore something else."[7] You still need to consider issues of valid-ity, reliability and generalizability and you must acknowledge the extent to which technical aspects of filming have influenced your impressions. As with any research involving qualitative data, it is important for you to make your values, attitudes, beliefs and assumptions explicit.

- **Decisions to focus on an individual can exclude interaction of others.** Classroom footage, for instance, which zooms in on one student who is responding well to a lesson may neglect to notice the 29 other students who are not engaged (or vice versa). Similarly the angle and position of the camera is critical. The preferred shot for research is one that is wide enough to capture all participants in a joint activity and narrow enough to see details of what they are doing, with the camera stationary and angled down slightly towards the participants.
- **Positioning of microphones can privilege certain voices or perspectives.** For instance, focusing on a teacher's voice can make a classroom seem unnaturally quiet while poor microphone location can pick up every cough and chair squeak, making a classroom seem chaotic.[8]
- **Ethical and legal issues** are paramount since participants are clearly identifiable in video data. This becomes particularly important if video data are used in a thesis, conference presentation or other publication. Generally it is legal to tape public behavior in a public space, but not private behavior (without permission) in private spaces or private conversations in a public space. Participants need to be free to refuse to participate, and understand that they can request destruction of the tape. Techniques such as distorting voices and "smudging" faces can preserve anonymity,[9] however you need to weigh up the benefits of presenting video in this way.
- **Introducing a camera will tend to change how participants behave.** Explaining the purpose of the taping, having the equipment in the context prior to filming and leaving equipment alone during taping can decrease this effect.
- **Video can quickly produce huge quantities of data**. Data reduction can become oppressively time consuming, with transcription of the audio alone taking up to 10 times the duration of the tape. It is common for researchers to collect too much video data without adequately planning how it will be used.
- **Don't expect a video masterpiece from your data collection phase.** Our familiarity with television and film impacts on our expectations of the quality of video. Technical considerations such as lighting, sound quality, level of activity and proximity influence our viewing and interpretation. There is often a temptation to expect a polished performance from our "actors."[10]

Getting the most from video recording

- Ensure good sound quality by positioning microphones as close as possible to the source. Try wherever possible to decrease ambient noise.
- Ensure video equipment is working well ahead of time. Try piloting the filming techniques (e.g. moving, zooming), noting the effect on perspectives.
- Start recording before participants arrive and stop after they have left, so that you don't miss the often critical "non-official" activities, providing you have permission.

- Use a camera operator to focus on particular events.
- Use tripods for smooth tracking when filming.
- Consider using multiple cameras if you need to focus on different aspects of the data collection context.
- Avoid glare and backlighting as much as possible.
- Make backups of tapes or video files before editing and use copies or "dubs" for analysis to minimize risk of loss or damage of original data.
- Methodically label or name tapes or files (date, place, tape number).
- Use multiple methods of observation and recording. On-the-scene observers almost always notice things that are not apparent in the video.[11]
- Take notes during and after sessions to collect information that might get lost. Video does not pick up or preserve broader contextual information, such as what occurred the previous day or the previous hour.
- Triangulate video data with other methods such as ethnographic or direct field observations, clinical interviews, journals, samples of work or photographs of fixed features.

Technical considerations in selecting video hardware and software

- Digital video editing requires lots of computer memory (both RAM and hard drive), particularly for longer footage.
- You will need a high-capacity backup system, either an external hard drive or a DVD recorder.
- Digital cameras generally use both USB or "firewire"[12] to download data directly (and quickly) to the computer. The latter provides a faster connection but a firewire card is required in your computer and is not always standard in the average computer;
- Digital editing software should allow clips to be converted into a common user-friendly format such as a Quicktime or .avi file format.
- It is advisable to plan a system or process to organize, manage and analyze your video data. This may require a simple database to manage files (see the section on data management databases in Chapter 4) and/or data analysis software which handles video data (see Chapter 11).

Feature Researcher: Video in Mathematics Education
Judith A. Mousley, Deakin University, Australia[13]

One of the areas of research which has developed a strong tradition in the use of video as a source of data is mathematics education. Judith Mousley's PhD research into mathematical understanding utilized video to inquire into the strategies that teachers use when interacting with students, including physical expressions, vocal features and linguistic characteristics, as well as conceptual, symbolic, pedagogical and organizational approaches such as group work or structuring of space.

(Continued)

One of the advantages of using video, for Judith, is that it enables rich and complex data to be revisited many times and examined through different lenses or for various purposes. Because of the complexity of Judith's analysis, she converted her video data to alternate formats such as audio only, video only, photo frames and transcripts. Judith found benefit in the process of transcription, as it gave her the opportunity to deliberate on data, to engage more deeply with the dynamics and to make connections between evidence of students' and teachers' meaning making and how assumptions affected the teachers' practice.

Judith's analysis strategy involved coding "snippets" of video that seemed relevant to the research question and literature into pre-determined and emerging categories. Judith utilized a spreadsheet into which a link was pasted to the video snippet itself, such that clicking on the hyperlink would play the relevant snippet. The spreadsheet also recorded notes on the origin of the video excerpt, its categorization, the question which had been asked and a short descriptor along with diary notes, each in a separate column.

As Judith highlights, being able to capture and present the look on a child's face as they worked out an answer to a mathematical problem is far more powerful than a text transcript could communicate.

Images as a data source

Still images can, like video, be a valuable data source, either in their own right or in combination with other methods. Stills can be extracted from video or taken using a digital or 35-mm camera. Of course, image data need not be limited to photos. Participants may be asked to produce drawings which can then be scanned to digital format or be produced by other means such as concept mapping. Many of the comments made in relation to video also apply to photos. Rather than providing further advice, we include an example of how images can be effectively used as a source of data in research.

Feature Researchers: Concept Mapping as Data Collection

Mike Keppel et al., Hong Kong Institute of Education[14]

Mike's research team at the Hong Kong Institute of Education has conducted research into the theories of teaching and learning that influence how pre-service teacher educators use technology-enhanced environments. They have used Inspiration, a mind mapping and visualization program (see Chapter 3) in their interviews with university staff.

Combined with video-based interviewing, the concept mapping software is used to capture teacher educators' ideas about their learning design. Figure 10.1 illustrates an example of such a concept map. As part of the interviewing process the

(*Continued*)

mind mapping software is used as a prompt for articulation and exploration. By using the hyperlinking features of Inspiration, the researchers are able to insert links to video files or other documentation that relate to the interviewee's concept map.

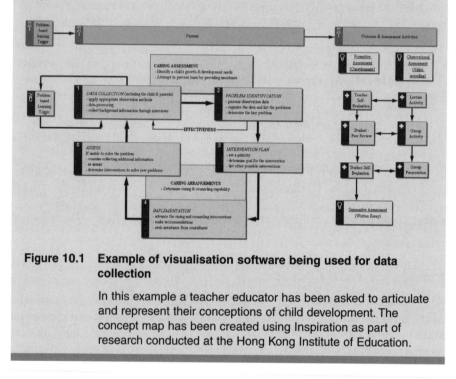

Figure 10.1   **Example of visualisation software being used for data collection**

In this example a teacher educator has been asked to articulate and represent their conceptions of child development. The concept map has been created using Inspiration as part of research conducted at the Hong Kong Institute of Education.

A range of software to support use of multimedia data is provided in a table at the end of this chapter.

Computer-based data collection

Collecting data through direct input into a computer can prove very efficient in certain research contexts, as there is no need to reenter the data for analysis, hence reducing time and decreasing the risk of inaccurate data entry. For example, participants in a focus group or workshop setting might be asked to vote on particular issues, rank items in order of preference or respond to multiple choice questions or an open-ended question. By respondents being able to interact directly with data input software, they can maintain a greater degree of anonymity and/or privacy, which may be important in some areas of sensitive research.

Being able to run such software on a laptop provides portability in the field and an increasing range of software is also compatible with palmtops/PDAs.

Another hardware solution is the use of electronic wireless keypads, portable keyboards or other response devices (for an example, see Impact Explorer or Perception Analyser, programs listed at the end of this chapter).

Behavioral observation software

As well as software or hardware systems that allow research participants to contribute data first-hand, you can also use computer-based data input software to assist you to record observations, for example of human or animal behavior in field-based, clinical and experimental settings. This software, sometimes called behavioral observation or notational analysis software, is most frequently used for real-time collection and analysis, but can also be used when analyzing video, after the event.

To use the program, you would create categories for the type of behaviors you are interested in recording (e.g. bird returns to nest; child raises hand) and assign each type of behavior a particular key stroke (as illustrated in Figure 10.2). When making observations, you press the relevant key when the behavior starts and again when it stops. The program records the start and stop times, providing time-based information for particular events (e.g. how long the bird stayed at the nest; how long the child's hand was raised before being acknowledged). The software allows you to record multiple events simultaneously and record narrative field notes at the same time.

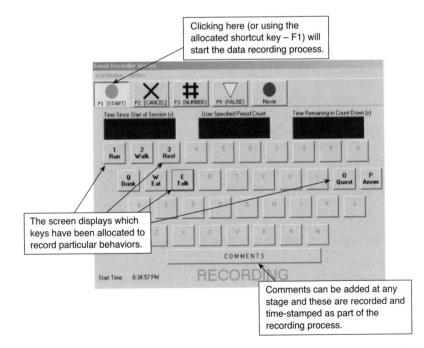

Figure 10.2 Example of behavior observation software data entry interface

The screen indicates which keys are mapped to which behaviors under observation. Example is from BEST.

Behavior observation software can be used in both quantitative and qualitative research, as it has the capacity to collect and (sometimes) analyze descriptive and predictive statistics (see Chapter 11), record qualitative comments and facilitate sequential analysis. While this software has been widely adopted in sport and exercise science, it also has applications in contexts such as analysis of teaching methods, observation of children's behavior at play, analysis of factory work practices or studying animal mating behavior.

Feature Researcher: Using behavior observation software to research sports coaching

John Hammond, Southern Cross University, Australia[15]

John's research aimed to compare swimming coaches' espoused values with their actual teaching practice. To do this, he needed to observe and record behavior during coaching sessions in some detail. Observation promised to be a complex process, as it was difficult for the researchers to assess behaviors in a context where interactions between coach and learners were changing constantly. John decided that computer-based recording would be most appropriate as it allowed for real-time collection of data and would be more accurate and faster than hand coding. It also provided continuity and consistency across observed swimming lessons.

To begin the data collection process, coaches first completed a questionnaire, with follow-up in-depth interviews aimed at eliciting their perceptions and attitudes regarding the skills and understanding they were teaching. Customized software (using hypertext technology) was developed, based on an analysis of themes from the questionnaires and interviews, with each type of coaching activity represented in a grid. For the purposes of analysis the behaviors were grouped under categories (e.g. water adjustment, stroke coordination).

Swimming lessons were then observed and videoed, with one person operating the camera and another inputting data directly on to a laptop running the software. As each observed behavior type began and ended, the operator clicked to record timings. Nine lessons, each involving 2–3 children per lesson, were observed and recorded for three instructors.

While coaches espoused buoyancy, water adjustment and safety to be of greatest importance, analysis of their teaching indicated that stroke coordination occupied 45% of their time, followed by safety and water adjustment. Buoyancy occupied the least amount of coaching time.

Another form of computer-based behavior observation software is specifically designed for research into human interaction with computers. These programs unobtrusively collect data as participants interact with a piece of software, capturing each keystroke and mouse click and attaching time data to significant events.[16] The researcher can then play back and observe the participants' interactions with the screen. Examples include WatchIt, WinWhatWhere, Historian and ScreenCam.

Techniques also exist for collecting and recording observational data online. For example, research participants may be asked to perform certain activities online, such as play an interactive game, engage with others in a discussion area or interact with a website. Online "experiments" can also be conducted by providing text, audio or video and gauging participants' reactions or by recording interactions between participants (see below for more on ways to collect data online). These techniques are ideal for linguistic observation, although it is also possible to observe using webcams.

Human movement recognition systems

Sometimes referred to as "augmented reality user interfaces," these programs traditionally involve placing markers on the body (usually human, but potentially animal), and the software monitors the body's movement and then digitally analyzes and/or represents it on screen. Some systems overcome the need for markers and input is via computer-analyzed video of whole body movement.[17] While these systems are widely used in sport and exercise science and some branches of medicine, they also provide potential in areas where detailed movement analysis is required such as music teaching and performance.

Repertory Grid Software

Researchers working with personal construct theory[18] use specially designed software which has the potential for broader application. Repertory Grid software is designed for use in an interview context, although it can be set up for self-directed use by a research participant. Essentially this software supports two main phases of data collection:

- In the **knowledge elicitation phase** the software prompts respondents through a series of compare-and-contrast questions established by the researcher. Generally this involves presenting a series of triads of concepts, one triad at a time. For each triad, the participant is asked to identify an attribute that distinguishes the two most similar members of the presented triad from the third outlying member. The discriminating construct is recorded by the software as representing "similarity" and the opposing construct is recorded as the "contrasting" construct. For example, a researcher might be investigating how people construct disease. The software might present triads such as "cancer, multiple sclerosis, hemophilia" and the respondent might make differentiations such as "life threatening" or "curable." Presentation of triads is repeated until no new constructs emerge.
- In the **rating grid phase** the software uses a matrix to challenge the interviewee to refine their grid.

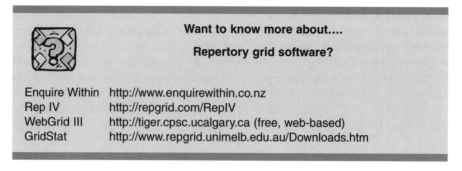

A range of examples of computer-based data input systems is provided in a table at the end of this chapter.

Simulation software

Simulation is a particular type of modeling which provides new ways of understanding complex behavior patterns. Rather than collecting data that is "out there," simulation generates data from within its own experimental modeling system. In simple terms, simulation software enables a researcher to enter into the program particular rules or criteria that govern how agents (such as molecules, bees or people) might behave and the environmental factors that might impact on them. The software then models interactions over time as parameters are changed and different outcomes can be observed. While simulations have been widely used in the natural sciences and economics, they are being adopted by social researchers in such diverse areas as sociology, political science, anthropology, geography, archaeology and linguistics. Simulations can be used for:[19]

- **enhancing understanding of behaviors** (for example, mating patterns of animals or people);
- **policy development** (for instance, modeling the impact of a health care reform or the future of aged care);
- **prediction**, through the ability to simulate the passing of time and gain an insight into a possible future (for example to predict population changes based on age-specific fertility and mortality rates);
- **replicating or substituting for human capabilities** (for instance to simulate the expertise of geologists or doctors);
- **training and assessment** (such as flight simulators for training air pilots);
- **entertainment**, with well known games such as Maxis' SimCity.

There is a range of software tools designed to support simulation and each can differ in terms of the number of levels of agent interaction they can model and whether they incorporate communication between agents.

Want to know more about...

Simulation methods and software?

- Gilbert and Troitzsch (1999) is an excellent resource.
- Social researchers interested in knowing more about simulation methods should consult The University of Surrey's Centre for Research in Social Simulation (CRESS) (http://cress.soc.surrey.ac.uk).
- Examples of simulation software include DYNAMO, DYSMAP, ithink, Magsy, Mimose, Powersim, SDML, SimPack, SIMPROCESS, SIMSCRIPT, Stella, Swarm, Vensim, Catpac and Galileo.

Collecting data online

Now that the population with access to the Internet is no longer limited to "well-educated, high-earning technically-proficient males from computer, academic or other professional fields"[20] it has become a valid means of collecting research data in its own right. In fact, the Internet allows research with populations previously difficult to reach and has the advantage of enabling the collection of data which is already in a digital format, facilitating data organization, management and analysis. In this section we offer tips on making the most of these methods and highlight some of the issues you need to consider when collecting data online.

Online surveys

There are three main ways that surveys can be conducted online: e-mail surveys; web-based surveys; or a combination of both. **E-mail surveys** include a series of questions in either the body of the e-mail or in an attachment and are generally linear and text based, with limited formatting. They are useful for closed populations, such as an organization in which all employees use e-mail and the same word processing program.

Web-based surveys include a series of questions on a webpage, with form fields, check boxes or similar interactive elements to collect responses. Images, audio or video material can be included as part of the survey, and they can be interactive and/or nonlinear. For example, respondents could be asked to visit a website and provide comments on their experience. Questions can also be customized for different respondents, e.g. males might be presented with a different set of questions from females. Web-based surveys can be promoted via e-mail, discussion groups, newsgroups or traditional media such as pamphlet, poster, television or radio. They can be checked automatically for missing responses and data can be dropped back into a database ready to be analyzed, which is more difficult to do with e-mail surveys.

Combined online surveying methods might involve you e-mailing your potential respondents and either sending them a hardcopy survey or inviting them to go to the website. You could also use a website to attract interest in your research, and then ask people to provide an e-mail address if they are interested in participating. There is some evidence that response rates for combined surveys are higher than those for e-mail or web-based surveys alone.[21]

Advantages and disadvantages of conducting surveys online
There is no doubt that technology that permits constructing, distributing and managing surveys online has taken much of the tedium and uncertainty out of conventional paper-based survey methods. However, such surveys also have issues associated with them that do not arise with traditional methods. Consider these advantages and disadvantages:[22]

- **Time.** Online surveys can be less time-consuming than print-based surveys in terms of distribution and response time. They may not be as timely, however, as phone surveys. There is some evidence that respondents will either respond immediately or not respond at all.
- **Cost.** Online surveys can be cheaper to conduct although there are still costs associated with programming, hosting and testing. Cost-effectiveness may be dependent on sample size.
- **Data entry and processing.** Online surveys can eliminate the need to reenter data, thus avoiding transcription errors and reducing data processing time. This is particularly valuable for open-ended questions.
- **Response rates.** Nonresponse to survey items may not be as low as other methods, and there is some evidence that respondents provide longer responses online than when asked to hand write.
- **Distribution.** Web-based surveys in particular have uncontrolled distribution. Although you can attempt to limit access to specific groups (e.g. through password access) or to prevent multiple access by the same respondent, determined computer-savvy individuals can find ways to overcome these safeguards.
- **Formatting.** If you attach a word-processed survey to an e-mail, there is no guarantee that it will be readable by all potential respondents, and even if the file format is readable, the formatting may be lost or scrambled.[23]
- **Access.** Online surveys cannot be used for populations who do not have access to the Internet or are not computer literate. Care is needed in generalizing or making inferences from the sample.
- **Spam.** In some circumstances e-mail surveys may be considered as spam. It can also be difficult for researchers to distinguish their surveys from the flood of online commercial marketing that comes through the Internet. Ethics approval and conduct, including informed consent, is imperative and it becomes very important to consider how you promote and distribute your surveys.

Tips on conducting online surveys

- Remember to include a brief statement at the beginning of the e-mail to specify that after a given date it is too late to respond, and make sure you clearly state your professional affiliations.
- Design your questionnaire using formatting that will not be disrupted when distributed.
- Aim for simplicity and clarity in layout and presentation.
- Keep software requirements as low-tech as possible.
- Pilot the survey across different platforms (Windows, Mac, etc.).
- Remember that you still have to have ethics approval to conduct an online survey.

Online interviews

As one of the most commonly used techniques for qualitative data collection, interviews are traditionally carried out face-to-face or by telephone. However, technology now makes it possible to conduct interviews online. Online interviewing can be done through e-mail, discussion boards or through live chat.

- **E-mail interviewing** involves sending questions to one or a few interviewees at a time, waiting for their response before clarifying the question, asking for more information or sending the next question. In this sense it is useful for follow-up questions or interviewing over a longer period of time where considered responses are required.
- **Discussion board or blog-based interviewing** is similar to e-mail interviewing except that messages are archived and retained as a discussion thread on a webpage which may (or may not) be accessible to other researchers, participants or the public.
- **Synchronous chat interviewing** is more immediate and questions and responses can flow more readily as in face-to-face conversation. While text-based chat is slower and reliant on participants' typing capabilities, voice and/or video-based synchronous technologies can provide an environment very similar to the face-to-face interview (see Chapter 6 for more details).

Issues to consider when deciding on an interview strategy
If you need to make a decision about which interview approach may best suit your research needs, consider the following factors:[24]

- **Cost**. Online interviewing is less expensive than face-to-face in terms of travel and researcher time, particularly for overseas interviews. While telephone interviewing is less expensive than traveling to meet an interviewee, international phone costs can also mount up (although Internet telephony, discussed in Chapter 6, may overcome this problem).
- **Time and convenience.** Coordinating a time and place for a face-to-face meeting can be problematic, particularly when you are interviewing busy professionals. Similar issues occur with synchronous online interviewing, as a mutually appropriate chat time can be difficult to organize. Asynchronous communication overcomes these issues, and is particularly useful if you need to communicate across different time zones.
- **Transcription.** E-mail or text-based chat eliminates the expense of transcription. Audio or video online interviewing also has the advantage of being able to be digitally recorded and interviews are thus more easily transcribed.
- **Language and translation issues**. If you are conducting face-to-face interviews with people who speak other languages you will need an interpreter, while interviewing online allows the use of translation software (see Chapter 6), although checking for accuracy with a native speaker would always be advisable.
- **Technology skills and literacy.** Online interview techniques rely on computer skills and equipment access as well as reading and writing ability, which could affect the representativeness of your sample.
- **Research requirements.** Perhaps most importantly, what you are exploring in your research must be paramount in your decision. For instance, if non-verbal cues, spontaneous responses and the personal connection you make with your interviewees are important for your research, then it would be hard to go past face-to-face interviewing. On the other hand, if the information you are seeking is controversial or very personal (such as involvement in illegal activities), your interviewees may feel more comfortable with the professional distance and anonymity that online interviewing can offer (as illustrated in the case study below).

Online focus groups

Just as interviews can be conducted online, so too can focus groups. Focus groups can use asynchronous technology (such as with discussion boards, mailing lists or blogs) or synchronous technology (such as text, audio or video chat). Sharing many of the strengths and issues of online interviewing, online focus groups work particularly well for bringing together people from diverse locations or dealing with personal or controversial topics, as the following case study demonstrates very well.

Feature Researchers: Virtual Focus Groups

Lyn Turney and Catherine Pocknee
Swinburne Institute of Technology, Australia

Lyn and Catherine's research[25] investigated the effectiveness of "virtual" focus groups in research involving difficult-to-access populations and sensitive topics. They conducted three online focus groups to explore public attitudes to a range of new technologies, in particular DNA paternity testing and stem cell research.

The virtual focus groups were made up of participants who had a stake or special interest in the technologies – men's rights activist leaders; mothers whose estranged partners had denied paternity; and a patient group who had a medical condition that might be helped or cured by stem cell research. All involved difficult-to-access populations whose participants were geographically separated from one another. Given the sensitive and emotionally charged nature of the topic, recruitment of participants was a delicate matter, and some of the approaches which were employed included online chat sites and e-mail as well as directly contacting relevant organizations.

The online focus groups were conducted using discussion boards provided by Blackboard (http://www.blackboard.com), a learning management environment which was already available within the University. Participants had password access to the site and each used a pseudonym in their discussions. A series of text-based questions were posed which gave the participants the opportunity to respond in text format. Participants were able to read others' responses and make comments.

The advantages of using online focus groups in this context included:

- participants being prepared to challenge each other if they disagreed, which isn't always easy face-to-face;
- participants giving more distilled and in-depth responses because they had the opportunity to reflect on their answers;
- the moderator being less interventionist and less directive than in conventional focus groups, with more opportunity to observe, "listen" and insert probes and additional questions;
- the ability of participants to be involved anonymously in research in the comfort and privacy of their own homes, particularly those who were isolated, lacked mobility or were sensitive about airing their views.

A range of examples of survey software is outlined in a table at the end of this chapter.

Data from the Internet: some examples

The Internet can not only be used for collecting data, it is also a vast source of primary data in its own right. While much of this data is often specific to particular disciplines, we provide here a glimpse of the range of sites from which data is readily accessible.

Statistics are one obvious example of this. There are websites produced by governments, organizations and national and international agencies which provide excellent access to statistical data, often including census data. Generally such data are provided in a variety of forms, both collated and partially analyzed (such as in discussion papers or fact files) and in "raw" format (commonly in spreadsheet format) Examples are given in Table 10.1.

Table 10.1   Examples of online statistics sites.

British Government statistical service	http://www.statistics.gov.uk
British Office for National Statistics	http://www.ons.gov.uk
Population Index on the Web	http://popindex.princeton.edu
United Nations – Statistics Division	http://unstats.un.org/unsd
World Population Economic Data and Trends, US Census International Database	http://gsociology.icaap.org/dataupload.html
Asian Development Bank	http://www.adb.org/Statistics

Digital repositories or archives are maintained by many major libraries and institutions as well as universities. They are commonly used for digitization of historical documents such as written and spoken words, sound recordings, still and moving images, prints, maps and sheet music (see Table 10.2).

Table 10.2   Examples of digital repository and archive sites.

National Digital Library Program (U.S. Library of Congress)	http://memory.loc.gov/ammem
The Avalon Project (Yale Law School)	http://www.yale.edu/lawweb/avalon/avalon.htm
Global Gateway	http://international.loc.gov/intldl

There are many other types of primary (and secondary) data that can be accessed online, however it is beyond the scope of this book to do this diversity justice. By way of illustration, see the examples below in Table 10.3.

Table 10.3 Other examples of online primary and secondary data.

History and visual arts. Access to fine and contemporary art images and data about those images

The Louvre	http://www.louvre.fr/ Contains a virtual tour of the gallery as well as several databases providing access to information displayed on labels that accompany works of art, authoritative commentary and analysis by the curators and staff
British Museum	http://www.thebritishmuseum.ac.uk/world/world.html The Museum's brief is to illuminate the history of cultures for the benefit of past and future generations. The collection (both historic and contemporary) is accessed by country, then the type of material that is held
Fine Arts Museums of San Francisco	http://www.thinker.org Try searching the ImageBase and try the ZOOM feature. It contains over 82,000 images

Genealogical (family) history

Family Search	http://www.familysearch.org Claims to be the largest collection of free family history, family tree and genealogy records in the world
Convict database	http://www.fremantleprison.com/history/history6.cfm A database allowing you to look up information about individual convicts sent to Australia
InGenaes	http://www.ingeneas.com An Ottawa-based organization that specializes in Canadian passenger records, immigration lists and other documents

Geography

Google earth	http://earth.google.com Provides satellite imagery and maps. Enter your sets of coordinates and literally "fly" from place to place around the world
USGS Map database	http://ngmdb.usgs.gov This is a national (U.S.) data base of close to 100,000 maps on topics such as geology, hazards, earth resources, geophysics geochemistry, geochronology, paleontology, and marine geology
The Atlas of Canada	http://atlas.gc.ca/site/english/dataservices/free_data.html Base map components are available in five scales

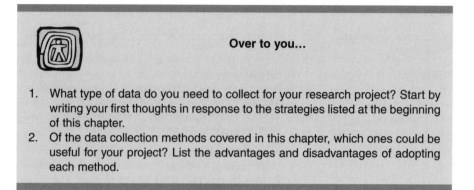

Over to you...

1. What type of data do you need to collect for your research project? Start by writing your first thoughts in response to the strategies listed at the beginning of this chapter.
2. Of the data collection methods covered in this chapter, which ones could be useful for your project? List the advantages and disadvantages of adopting each method.

Notes

1 Stevens and Asmar 1999, p. 38.
2 Patton 2002, p. 380.
3 Stockdale 2002.
4 This summary draws partially from Stockdale 2002 and Brown 2002, two references well worth further consultation.
5 Brown 2002.
6 Information in this section is derived from a range of relevant references including: Hall 2000; Lesh and Lehrer 2000; Roschelle 2000; and Brown 2002.
7 Hall 2000, p. 659.
8 Roschelle 2000.
9 Brown 2002.
10 Lesh and Lehrer 2000.
11 Lesh and Lehrer 2000.
12 Firewire is a term used by Apple (Sony use the term iLink) that applies to ISO IEEE1394 data transmission standard.
13 For further details see Mousley 1998, 2000.
14 For more information about Mike's research see Keppell et al. 2005.
15 Hammond 2004.
16 For further information see Edyburn 1999.
17 Green 2004.
18 Based on the work of George Kelly 1955. The underlying principle of this theory is that people are capable of applying alternative constructions (meanings) to any events in the past, present or future and that individuals interpret the world in terms of their own personal set of constructs – bipolar abstractions that a given individual uses to distinguish between similar and different elements in the world. Essentially the theory is an attempt to explain why people do what they do. The extent to which two individuals share a similar set of constructs indicates the extent to which they experience and understand the world in similar ways.
19 These examples are drawn from Gilbert and Troitzsch 1999, which provides a detailed discussion of simulation and simulation software.
20 Hewson et al. 2003.
21 Schonlau et al. 2001.
22 Derived from Schonlau et al. 2001.
23 Coombes 2001.
24 Drawn partially from Chen and Hinton 1999.
25 Turney and Pocknee 2005.

Examples of software to support use of multimedia data.

Software	Manufacturer/developer	Platform	Website	Licensing	Demo on website?	Notable features
AnnoTape	AnnoTape	Windows Mac	http://www.annotape.com	Commercial	✓	Records, analyzes & transcribes audio, video, image and text data, negating the need for transcription
Audacity	Audacity	Windows, Mac, Linux	http://audacity.sourceforge.net	Free (Open source)	✓	Records live audio, converts tapes and records into digital format; edits Ogg Vorbis, MP3 and WAV sound files; cuts, copies, splices and mixes sounds; changes the speed or pitch
Audio Recorder Pro	EZ SoftMagic	Windows	http://www.ezaudiorecorder.co	Shareware	✓	Records from a sound card; microphone; streams audio from the Internet; external input devices (CDs, LP, cassettes and phone); and applications e.g. WinAmp and Media Player
OSS Audio Extractor	One Stop Soft	Windows	http://www.onestopsoft.com/mi-a-extr.html	Commercial	✓	Extracts audio from videos. Saves in a range of formats
Direct MP3 Splitter Joiner	My Music Tools	Windows	http://www.mymusictools.com/splitter_joiner_24	Shareware	✓	Joins or splits MP3 or WAV files and performs basic editing e.g. trimming or removing silence. Includes editing, adjustable playback speed, automatic track numbering and pause detection
Transana	David Woods	Windows	http://www.transana.org	Freeware (Open source)	✓	Transcribes & analyzes audio & video. Assigns keywords to clips, arranges and rearranges collections, explores relationships between keywords and allows you to share analysis with colleagues

Examples of software to support use of multimedia data. (*Continued*)

Software	Manufacturer/ developer	Platform	Website	Licensing	Demo on website?	Notable features
Quickscribe	Quickscribe	Windows	http://www.quikscribe.com	Commercial	✓	Digitally dictates and transcribes. Is controlled via an external handheld device with a built-in microphone. Instant undo, redo and editing. Recognizes spreadsheets, e-mail addresses & URIs
F4	Dresing and Pehl	Windows	http://www.audiotranskription.de/english/f4.htm	Freeware	✓	Transcription software. Can be used with or without a footswitch. Facilitates play, slow-forward, automatic rewind of a few seconds when stop is pressed; has volume control and record
Listen&Type	NattaWorks	Mac	http://www.nattaworks.com/english.html	Shareware	✓	Transcription/dictation tool. Types while you listen to a sound file. Start, stop, rewind with keyboard shortcuts
Switch	NCH	Windows, Mac, Linux	http://nch.com.au/switch	Commercial	✓	For conversion of audio files between different formats
InterClipper	DocuMat LLC	Windows	http://www.interclipper.com	Commercial	By order	Records video (or audio) directly to computer. Accesses any point without rewinding. Bookmarks sections while recording or on playback. Organizes clips in a searchable database

Examples of computer-based data input systems and survey software.

Software	Manufacturer/ developer	Platform	Website	Licensing	Demo on website?	Notable features
Perception analyser	MSInteractive	Windows	http://www.perceptionanalyzer.com	Commercial	✗	Handheld device relays responses to computer. Used in academia, market and public opinion research
Impact Explorer	Banxia	Windows	http://www.banxia.com/impact	Commercial	✓	To gather data or focus discussions. Can be used with wireless keypads
Survey Select	Survey Connect	Windows	http://www.surveyselect.com	Commercial	✓	Designs, administers and analyzes surveys
SurveyWin	David Hull	Windows	http://www.raosoft.com	Commercial	✓	Designs, collects and analyzes electronic or paper survey data
MaCATI	Senecio Software	Macintosh	http://www.senecio.com	Commercial	✓	Creates and edits questionnaires, collects and analyzes data. For telephone or mail surveys and polling visitors to a website
StatPac	StatPac Gold	Windows	http://www.statpac.com	Commercial	✓	Designs, creates, delivers and analyzes surveys. For online surveys, telephone interviewing (CATI) or paper questionnaires
BEST	Tom Sharpe (SKWare)	Windows	http://www.skware.com	Commercial	✗	Data collection and analysis of both qualitative and quantitative data. Has modules for video, handheld hardware and environments where the researcher is not present to collect data
EthoVision	Noldus	Windows	http://www.noldus.com	Commercial	✓	Video tracking system for recording movement and social interaction of animals

Examples of computer-based data input systems and survey software. (*Continued*)

Software	Manufacturer/developer	Platform	Website	Licensing	Demo on website?	Notable features
Galileo	Galileo Company	Windows	http://galileodownload.2ya.com	Commercial	✓	Measures attitudes and beliefs of individuals and groups. Automates questionnaire design and uses algorithms to develop strategies to change attitudes and beliefs precisely
Observer	Noldus	Windows	http://www.noldus.com/site/doc200401012	Commercial	✗	Event recorder for the collection, analysis and presentation of observational data. Can connect directly to a video camera
Surveylogix	Sparklit	Web-based	http://www.surveylogix.com	Commercial	✓	Creates and distributes surveys via Web or e-mail. You pay for the amount of time your survey is active
Sphinx	Sphinx Development	Windows	http://www.sphinxdevelopment.co.uk	Commercial	✓	Questionnaire design, internet surveys and qualitative and quantitative analysis
NetVis	Jonathon N. Cummings	Windows	http://www.netvis.org	Freeware Open Source	✓	Analyzes and visualizes social networks using data from online surveys, and electronic discussion groups
Zoomerang	MarketTools	Web-based	http://info.zoomerang.com	Commercial	✓	Online survey software. Uses templates to produce questions. E-mail or Web-based promotion. Displays results graphically

Chapter 11

Managing Data Analysis

Collecting data "out there" in the field can be one of the most enjoyable parts of the research process. Analyzing and making sense of the data you collect, however, can sometimes be the most challenging research task. In this chapter we focus on the organizational and management issues which impact on data analysis and more specifically the software which is available to support this process. It is beyond our scope to address specific analysis methods or discipline specific applications in any depth and there are many publications which perform this role very well. Rather, we provide you with an informative and accessible introduction upon which you can develop your data analysis strategies.

For convenience, the chapter is divided into two sections: qualitative data analysis and quantitative data analysis. The depth of our treatment of the two sections differs because processes involved in qualitative data analysis require a different type of understanding than those for quantitative analysis. If you are doing so-called "mixed methods"[1] research, both sections of the chapter will be relevant to you.

Specifically, we consider:

- qualitative data analysis strategies associated with different research approaches;
- how qualitative data analysis is done both with and without technology;

- the different types of qualitative data analysis software packages and how to make a decision about their use;
- how to plan, organize and manage quantitative data analysis;
- fundamental statistical concepts that lie behind quantitative data analysis technologies;
- how to decide what level of statistical analysis is appropriate for your research.

Qualitative data analysis

Qualitative data is nonnumerical, mostly in the form of text, but may also include other formats such as images, video or audio. By its very nature it is often voluminous, unwieldy and time-consuming to organize and analyze. Qualitative data analysis involves both conceptual operations and mechanical tasks.[2] It is a dynamic, intuitive and creative conceptual process of inductive reasoning, thinking and theorizing.[3] But it also requires a wide range of activities such as organizing, storing, reproducing and retrieving data. "Data don't become manageable in the analysis process because there is less to deal with; they become manageable because they are organized."[4] Without good organizational systems and strategies, qualitative data analysis can be incredibly difficult, inefficient and, in some cases, impossible.

Approaches to qualitative research and analysis

The range of approaches to qualitative research is diverse and each arises from different epistemological and methodological understandings. Analysis of data in ethnographic research, for instance, will differ significantly from that in discourse analysis, symbolic interactionism, content analysis, case study research or action research. While it is not our intention here to explore these different approaches in any detail, it may be useful to locate your research project within one of the following three main groups (noting that there is often overlap and that research does not always fit neatly into any one category).[5]

Language-oriented research approaches are interested in the use of language and in the meaning of words. Analysis may involve studying language as communication or culture. Examples include content analysis, discourse analysis, ethnoscience, structural ethnography and symbolic interactionism. In this type of research, analysis will involve:

- locating individual words and phrases to determine whether, and how often, particular words or phrases are used, whether they are used in proximity with each other and/or whether synonyms are used;
- creating word lists and/or counting the frequency of the occurrence of words to study the vocabulary used, or to pick out words of interest and locate their context;
- creating indices or concordances (a little like making an index for a book) where words can be compared across texts and their locations can be taken into consideration.

Descriptive/interpretive research approaches seek to gain insight into the human phenomenon or situation under study and to provide a systematic and illuminating description of the phenomenon, but don't explicitly aim to generate theory. In this type of research, analysis will involve:

- examining a text for topics or themes;
- breaking the text into segments that represent instances of that theme, and attaching to each a keyword or code;
- bringing together segments of text that deal with the same theme, i.e. retrieving groups of "like" data.

Theory-building research approaches allow researchers to seek connections within the data and aim to arrive at theories to explain the connections. In this type of research, analysis will involve determining whether the data possess discernable structures or whether links exist between/among categories, with the purpose of making propositional statements or assertions regarding the underlying principles.

In general, qualitative data analysis thus involves researchers engaging closely with their data, whether it is in the form of text, audio, images or video, to:

- locate or identify patterns, themes or underlying meaning in their data;
- make comments or notes about what is being implied or said;
- mark or extract segments of data which represent meaningful units, such as a quote, video extract or audio clip; and/or
- attach extracts to categories (coding and categorizing), while maintaining a connection to the original source (categories might be developed *before* interacting with data or, if using "grounded theory",[6] will *emerge* from the data themselves).

While there is no one "right way" to analyze qualitative data, good qualitative data analysis practice is systematic and comprehensive, without being rigid or formulaic. The process has been described as one of "intellectual craftsmanship."[7]

Doing qualitative data analysis manually

Qualitative data analysis was undertaken long before computers were around and is still conducted without the aid of technology by some researchers. If you were conducting qualitative data analysis in this way you would typically do the following:[8]

- Make multiple copies of the original data (such as your interview transcripts) by photocopying.
- Read transcripts closely and cut them up into extracts according to topic or theme. Because one segment of text might relate to two or more themes, multiple transcript copies are required.
- Include source information on every extract since it is difficult to locate the original context of the quotes once transcripts are cut up. Some

researchers number each transcript page and each line of text before photocopying, to enable any extract of data to be represented by three figures: the document number, page number and line number.

• Sort these segments of paper into different piles or folders, or perhaps paste them on cardboard or pin them on boards or walls.

Clearly, having a transcript in digital format means that it is a small step to using the cut, copy and paste facilities provided by word processors, which leads us to consider the more basic forms of computer-assisted data analysis in the following section.

Qualitative data analysis using computer technology

While a variety of readily available software (including word processors, spreadsheets and database programs) can be used to organize and manage analysis, Computer Assisted Qualitative Data Analysis Software (CAQ-DAS)[9] is designed specifically to meet the needs of qualitative researchers.[10] Such software essentially supports the coding, categorization, organization and retrieval of data, providing enhanced flexibility and helping you to manage notes or memos made during analysis.

Qualitative data analysis doesn't necessarily need to be done with complicated software. For instance, by embedding small codes or symbols in your word-processed data (such as an interview transcript), you can then use the Find function of the word processor to relocate excerpts related to particular themes. You can also perform a simple count of the number of instances of that code (see Figure 11.1).

Figure 11.1   Simple example of the code and retrieve process

In this example the researcher has embedded symbols (for instance XX or $$) into a transcript document to mark passages representing particular ideas or themes. Using the Find function of word processing software allows you to return quickly and easily to each instance of the theme or to perform a simple word count.

CAQDAS facilitates this process but in more sophisticated ways, enabling you to perform more complicated data analysis. The process is similar, except that the categories you establish are recorded by the software.

Codes or categories can still be developed prior to analysis or during data analysis for a grounded theory approach. As you work through the text (or other form of data), you highlight sections (for example a phrase or quote) and then instruct the software to associate each extract with a particular category (or theme), which may also have an associated code, as illustrated in Figure 11.2.

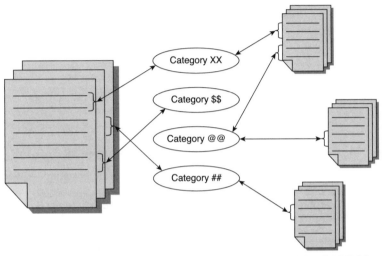

Figure 11.2   The 'code and categorize' process performed by CAQDAS

In this example four categories have been established by the researcher. As you read through your transcript you select segments of text and allocate each to a category. A segment of text can be allocated to more than one category.

Many programs also allow the recording of specific information about the documents (e.g. interview transcripts) themselves, for instance the age, gender, marital status or occupation of the interviewee, the date of the interview or the interviewer's name (as indicated in Figure 11.3). Analysis and reporting of data can then be based on this demographic information (metadata).

Qualitative data analysis software

Broadly speaking, there are five types of CAQDAS:[11]

- **Text retrievers**. These specialize in finding all instances of words or phrases, marking or sorting found text into new files, or linking annotations and memos to the original data. Some count the words, display the words in their context, and create word lists and concordances (organized lists). Some programs build an index which speeds searching processes. Text retrievers will normally incorporate the use of Boolean logic, phrase and truncation searching (see Chapter 7). Examples include INTEXT, WordSmith and VBPro.

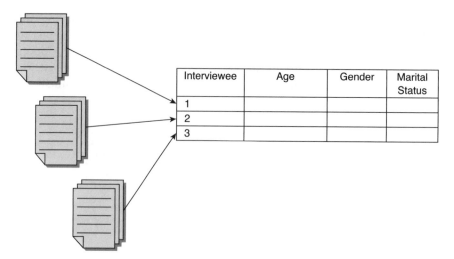

Figure 11.3   Additional data about transcripts as managed by CAQDAS

CAQDAS can also manage demographic or other metadata. For example, you might record information such as age, gender or marital status about each interviewee and associate each transcript with this information

- **Textbase managers.** These organize, sort and make subsets of data (text, pictures, audio or video). Some have hypertext capabilities. Unlike databases, these programs work with "free text" or text which hasn't been restricted into fields. Examples include AskSam and other data management systems described in Chapter 4.
- **Code and retrieve programs**. These allow you to interact with word-processed text, sound or video files and assign segments to codes. The software is then asked to retrieve codes or combinations of codes and display them together with the data assigned to them. Examples include Kwalitan and Ethnograph.
- **Code-based theory builders.**[12] These have the same capabilities as code and retrieve programs, but provide additional features that allow you to explore relationships between concepts or text segments, make connections between codes to develop higher order classifications and categories or to formulate propositions or assertions. Such approaches are particularly useful if you are using a grounded theory approach. Examples include Aquad, Atlas.ti, HyperRESEARCH, NUD*IST and NVivo.
- **Conceptual network builders**. These are also theory-building programs with an extra facility to work with graphic networks, normally represented by rectangular nodes with connecting lines, representing relationships between data. Note that some graphic programs, while not

specifically developed as qualitative data analysis programs, have features such as text in nodes, pop-up menus, outlining and hypertexting which means that they can also be used as conceptual network builders (see the section on visualization and mind mapping software in Chapter 3). Examples include NUD*IST, NVivo and Atlas.ti.

While we have suggested examples of software in each of these categories, the divisions between the categories are not always distinct, and many programs perform multiple functions. A more extensive list of CAQDAS is provided at the end of this chapter and we also advise that you consult the manufacturers' websites that we list.

Arguments for and against the use of CAQDAS

In making the decision about whether to use software for your qualitative data analysis, you are bound to encounter diverse advice.

> Some researchers harbor a secret desire that a computer will somehow do away with the need to engage with the data – that the computer will distinguish the important bits and then make all the links between these bits. For another group of researchers, it is the underlying fear and anxiety that the computer will indeed take over the data and do things to it![13]

Unfortunately you may be presented with only one side of the argument, either from your supervisor or peers, and thus you may be denied the opportunity to try CAQDAS out for yourself. We present here some of the general arguments for and against the use of CAQDAS, both from the literature and our own experience. These points will assist you to reach an informed personal decision about its value to your research[14]:

- Some researchers associate computers with positivistic (quantitative) forms of research. As we identified above, there are many types of qualitative research, each with distinct epistemological and methodological frameworks. Some types of CAQDAS are more appropriate to some forms of research than others, for example, the more automated capabilities of text retrievers will be inappropriate for many types of qualitative studies.
- Some people claim that using a computer "distances" the researcher from their data[15] or that it will "take over" the analysis and researchers will not be aware of the process by which conclusions are reached. However, using CAQDAS does *not* mean that you stop having ideas about, engaging with and getting to know your data, nor does it mean that the computer will take your research in directions you don't intend it to go.[16] All the software does is follow your instructions; *you* are the one who does the thinking, judging, deciding and interpreting.
- Critics claim that CAQDAS contains assumptions that bring bias to research results. Really, using CAQDAS is not substantially different

from traditional analysis using scissors and piles of paper. There are many opportunities for assumptions and biases to influence any type of research, qualitative or quantitative, manual or technology based.

- Having access to CAQDAS can lead researchers to collect and analyze large volumes of data, simply because the computer makes this easier. In some research, such breadth is appropriate. However, CAQDAS can also make it easier to locate and focus on small but significant pieces of data. It is really up to you to use it in a way that is appropriate to your methodology and research questions.
- Critics state that CAQDAS encourages "quick and dirty" research with premature theoretical closure. While some researchers may do this, with or without software, CAQDAS encourages you to "play" with your data, try out new analytical approaches, perform much more detailed coding and categorizing and thus facilitates a greater depth of analysis.
- Some people think using CAQDAS will save them time. This isn't necessarily the case. It can certainly save you time spent in many of the more mundane organizational and data management processes, however the time spent on conceptual analysis is not likely to be significantly different.

There are, of course, projects when CAQDAS is less appropriate and/or might be described as "overkill." Ultimately, we recommend that your choice between manual methods (or at least word-processor facilitated approaches) and CAQDAS should depend on:

- **The theoretical and methodological underpinnings** of your research. You need to consider the type of analysis required to answer your research question or address your research topic.
- **The size of the project and the amount of data you will generate**. If your research involves a small amount of data which does not need to be analyzed in great depth it may be just as easy to analyze "by hand."
- **The depth and complexity of the analysis you wish to perform**. Often researchers use CAQDAS and then find that the analysis they perform falls short of the software's potential. If you are really just doing less in-depth analysis then it may be quicker and easier to do it manually.
- **The format of the data**. If the project involves large amounts of untranscribed data then you will need to weigh up the benefits and pragmatics of converting it to an electronic format (note that some software can handle digital audio and video files).
- **The funds available** for purchasing software.
- **Your inclination, interests and expertise**. There is certainly an investment of time required to learn any new program. However, familiarization with CAQDAS is an important aspect of research training. It can be worth the effort to build your research repertoire.

The "code and categorize" process using CAQDAS
When using CAQDAS to code and categorize your data, you would gener-ally work through a series of "steps" which we outline below. In reality, however, the analysis process is never as linear or as simplistic as this implies. Most qualitative researchers work through an iterative and cyclical process, reporting on their initial coding, but then going back and creating new categories and re-coding their documents.

- **Begin by setting up a new file** (your project) and importing documents into the project. These documents might be text files, video or audio clips or images. Sometimes the software requires these documents to be in a certain format such as a .txt or .rtf document.
- **Associate each document with particular characteristics** if you wish your analysis to account for demographic data or other metadata (data about your data). For instance, you might want to report on an interviewee's gender, age, nationality, organization or other characteristics. The pro-gram thus associates each document (the transcript or video) with its particular "characteristics" (as illustrated in Figure 11.3).
- **Specify the categories into which the data will be coded**, either at the outset or, if you are using a grounded theory approach, as you interact with your data. Most programs allow categories within categories (some-times referred to as nodes and sub-nodes). These categories can continue to be changed or added to as your analysis progresses.
- **Read through (or listen to or view) your data**. While you are doing this you are likely to be selecting chunks of data which relate to a particular theme and allocating them to categories (as described above).
- **Record notes and memos** as you reflect on your data to remind yourself of thoughts and insights.
- **Report on your data analysis**. Often this will mean that you want to see the content of a particular category. Many software packages also allow you to report on the combinations of categories, for instance, where a piece of data has been coded into more than one category.

What to look for in CAQDAS
There is a wide range of CAQDAS available on the market, a selection of which is detailed in the table at the end of this chapter. If you choose to use this software, make sure you take account of the following factors[17]:

- **Your theoretical approach**. The analysis approaches used by each pro-gram will lend themselves in varying degrees to particular theoretical perspectives.
- **Whether the software supports data other than text** (e.g. images, video, audio).
- **The way data needs to be entered**. Most programs allow you to import data from a word processor, while some require data to be entered directly. Some support the coding of webpages (.html format).

- **The flexibility offered in terms of "chunking" data**. Some programs require you to divide text data into pages, paragraphs or lines, which then form the unit of analysis, while others allow completely free-form chunking. Some programs allow chunks to overlap, while others don't.
- **The degree of flexibility**, particularly when modifying coding.
- **The ability to record memos and/or annotate specific codes or chunks of data.**
- **The facility to form connections between data or between categories.** Some programs permit hyperlinking, allowing you to navigate through the data more easily.
- **Search and retrieve capabilities**, including whether they use Boolean logic or wildcards (see Chapter 7).
- **The ability to save the results of searches**, perhaps as new data categories.
- **Theory-building capabilities**, enabling you to test "if … then" propositions or hypotheses.
- **The ability to display the analysis in graphical formats.**
- **Whether it permits use on a network and/or collaborative analysis** by a team of researchers.

More tips on using CAQDAS

- **Get in and try it out.** Often the best way of learning to use CAQDAS is to try out some "real" research data that provides you with a context for meaningful analysis. You don't necessarily need to know all the features of the software before you give it a go. "So long as you know that you will not create future problems, or limit future choices, you can get on with a project and get to know the software as you go."[18]
- **Prepare your documents (e.g. transcripts).** The use of paragraphs or formatting to differentiate sections warrants some forethought. Some programs (for instance NVivo) make use of styles (see Chapter 12) and although these can be allocated once the document is imported, it is wise to use styles when preparing your transcripts and documents. In many programs features such as footnotes, tables, pictures and columns are not recognized during import and should be avoided.
- **Code concurrently with other tasks** such as reflective writing, brainstorming or going back to literature. Constantly returning to the research question and asking why you are coding the data and how it is relevant to the research is critical.

(Continued)

- **Allow plenty of time for coding.** How long this takes will depend on:
  - what your project is about;
  - the complexity of the questions that have been asked;
  - your timeframe for the project;
  - your methodological approach;
  - whether you are familiar with the data and the tool you are using.

Coding based on broad themes might take 2 hours for every hour of data, but micro-coding in fine detail might take 6–12 hours for every hour of data.[19]

Want to know more about...

Qualitative data analysis software?

There are a number of seminal and more recent publications which explore computer-assisted qualitative data analysis processes in significant depth.[20]

- A key resource is the CAQDAS Networking Project website, located at http://caqdas.soc.surrey.ac.uk, which includes an excellent bibliography, online articles, descriptions of various software products and a discussion list.
- One journal which frequently carries articles on the use of CAQDAS is: *FQS: Forum: Qualitative Social Research* http://www.qualitative-research.net
- A selection of software that provides data analysis functionality for use with multimedia data such as audio or video is listed at the end of Chapter 10.

Quantitative data analysis

While qualitative data analysis is concerned with nonmeasurable aspects of data (particularly text, audio, video and image data), quantitative analysis deals with data that *is* quantifiable, i.e. it can be measured in numerical terms (which some "qualitative" data can be as well, of course[21]). It is the approach inherent in your research design, i.e. *how* you collect, measure and treat your data, more than *what* you actually collect, that determines what sort of analysis you perform.

It is far beyond the scope of this book to discuss in any depth the range of statistical concepts, processes or tests, and there are many books and websites which already do this in great detail (see some suggestions later in this section). Rather, in keeping with our focus on the organizational and management issues that impact on analysis, we focus on aspects you need to consider in planning your quantitative study; outline the range of technological tools available to support quantitative research; and summarize what issues you should consider when deciding on the most appropriate statistical software to use. However, before we do this it is important to review some of the fundamental statistical concepts necessary to understand before you can make your planning decisions. If you already have an understanding of statistics, this section can be skipped.

Fundamentals of statistics

In this section, we cover briefly some of the foundational concepts you need to understand if you intend to use quantitative (statistical) methods.

Statistics is a branch of applied mathematics concerned with the collection and interpretation of quantitative data. It uses probability theory to estimate population parameters. There are two main types of statistics, associated with different methods:

Descriptive statistics is the branch of statistics that includes the many and varied techniques used to summarize data. These include: tabular descriptions (e.g. using a simple table), graphical descriptions (e.g. a pie chart or a histogram), and summary statistics (e.g. calculating mean, medium or standard deviation).

Inferential statistics, on the other hand, covers numerical techniques for drawing conclusions about a population, based on information drawn from a sample of that population. There are two branches of inferential statistics: parametric and nonparametric.

- **Parametric statistics** is the subbranch of statistics that uses families of probability distributions, the best known example being the normal distribution, for hypothesis testing. Basically, assumptions are made that the distribution of the variables being tested belongs to certain known probability distributions.
- **Nonparametric statistics**, on the other hand, is the subbranch of statistics that is applied when populations are not normally distributed or where there are severely skewed data. For this reason it uses what are known as "distribution-free" tests. In general, as nonparametric tests require fewer assumptions than similar parametric tests (that is they have less information on which to determine significance), they are less powerful. Of course, a parametric test where the sample distributions do not meet the distribution assumptions of the test will yield questionable results. Better to use a less powerful test that is valid, than a more powerful test that is not valid.

The various statistical methods are summarized in Figure 11.4. Fundamental mathematical terms that form the foundations of statistical analysis are defined in Table 11.1.

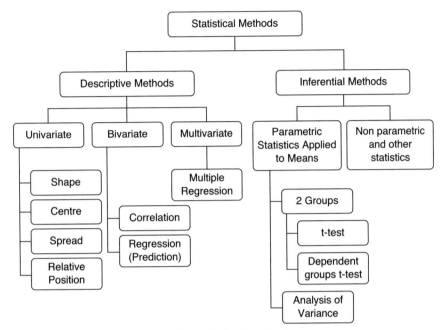

Figure 11.4   A classification of statistical methods

Table 11.1   Definitions of statistical terms.

Term	Meaning	Examples
A constant:	An attribute that does not vary	$1=100 cents
A variable	An attribute that has two or more divisions or characteristics (opposite to a constant)	Gender, age, income
▪ A discrete variable	One that is measured as a unit and cannot be subdivided	The number of children in a family
▪ A continuous variable	A variable that can be subdivided, i.e. it can take on any value in a line interval	Income; height; length
A case	An entity that displays the characteristics of a given variable	A family has an average annual income
A population	The set of all cases of interest	Total number of families in the country
A sample	A set of cases selected in some way (usually randomly) from the population	1000 families selected from across the country

Table 11.1 (*Continued*)

Term	Meaning	Examples
Measurement	The process of recording the level of a variable in individual cases (there are four types, as defined below)	Determine and record the number of children in each family
▪ Nominal (or categorical) scale	Numerals or names are assigned to cases as labels only and these numerals cannot be mathematically manipulated (e.g. added, multiplied etc.) A "dichotomous scale" occurs when there are only two labels	Postcodes or 1 = Female 2 = Male
▪ Ordinal (or rank) scale	Numbers are assigned to objects that represent rank order (comparisons can be made between cases but even simple mathematical addition cannot be applied)	1 = low income; 2 = medium income; 3 = high income
▪ Interval scale	Numbers assigned to objects that have all the features of ordinal measurements plus equal differences between measurements represent equivalent intervals	Measurements on a temperature scale
▪ Ratio scale	Numbers assigned to objects have all the features of interval measurement and also have meaningful ratios between arbitrary pairs of numbers (mathematical operations such as multiplication and division are therefore meaningful)	Length in meters

Want to know more about....

Statistical analysis?

There are many general texts which deal with statistics and statistical analysis. One highly respected seminal work is David Sheskin's *Handbook of Parametric and Nonparametric Statistical Procedures*[22] which provides details on over 100 tests. There is also a considerable amount of material freely available on the Web, for example:

- Carnegie-Mellon University's StatLib, http://lib.stat.cmu.edu providing hundreds of links to news, software and data sites relevant to the statistical community

(*Continued*)

• The University of Florida's WWW Virtual Library Statistics	http://www.stat.ufl.edu/vlib/ statistics.html
• The University of Newcastle (Australia)'s Surfstat providing an online text in introductory statistics	http://www.anu.edu.au/nceph/ surfstat
• Clay Helberg's Statistics. Many useful links on book, Web resources and software sites	http://my.execpc.com/~helberg/ statistics.html
• Robert Niles's Statistics every writer should know	http://nilesonline.com/stats
• Easton and McColl's Statistics Glossary	http://www.stats.gla.ac.uk/steps/ glossary
• GASP – the Globally Accessible Statistical Procedures initiative is designed to make statistical routines available via the Web	http://www.stat.scarlina.edu/rstch/ gasp

Planning your quantitative study

The key to any successful research analysis is planning. This is particularly important when considering a study that will use statistical analysis, as how you sample, collect and measure your data will determine your choice of statistical method. Statistical analysis *is not* something you deliberate on after you collect your data; it is something that is considered early (before you start) and should be seen as an integral part of your research planning. Thinking through your data analysis should not be just a straightforward linear process but rather should involve repeated "forwards and backwards" thinking. This can aid in detecting problems before the collecting and analysis phases of the study begin. It is much easier to fix a problem in the planning stage than after an experiment is underway or much of the data is collected. It is advisable to design your data analysis approach in consultation with an experienced statistician or researcher. Methodologist's Toolchest, discussed in Chapter 4, is also a useful tool in planning your statistical analysis.

Consider these questions as a guide to planning a hypothesis-testing quantitative study (see the following section for further explanation of some of the basic concepts referred to in Table 11.2).

Table 11.2   Questions to consider when planning your study.

Intent	**What is the intention of your study?** What are you collecting data for? What questions are you asking? Can these general questions be used to generate formal hypotheses? What data do you need to collect? No matter how accurate your measurements or how sophisticated your statistical analysis, it will not produce an appropriate or quality outcome if your original questions/hypotheses make no sense
Sampling	**What sampling decisions do you need to make?** Who or what is your population? How will you ensure your sample is representative and of a suitable size for statistical testing so that you can confidently generalize from your findings?
Measurement	**What sort of measurement will provide the appropriate data?** Can measurement be done reliably? Are your measures valid in terms of the overall research design and research questions? Will the measurements you intend to take be able to detect the difference you need to detect (i.e. is your measuring equipment appropriate to the task)?
Formatting data	**How will you format your data?** Will you set out your data in a flat file (one row per subject, all data in one row) or long file format (each measurement has its own row)? Is the format you will be using for entry also the format your analysis procedure will need? Do you need to consider *data transformation* issues such as the need to export your data from a relational database to a flat file format, as is required for importation into a statistical package?
Security	**What do you need to do to back up your data?** How many secure locations are appropriate in case of fire, theft, computer failure, etc.? What confidentiality issues do you need to take into account?
Analysis	**What are the appropriate and valid statistical tests that can be applied to the data?** What sort of analysis is appropriate to the measurement scale? Will the data meet the various assumptions that underpin the tests applied?
Presentation and reporting	**How will the data and results be displayed and summarized?** This should be planned as an integral part of the data analysis process and be designed with the audience (thesis examiners; type of journal) in mind

Software for analysis of statistical data

There is a large range of software packages specifically designed to analyze quantitative data. They vary in the number of features offered; the platform(s) on which they run; whether they are "add-ins" to be used with other software; and whether they are Web-based packages or stand-alone programs. Whatever software you choose to use, it is wise to set its structure up in advance of your actual data collection and run some trial data (ideally a pilot study) through it. This gives you the opportunity to test and refine your analysis structure and understand how the software will present results.

Spreadsheets

In Chapter 2 we outlined how spreadsheets work and the basic features they offer. Spreadsheets are ideally suited to managing and processing numerical data, and they can be used for certain types of quantitative data entry and analysis. While standard spreadsheet programs on their own are not (generally) nearly as powerful as specialized statistical packages, they can perform a range of statistical functions, particularly with the inclusion of various so-called "add-ins," examples of which are included in Table 11.3.

Table 11.3   Examples of statistical add-ins for Microsoft Excel.

Analyse-it®	http://www.analyse-it.com	Includes over 30 parametric and nonparametric tests, including descriptive statistics, box-whisker plots, correlation, multiple linear regression analysis, ANOVA (analysis of variance) and chi-square statistics for general statistical research. A separate package is available for clinical method evaluation
Lumenaut	http://www.lumenaut.com	Aimed at business applications. Includes regression, logistic regression, decision trees and some time series and a new Monte Carlo Simulation package for risk analysis
NeuroXL	http://www.neuroxl.com	This pair of programs (Classifier and Predictor) provides a neural network tool to carry out classification, forecasting and estimation tasks
UNISTAT	http://www.unistat.com	Available as a stand-alone package or Excel add-in. Includes logistic regression, classification and clustering. Available in limited and light editions with an optional "Analysis of Bioassays" module
XLSTAT	http://www.unistat.com	Includes logistic and probit regression, nonlinear regression, multiple regression and so on
WINSTAT	http://www.winstat.com	Provides a range of statistics add-ins

Want to know more about ...

Spreadsheet add-ins?

Rodney Carr of Deakin University, Australia provides Excel workbooks for basic statistical analyses. Note the disclaimers.
http://www.deakin.edu.au/individuals-sites/?request=~rodneyc

Web-based statistical programs

You probably will not be surprised to know that the Web offers a whole new way to analyze quantitative data, an example of which is provided in the feature below.

Feature Website: StatCrunch

http://www.statcrunch.com

StatCrunch[23] (formerly Webstat) is a statistical data analysis package for the World Wide Web. You need to register to use it but registration is free. StatCrunch allows you to upload data in the form of text or Excel files from your own computer and it will then analyze the data with a full range of numerical and graphical methods. It can even produce interactive graphics for exploratory analysis and compute mathematical expressions. StatCrunch also provides an HTML output that can be copied and saved back to your own computer.

Commercial and shareware stand-alone packages

There are also many commercial and shareware programs available which are specially designed for statistical analysis, and are thus (generally) more powerful and flexible than spreadsheets. While there will be an investment in time to familiarize yourself with any such program, it is an important research skill to develop and include in your research skills portfolio. Some packages are designed for general use, while others are tailored for particular purposes or disciplines (examples of quantitative data analysis software are listed in a table at the end of this chapter).

Choosing statistical analysis software

It is difficult to give clear guidance on how to choose an appropriate statistical package for your research, as so much depends on the research culture and context in which you are operating and your specific disciplinary needs. If it is available, it is always useful to seek advice from a professional statistician, but keep in mind they are likely to recommend the more powerful packages, which may not be the easiest to use. The final decision will often involve weighing up a range of factors including:

- appropriateness for the study (i.e. just how sophisticated an analysis do you want to carry out?);
- cost and availability of the software (many universities have site licenses);
- how easy it is to use and how much training is required to use it;
- your previous experience;
- whether you can run it on the computer you have access to;

- whether the package has been used in similar studies;
- the special features of the package (such as might be applicable to certain research problems or discipline areas).

If you are an inexperienced researcher you may be facing a decision as to whether your spreadsheet application (possibly with some add-ins) will be adequate for your research requirements, or whether you need to learn to use more advanced software. Spreadsheets may be more useful if:

- **Your research only involves a small amount of simple quantitative analysis**. This might apply where you are essentially using qualitative methods, but you may wish to include some descriptive statistics on the average age of your participants, or the frequency of responses to certain categorical questions (for example, the number of responses to a yes/no or multiple choice question included in an otherwise qualitative survey or interview).
- **You are unfamiliar with quantitative software** and more comfortable entering your data in a spreadsheet program *or* you (or someone working with you) are entering data on a computer which does not have a statistical package installed. Remember that all spreadsheets can easily export data to a format which can be imported relatively easily into most statistical packages.
- **You wish to use the formatting features of a spreadsheet to enhance accuracy** in your data entry. For instance, we find it useful to use color in blocks of rows or columns to identify groups of questions, and ensure data entry is "matching up" with the correct cells. When you export the data, these formatting conventions are removed.
- **You only want to perform basic statistical functions**, and feel confident using functions and formulas in spreadsheets (as described in Chapter 2). You can perform analysis using the many built-in functions, but this *does* mean that you need to understand the statistical functions you select, and how they should be applied to the data. You must take particular care that your use of functions is accurate.

 Over to you...

1. If you are doing a qualitative project, which broad research category does it fall into? What data analysis approach seems most appropriate?
2. What do you need to make the decision as to whether to use CAQDAS or not?
3. If you are doing a project that is suitable for quantitative analysis, have you considered the questions raised in Table 11.1?
4. What factors do you need to take into account in choosing your statistical analysis tools? Is the level of sophistication of your chosen tool appropriate to the level of analysis your research requires?

Notes

1 In fact, the popularization of mixed methods research (Tashakkori & Teddlie 2003; Johnson & Onwuegbuzie 2004) means that many researchers will involve themselves with both analysis approaches.

2 Tesch 1991.

3 Basit 2003.

4 Tesch 1990, p. 139.

5 Derived from Tesch 1991.

6 Glaser and Strauss 1967.

7 Tesch 1990.

8 Bogdan and Biklen c.1982 were among the first (and still few) authors to describe in a structured way the processes which researchers use when manually analyzing qualitative data.

9 The term was first employed by Fielding and Lee 1991, 1998. As they point out in their latter work, it is a nice pun on "cactus," being somewhat symbolic of the historically thorny issues surrounding the use of computers in qualitative research.

10 There are a number of books and papers available which detail the advantages, issues and process of using CAQDAS, for example, Tesch 1990; Fielding and Lee 1991, 1998; Weitzman and Miles 1995; Popping 2000; Weitzman 2000. We will not attempt to compete with the level of discussion and analysis these books provide. If you are intending to use CAQDAS then you would be well advised to consult such references.

11 Derived from Fielding and Lee 1991; Weitzman and Miles 1995; Popping 2000; Stroh, 2000.

12 It is important to clarify the term "code-based theory builders." As Weitzman and Miles 1995 have pointed out, "No program actual builds theory for you, nor would you want one to. Computers don't think, and they can't understand the meaning of your qualitative data. But programs differ in the amount and kind of support they offer to your theory-building efforts."

13 Gahan and Hannibal 1998, p. 1.

14 These points are derived from a range of excellent sources including Tesch 1990; Fielding and Lee 1991, 1998; Seidel 1991; Gahan and Hannibal 1998; Stroh 2000; Coombes 2001; Bong 2002; Basit 2003.

15 Fielding and Lee's 1998 discussion of this issue, and what it means to be "close to your data" is particularly pertinent.

16 Gahan and Hannibal 1998.

17 Partially derived from Weitzman and Miles 1995 and Stroh 2000.

18 Bazeley and Richards, 2000.

19 Marshall 2003.

20 For instance, Tesch 1990; Fielding and Lee 1991, 1998; Denzin and Lincoln 1994; Miles and Huberman 1994; and Lewins and Silver 2005.

21 The statistical analysis of textual data is considered at some length by Popping 2000.

22 Sheskin 2000.

23 A full outline of the package is contained in an article in the *Journal of Statistical Software* at http://www.jstatsoft.org/v09/i05/scjss

Examples of qualitative data analysis software.

Software	Manufacturer/ developer	Platform	Website	Licensing	Demo on Website?	Special features
AnSWR	Centres for Disease Control	Windows	http://www.cdc.gov/hiv/software/answr.htm	Freeware	✓	For large-scale, team-based analysis that integrates qualitative and quantitative techniques. Provides control over the level of access team members have (e.g. reporting, coding, administration); monitors team members' responsibilities
AQUAD	Gunter Hubert		http://www.aquad.de/eng	Commercial	✓	Analyzes video and audio data without transcription. German but available in English. Manual on website
Atlas.ti	Scientific Software Development		http://www.atlasti.de (click on the English link)	Commercial	✓	For text, audio and video analysis. Uses an external database structure (data files are not copied into the project). Displays documents, quotations, codes and memos in tiled windows. No limits on text unit length. Allows free (uncoded) quotations and hyperlinking between quotations and text. Documents can be organized into subsets. XML export facility. 📖
Catpac	Galileo Company	Windows	http://www.terraresearch.com	Commercial	✗	Automatic text analysis system which claims to "read any text and summarize the main ideas." Performs cluster analysis and generates perceptual maps

Entries marked with 📖 have a detailed review at http://caqdas.soc.surrey.ac.uk

Examples of qualitative data analysis software. *(Continued)*

Software	Manufacturer/ developer	Platform	Website	Licensing	Demo on Website?	Special features
C-I-SAID	Code-A-Text	Assume Windows	http://www.code-a-text.co.uk	Commercial	✗	For text, audio or video. Qualitative analysis within a quantitative analytic framework. Open-ended coding, comments and annotations. Categorical or numerical rating scales. Has an acoustic manager (measuring volume, pitch and speed of speech) that generates statistics. Produces reports, tables, charts and statistics as well as qualitative output
Diction	Roderick Hart	Windows	http://www.dictionsoftware.com	Commercial	✓	Determines the tone of a verbal message by searching for five general features: certainty, activity, optimism, realism and commonality. Reports on text processed and prepares numeric data for statistical analysis
Ethnograph	Qualis Research Associates	Windows	http://www.qualisresearch.com	Commercial	✓	Helps search and note segments of interest within data, marks them with code words and runs analyses
EZ-Text	Centres for Disease Control	Assume Windows	http://www.cdc.gov/hiv/software/ez-text.htm	Freeware	✓	For semi-structured data (e.g. from questionnaires). Templates facilitate entry of data, which can then be searched. Export, import and merge capabilities. Manual available on website

Entries marked with ▭ have a detailed review at http://caqdas.soc.surrey.ac.uk

Examples of qualitative data analysis software. *(Continued)*

Software	Manufacturer/ developer	Platform	Website	Licensing	Demo on Website?	Special features
General Inquirer	Philip Stone, Uni. of Maryland	Windows, Mac, Unix or Linux	http://www.wjh.harvard.edu/~inquirer Web-based version at http://www.webuse.umd.edu:9090	Web-based version Free	Used via Website	Java-based content analysis of text. Dictionaries (it comes with two that are customizable) assign words to researcher-defined categories (e.g. the word "money" might be assigned to the "wealth" category). Outputs in spreadsheet format
Hyper- RESEARCH	Research Ware	Windows, Mac	http://www.researchware.com/hr	Commercial Free Teaching Edition	✓	For text, graphics, audio and video. Memoing, autocoding and graphical representation of coding. A hypothesis tester applies rule-based "expert systems" techniques to analyses of data. Supports group work. Tutorials available on website. 📖
INTEXT	Social Science Consulting	MS-DOS	http://www.intext.de	Freeware	✓	For linguistic analysis of text. Works with word lists, word sequences and word permutations. Identifies morphological, lexical and syntactic patterns and builds concordances. Coding can be automatic or interactive. German but available in English. Manual on website. (See also TextQuest for Windows version)
Kwalitan	V. Peters, Uni. of Nijmegen	Windows	http://www.kwalitan.net/engels	Commercial	✓	Code and categorize functionality and text searching. Exports data in qualitative or quantitative. matrix format

Entries marked with 📖 have a detailed review at http://caqdas.soc.surrey.ac.uk

Examples of qualitative data analysis software. *(Continued)*

Software	Manufacturer/ developer	Platform	Website	Licensing	Demo on Website?	Special features
MaxQDA	MaxQDA	Windows	http://www.maxqda.com	Commercial	✓	Creates a hierarchical coding system with up to 10 levels and attaches a relevance weighting to text segments. Text can be imported from the Internet by drag-and-drop. ▯
NUD*IST	QRS International	Windows	http://www.qsrinternational.com	Commercial	✓	For large-scale projects with large amounts of plain text data. Minimum text unit is a paragraph (or a line if each ends with a carriage return). Uses a tree-like structure of "nodes." Comparisons to NVivo on the QRS website. ▯
NVivo	QRS International	Windows	http://www.qsrinternational.com	Commercial	✓	For fine-grained analysis. Minimum text unit is one character. A Model Explorer provides more flexibility than the node hierarchy in NUD*IST. Merge for NVivo allows you to align, compare, assess and merge results from two or more NVivo projects. Comparisons to NUD*IST on the QRS website. ▯
Qualrus	Idea Works	Windows	http://www.ideaworks.com/Qualrus. shtml	Commercial	✓	Analysis of text, graphics, video and audio. Drag-and-drop text segments between coding "stacks." Memos can be attached to any object. Enables Boolean and semantic searches and visually presents relationships among codes. HTML output. Can be customized. ▯

Entries marked with ▯ have a detailed review at http://caqdas.soc.surrey.ac.uk

Examples of qualitative data analysis software. (Continued)

Software	Manufacturer/ developer	Platform	Website	Licensing	Demo on Website?	Special features
QDA Miner	Provalis Research	Windows	http://www.provalisresearch.com/ QDAMiner/QDAMinerDesc.html	Commercial	✓	Text management and analysis. Examines the frequency of manually assigned codes and the relationship between those codes and other categorical or numeric variables. Integrates with WordStat (for text-mining) and Simstat (for statistical analysis). 📖
SignStream	Unknown	Mac	http://www.bu.edu/asllrp/Sign Stream	Shareware	✗	For analysis of linguistic data captured on video. Specially designed for use with sign language but has wider applications
TAMS and TAMS Analyser	Matthew Weinstein	Mac	http://tamsys.sourceforge.net/osxtams	Freeware (Open source)	✓	Text Analyze Markup System for identifying themes in texts (webpages, interviews, field notes)
TextAnalysis	Megaputer Intelligence	Windows	http://www.megaputer.com/products/ta	Commercial	✗	Determines what words and word combinations are most important in text context. Labels each concept as a node and assigns a numeric semantic weight. Produces a graphic Semantic Network
Textpack	ZUMA	Windows	http://www.gesis.org/en/software/ textpack/	Commercial	✓	Produces automatic quantitative analysis of text using both a dictionary approach and/or an empirical approach. Output can be exported to statistical packages

Entries marked with 📖 have a detailed review at http://caqdas.soc.surrey.ac.uk

Examples of qualitative data analysis software. (Continued)

Software	Manufacturer/ developer	Platform	Website	Licensing	Demo on Website?	Special features
TextQuest	Social Science Consulting	Windows	http://www.textquest.de	Commercial	✓	Updated version of the open source program INTEXT. One module computes readability coefficients and lists sentences which are longer than a set number of letters or words
Transana	David Woods	Windows	http://www.transana.org	Freeware (Open source)	✓	Transcription and analysis of audio and video data. Assigns keywords to interesting clips, arranges, rearranges and creates complex collections of interrelated clips. Explores relationships between applied keywords. Multiuser version allows sharing data and collaborative analysis
VBPro	Mark Miller	Windows	http://mmmiller.com/vbpro/vbpro.html	Freeware	✓	Creates frequency lists of words, finds and tags key words and phrases in context, codes units (sentence, paragraph, or user defined case) for frequency or presence/absence of categories of selected words and phrases, maps terms in a multidimensional space in which the proximities are indicative of the degree to which terms co-occur

Entries marked with 🕮 have a detailed review at http://caqdas.soc.surrey.ac.uk

Examples of qualitative data analysis software. *(Continued)*

Software	Manufacturer/ developer	Platform	Website	Licensing	Demo on Website?	Special features
WordSmith	Mike Scott Provalis Research	Windows	http://www.lexically.net/wordsmith	Commercial	✓	Lists words or word-clusters, sets out in alphabetical or frequency order. A concordancer allows you to see any word or phrase in context. Finds the key words in a text. Used by Oxford University Press for lexicographic work in preparing dictionaries
WordStat	Provalis Research	Assume Windows	http://www.provalisresearch.com/wordstat/wordstat.html	Commercial	✓	Categorizes text using a dictionary approach, text mining or manual coding. Uses graphical tools to explore the relationships between the content of documents and information stored in categorical or numeric variables such as gender or age. Uses hierarchical clustering, multidimensional scaling, correspondence analysis and heatmap plots to explore relationships
Xsight	QRS International	Windows	http://www.qrs.com.au/products/nvivo.html	Commercial	✓	Specifically designed for market researchers

Entries marked with 📖 have a detailed review at http://caqdas.soc.surrey.ac.uk

Examples of quantitative data analysis software.

Software	Manufacturer/ developer	Platform	Website	Licensing	Demo on Website?	Special features
AM	American Institutes for Research	(assume Windows)	http://am.air.org/	Freeware	✓	For analysis of data from complex samples, especially large-scale assessments. Excellent online manual
DataDesk	DataDesk	Windows, Mac	http://www.datadesk.com	Commercial	✓	Interactive graphical tools for analyzing and understanding data including exploring patterns, relationships, and exceptions. Performs many traditional statistics techniques
JMP	SAS Institute	Windows, Mac, Linux	http://www.jmp.com/software/	Commercial	✓	A structured, problem-centered approach for exploring and analyzing data. Dynamically links statistics with interactive graphics to let you visualize, explore and understand your data
Maple	Maplesoft		http://www.aplesoft.com	Commercial	✗	For research in mathematics, science and engineering. Combines numeric and symbolic calculations, explorations, mathematical notation, documentation, buttons and sliders, graphics and animations
Mathematica	Wolfram Research	Windows, Mac, Linux	http://www.wolfram.com	Commercial	✓	Wide range of statistics functions. Allows you to create "live" mathematical expressions (formatted in any typeface, size or style) which you can interact with or parse to other programs. A notebook function allows recording of calculations, code, results and graphics

Examples of quantitative data analysis software. (*Continued*)

Software	Manufacturer/ developer	Platform	Website	Licensing	Demo on Website?	Special features
mathStatica	MathStatica	Windows, Mac, Linux	http://www.mathstatica.com/	Commercial	✗	Used to solve algebraic and symbolic problems of interest in mathematical statistics. Compatible with Mathematica
MINITAB	Minitab	Windows	http://www.minitab.com	Commercial	✓	Comprehensive and relatively easy to use package. Ability to customize menus and toolbars. Multi-language versions
OpenStat	William G. Miller	Windows, Linux	http://www.statpages.org/miller/ openstat/	Freeware (Open source)	✓	Originally written as an aid for statistics courses in the social sciences, particularly in developing countries with limited resources. Performs a broad range of foundational statistical processes
SAS	SAS Institute	Windows, Mac, Unix	http://support.sas.com/software	Commercial	✗	Excellent analytical data manipulation and reporting capabilities. More suitable for advanced users
SPSS	SPSS	Windows, Mac	http://www.spss.com	Commercial	✓	Popular and widely used package which is relatively easy to use and performs a broad range of processes. Integrates with a range of related products for research planning (including determining sample size), data entry and reporting. Broad range of support available
Stata statistical software	StataCorp	Windows, Mac, Unix	http://www.stata.com	Commercial	✗	Integrated statistical package with a point-and-click interface, intuitive command syntax and online help. Good documentation

Examples of quantitative data analysis software. *(Continued)*

Software	Manufacturer/ developer	Platform	Website	Licensing	Demo on Website?	Special features
Statgraphics	Manugistics	Windows	http://www.statgraphics.com	Commercial	✓	Over 150 statistical procedures covering all major areas of statistical analysis. Documentation and "how to" guides on website
Statistica	StatSoft	Windows	http://www.statsoft.com	Commercial	✓	A suite of modules providing a broad range of data analysis, data management, data visualization and data mining procedures. Wide selection of predictive modeling, clustering, classification and exploratory techniques. Includes an electronic statistics textbook
SYSTAT	SYSTAT	Windows	http://www.systat.com	Commercial	✓	Widely used package providing a range of functions. SYSTAT also produce Sigmaplot for producing technical graphs and SigmaStat which provides expert system guidance on choosing correct statistical methods to analyze your data
UNISTAT	UNISTAT	Windows	http://www.pstat.com/unistat	Commercial	✓	Works as a stand-alone package or an Excel add-in. Includes a range of statistical processes including logistic regression, classification and clustering. Full and lite versions available

Examples of quantitative data analysis software. *(Continued)*

Software	Manufacturer/ developer	Platform	Website	Licensing	Demo on Website?	Special features
ViSta	Forrest W. Young	Windows, Mac, Unix	http://forrest.psych.unc.edu/research	Freeware (Open source)	✓	Performs univariate and multivariate statistical analysis. Constructs interactive, dynamic graphics that show you multiple views of your data. Versions in English, French and Spanish
WinIDAMS	UNESCO	(assume Windows)	http://www.unesco.org/idams	Freeware (Open source)	Via form	Developed by UNESCO for the validation, manipulation and statistical analysis of numerical data of any kind. Versions in English, French and Spanish

Chapter 12

Improving Your Writing Efficiency

The success or failure of any research project often hinges on how well it is written, i.e. how you communicate what you have done. It can also be the most frustrating and time-consuming part of your research. Many a superb research project has failed to reach timely completion because the researcher in question has not been either effective *or* efficient in organizing and managing their writing process. Writing is, of course, in major part a conceptual and intellectual endeavor, and in this book we don't venture into content aspects of writing. However, writing is also a technical and organizational process and a range of work strategies and management processes can help considerably in structuring and managing your writing to maximize productivity.

The tool you almost certainly will already use to aid your writing is a word processor. However, are you aware of the more sophisticated word processing features that can considerably enhance your research writing? Are you aware of how to customize your word processor or work with long documents and do you use features such as headings and styles, outline view, tables of contents, indexes, glossaries and multiple windows?

In this chapter we offer tips on how to:

- use the features of your word processor that assist the research writing process;
- improve the efficiency of your writing practice, including tips on how to overcome writers' block and manage the sheer volume of data;
- manage the editing process;
- improve collaborative writing strategies.

We also include a section on the advantages of writing for screen and in non-linear formats.

Word processing skills for research writing

While you will probably be familiar with most of the basics of using your word processor, learning to use more advanced features will be of great benefit if you need to:

- work with long documents;
- use specific formatting features;
- self-edit and write collaboratively with others;
- distribute letters and other documents;
- perform certain functions repeatedly.

While there is little point in us replicating information available in "how to" guides on using specific word processing software, in this section we provide general guidance on when advanced features can be beneficial for your research writing and offer more detailed guidance for some of the less well-known or more complex but highly beneficial features. In general, though, we trust in your capability to explore and/or consult the help features of your word processor program as you require.

Working with long documents

Researchers frequently find themselves working with very long documents. Your thesis will be one; however you may also produce reports or publish books throughout your research career. Such documents require particular word processing skills, some of which are outlined in Table 12.1.

Table 12.1 Advanced word processing features that assist with long documents.

Advanced feature	Explanation and tips for use in research
Master documents (file linking)	Any experienced researcher will emphasize that it is safest not to keep your entire document in one file – that is like putting all your eggs in one basket! However, separate files lead to issues with bringing your document together. Master documents and file linking are essential tools for producing a large document
Styles	Styles are foundational to other advanced features for working with long documents, including: • formatting headings; • numbering sections; • sequentially numbering tables and figures; • creating a table of contents
Headers and footers	Headers usually contain the name of your report or thesis,or the name of the chapter (for the latter you need to use file linking and/or section breaks, as explained below). Footers normally include the page number, but can also be used to include other temporary information such as the date the document was last printed (useful for keeping track of hardcopy drafts of your work)
Section breaks	You can insert breaks between different parts of your document so that particular sections can display differently.This is useful for: • each chapter of an unlinked document, enabling you to have different headers and footers for each section; • formatting a page or series of pages to print in landscape layout (sideways) rather than portrait; • using particular formatting such as page borders on only part of a document
Multiple windows	Creating a new window on your document, or splitting the one window into two sections, allows you to view different parts of the document at the same time and move quickly between them. This is particularly useful when you are shuffling content or comparing your arguments in different sections
Mirroring of margins	If you intend to print your document back-to-back and bind it then you should set the margins to "mirror" (usually found in File – Page Set-up). This means alternate left and right margins will be wider to allow for binding
Indexes and glossaries	Most word processors provide an automatic indexing function by which you can "mark" particular terms in your document and have appear in an index with the page number these terms automatically generated. A similar process can be used to generate a glossary, marking terms which are defined and explained in an appendicized section
Cross-referencing	If you use styles you will be able to cross-reference between parts of your document and have your word processor update such things as numbering or page location. For instance, rather than typing "see section 5.6" and then finding that as you edit 5.6 becomes 5.8, inserting a cross-reference to the heading of that section, with directions to display the section number, ensures the numerical reference will always be correct

Styles

Styles define the appearance of specified text within your document. They also ensure consistency and professionalism in layout and provide flexibility if you later want to submit to journals or other publications. When you apply a style to a heading or paragraph, you can control the appearance of all similar headings or paragraphs in one simple operation. For example, if your main headings are 14 point Arial, flush left, and bold, and you later decide you want your headings to be 16 point Arial and centered, you don't have to reformat every instance of a main heading in your document. Instead you simply change the properties of that style. Styles not only make formatting your research document much easier and more efficient, they also ensure consistency. Additionally, they serve as building blocks for outlines and tables of contents (described below).

Setting up and applying styles

Styles can usually be applied using a drop-down menu on your word processor's toolbar. The process is a little like changing a font (as illustrated in Figure 12.1). Simply highlight one of your headings and then select the appropriate level for that heading. For instance, Heading 1 could be your chapter heading, Heading 2 the larger sections within the chapter and Heading 3 the subheadings under Heading 2.

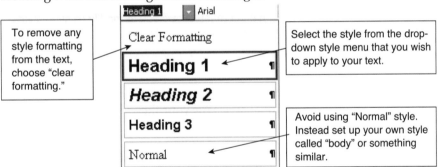

Figure 12.1 Apply styles from the drop-down menu

The appearance of your text can be formatted by selecting a set style from the drop-down style menu. This ensures consistency of headings (for example) across a whole document. Example is from Microsoft Word.

You can change the appearance of your styles at any time by modifying the style formatting rules. In Microsoft Word, for example, select "Styles and Formatting" from the Format menu, or use the following icon:. A drop-down menu for each style allows you to modify the style's formatting. Alternatively you can change the appearance of the heading in your document *first*, and then select "Update to Match Selection." All headings in your document that have been set to that style should change and thus be consistent. From this screen you can also set up your own "New Styles" (see Figure 12.2).

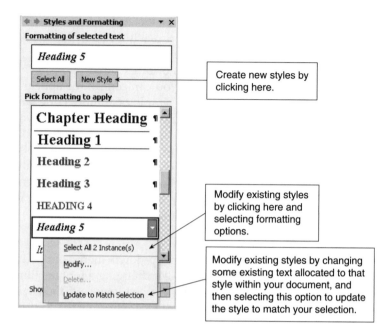

Figure 12.2   Options for modifying styles

The styles and formatting menu allows you to modify existing styles or create new ones. Example is from Microsoft Word.

While you may only think of using styles for heading levels, consider creating the following additional styles for your thesis or research report:

- **Body.** Set this style up for all your standard text. It is better to use your own style than the built-in "Normal" style, which cannot easily be modified.
- **Bullets and sub-bullets**. This will ensure consistency with indentation.
- **Quote.** Use for block quotes which require consistent indentation, perhaps using a smaller font or different line spacing.
- **Reference list.** This may require different indentation and potentially a smaller font.
- **Table text.** Often the size or alignment of text within tables is different from text in the body of your document.
- **Table headings and figure headings.** Formatting these with a particular numbered style (see below) will automatically number these sequentially throughout your document as well as produce a list of tables and figures at the beginning of the document with accurate page numbering.
- **Other styles of your choice.** Use these as required for particular features of your document such as text with borders.

Numbering headings using styles

Many long documents, including theses, use a number format for heading structures, for example, 1.0, 1.1, 1.1.1., 2.0, 2.1 and so on. Doing this numbering by hand means that you must either continuously make adjustments throughout your writing process or leave numbering until the end, which means you don't enjoy the benefits of numbering during your drafting phases. Your word processor can take care of the tedious numbering process, providing accuracy and continuously updating as you go.

Most word processors have a numbering feature (in Microsoft Word look under the Format menu). The "Outline Numbered" feature enables you to select the type of numbering you prefer, based on your use of styles (as illustrated in Figure 12.3). The "Customize" feature enables you to put your own text before the automatic numbering; a useful tip for numbering tables, figures or chapters.

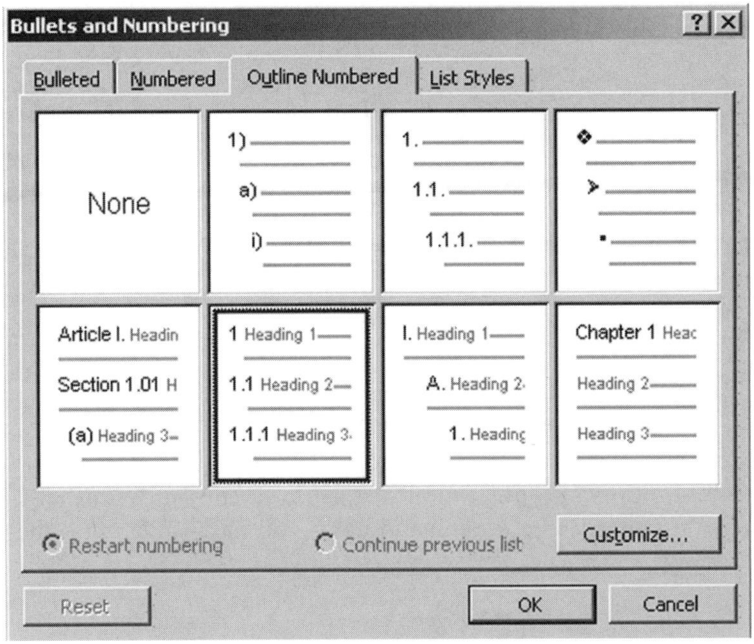

Figure 12.3   Formatting numbering using the outline numbering feature

This allows you to allocate automatic numbering to your heading levels. Example is from Microsoft Word.

Using Outline View with styles

If you have used styles to set out your document, you can then use the "Outline View" to review and restructure it. The outline function allows you to gain an overall impression of your document's structure (see Figure 12.4). By using the outlining toolbar you can then promote or demote headings and sections to a higher or lower level. You can also shuffle sections of your document around by dragging-and-dropping the headings displayed in the outline view so that the text associated with those sections will also move.

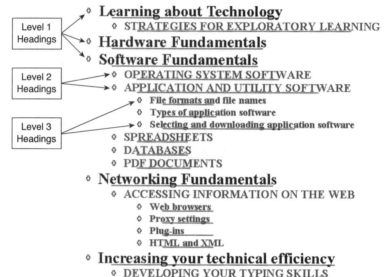

Figure 12.4   A document in outline view

In this example level 1, 2 and 3 headings are showing. However, these headings can be expanded to show other heading levels or the text within each section. Example is from Microsoft Word.

Some programs also allow you to view a document map that lists all headings on a separate task pane and helps you navigate around the document quickly.

Inserting Tables of Contents from styles

This is where word processors really come into their own. Creating tables of contents, indexes or glossaries are *definitely* not something you would choose to do manually if you have the option of using your word processor to generate them for you. If you have used the styles feature you can insert a table of contents automatically, and then just keep updating it as you progress through your thesis or report. (In Microsoft Word, look under the Insert menu – Reference – Index and Tables – Table of Contents). Note that you can specify how many heading levels display in your table of contents (you may not want all levels of subheadings to appear) and you can also customize the table of contents to include other style types.

You can also use styles to generate lists of tables and figures (as normally appear after the table of contents). By using a specific style for table titles or figure titles you can then insert a second and third table of contents (as above) based on these specific styles. (In Microsoft Word, Insert – Reference – Index and Tables – Table of Figures, then choose "Options" to select the style your list will be built on).

Copying styles between documents

If you are formatting a thesis or report that has separate documents for each chapter, it can be very useful to copy styles from one document to another. (In Microsoft Word, look under the Tools menu and select "Templates and Add ins"). The Styles Organizer allows you to move styles from one template or document to another (see Figure 12.5). You can also link a particular template to a document so that the moving of styles between documents occurs automatically, although this needs to be approached with some care.

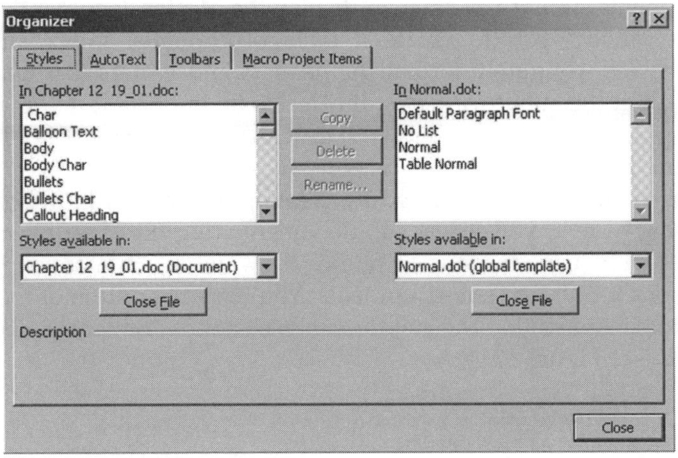

Figure 12.5   **Moving styles from one document to another using Styles Organizer**

By closing the normal.doc file and opening another established document or template, individual styles or all styles can be copied between files. Example is from Microsoft Word.

Using pre-setup templates

If you don't want to set up styles yourself, it is possible to use a preestablished styles template. Your word processor may provide some of these already or you might download or be given one by your university, a journal editor or a publisher. We suggest it is still important to know how to apply and modify styles as it is unlikely that any one template will meet all your personal or institution's requirements.

See the **Organizing and Managing Your Research Website**

for several templates for laying out a thesis or report.
http://www.sagepub.co.uk/phelps

Master documents (file linking)

If you create your long document with each chapter or other section as a separate file (as we suggest), then at some stage you will want to link them all together. While you *can* copy and paste each chapter into the one document, and proceed to format the whole document, you run the risk of having all of your work (including all your final editing) in one easily corrupted and difficult-to-navigate file. The "Master document" facility provided by many word processors allows you to keep each chapter separate, but draws them together *for display only* in a single document. You can continue to work on sub-documents, and at any stage re-display the Master document. A Master document allows you to create a table of contents, index and cross-references, and accurately format the headers and footers (e.g. page numbers) for all of the sub-documents. It can also be important if you are using bibliographic software (see Chapter 9) to achieve a single reference list based on citations in each separate document.

A Master document is formed by creating a new file. However, rather than typing in text, you insert sub-documents (the files you have already created). This is usually done in outline view, where the toolbar provides special icons for adding sub-documents. You have the option of locking the Master document so that the sub-documents cannot accidentally be moved or deleted (see Figure 12.6).

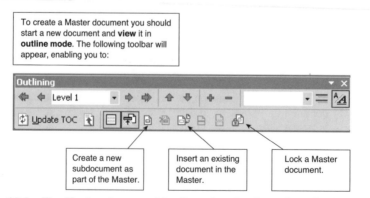

Figure 12.6 The Master document toolbar showing insertion of subdocuments

Existing documents can be added to a Master document, or new sub-documents can be created as separate files, but displayed in the Master. Example is from Microsoft Word.

Other useful formatting features

You no doubt use basic formatting devices such as changing fonts, changing font size, using bold or italics, changing line spacing or margins, etc. but you may not be familiar with all the formatting features that could be useful for your research. Table 12.2 offers a sample.

Table 12.2   Advanced formatting features useful for research.

Advanced feature	Explanation and tips for use in research
Footnotes and endnotes	Footnotes are numbered notes that appear at the bottom of pages while endnotes appear at the end of chapters or the entire document. They are used in research for referencing, to offer asides or to elaborate on points in the main text. Use of these is often discipline-specific (e.g. they are used widely in law for referencing), so be sure you are familiar with the protocols in your own discipline
Formatting tables	As well as setting out results, tables can also be used as a convenient layout device for positioning text or images on a page. The Table Autoformat feature (in Microsoft Word) assists in providing consistent formatting for your tables
Using symbols and signs	You may need to include symbols specific to your research, for example, numerical signs in mathematics; foreign language symbols; or symbols useful for surveys. Be aware that every font has its own set of symbols, so when you select "Insert – Symbol" (in Word) you can broaden the range by designating different fonts. Symbols which might be useful include: ❑ ✄ © ® ™ ☑ ☒ £ • ✓ µ í ä • • • • • •
Find and replace	While this is a commonly used feature, it plays an important role in research writing in ensuring consistency in spelling and formatting of terms. For instance, it can be useful when you decide to change the capitalization or hyphenation of terms
Creating hyperlinks	The ability to create a hyperlink is a skill that runs across many programs. Once you understand the process it is easy. Type in the text that you want to appear on your page, highlight it and choose "Insert – Link." If you are linking to a website, then copy and paste in the URI. If you are linking to one of your own documents, browse to select the file. The text will generally appear blue and underlined to signify a link

Editing tools

When you are writing up your research you are certain to do a lot of editing and re-editing of your drafts. You are also likely to seek feedback from others (including supervisors). At times you may also find yourself working collaboratively with peers on papers and other publications. The features in

Table 12.3 can help this process run smoothly without too much confusion as different versions and changes are made. See also Figure 12.7.

Table 12.3   Tools to assist with editing and collaborative writing.

Advanced feature	Explanation and tips for use in research
Highlighting tool	Use the highlighting tool to mark sections you want to return to. When you are editing on screen, different colors can signify different types of tasks, for example, paraphrase a quote, find a reference, check on the details, edit the section further or find a better way to express it. In collaborative writing a particular color might represent a task for each group member
Track changes	Turn on the "track changes" tool when you want your changes to be visible to your collaborator or supervisor (and they can do the same on your work). Deleted text will be shown as a strike-through or a box to the right indicating what has been cut, while new text will appear in a different color. The tool allows you and your collaborators to accept or reject changes. At any stage you can view your document in "final layout" (the editing will be hidden) or "with markup."
Comments	Use the "comments" tool (Insert – Comment in Word) for making notes to yourself, your supervisor or your collaborative writers about questions you have, points you need to return to, or tasks you want each other to perform. A small note appears in the right hand margin and you have the option to print with or without the comments (see Figure 12.7)
Managing versions	Some word processors provide a facility for automatically managing different versions of documents so that the most recent versions aren't overwritten by older versions. Use this to provide a safeguard against mistaken or later regretted deletion of text. Be aware that this can dramatically increase the document size and it may be preferable to manually archive versions (see Chapter 4)
Comparing and merging documents	If someone has made changes to one of your documents without tracking changes some word processing programs provide the facility to compare and merge documents. Most do this paragraph by paragraph, alerting you to any changes between the original and the newer version. This feature can also be useful if you aren't sure which of two files is the most recent or contains the changes you last made (look under the Tools menu)
Sound annotations	Some word processors allow insertion of audio comments, which may be preferable to typing feedback on your document. They require a microphone and can be used in the same way as inserting typed comments (see above)

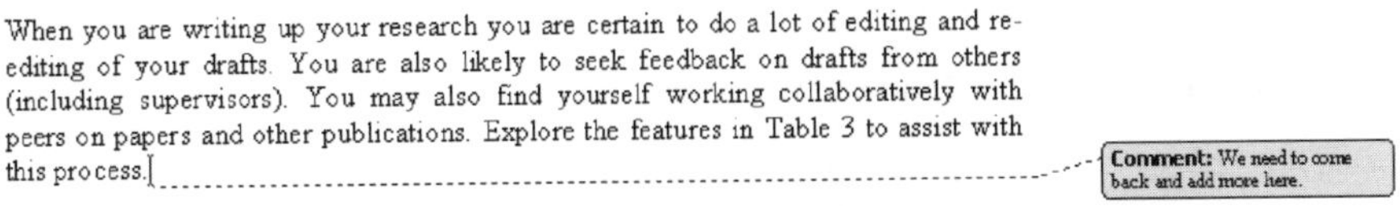

When you are writing up your research you are certain to do a lot of editing and re-editing of your drafts. You are also likely to seek feedback on drafts from others (including supervisors). You may also find yourself working collaboratively with peers on papers and other publications. Explore the features in Table 3 to assist with this process.

> **Comment:** We need to come back and add more here.

Figure 12.7   The comment feature, used to add margin notes to text

Example is from Microsoft Word.

Distributing letters and other documents

There are times when, as a researcher, you might need to do a mail-out (using either standard post or e-mail), for example, to distribute invitations to a group of people to participate in your research, to thank your intervie-wees for their participation, or to provide a paper to colleagues you met at a conference. Table 12.4 outlines word processing features that would be useful to you in this circumstance.

Table 12.4   Features for distributing letters and documents.

Advanced feature	Explanation and tips for use in research
Mail or e-mail merge	Use this feature (under Tools – Letters and Mailings in Word) to send correspondence to a group of people. You can either use an existing list, type in a new one (using a simple built-in database) or draw data from an existing database (such as the address book in Microsoft Outlook). Your word processor will drop the address details and salutation expressions (as per your directions) into your letter or e-mails, generating a batch of messages from your template
Envelopes and labels	Many word processors also facilitate printing of envelopes and labels. Through a process similar to mail merging (above) you can draw from a database and have the software position the text on the labels for you. This can be invaluable when distributing surveys or thank-you letters to research participants

Customizing your word processor for enhanced efficiency

It is likely that in the process of writing up your research you will find your-self performing certain functions repeatedly. To make your writing process more efficient, explore the tools in Table 12.5.

Table 12.5 Tools for customizing your word processor.

Advanced feature	Explanation and tips for use in research
Using Autocorrect	Use the Autocorrect feature (under "Tools" in Word) to set up your word processor to replace something that you type with an alternative word or phrase. This is useful not only for correcting habitual typing errors, but also for shortcuts that replace terms that you type frequently. For example, "att" might be set to expand to "attribution theory." Make sure that your shortcut terms are not familiar words or acronyms (e.g. "par" would not work as a shortcut for "participatory action research")
Allocating shortcuts	See Chapter 2
Adding icons to toolbars	See Chapter 2. This is particularly useful for frequently performed functions such as inserting a pagebreak
Managing dictionaries	Build a customized dictionary if you need to add words specific to your research but which don't appear in your word processor's dictionary. Add authors' names as well so that your spell-checker no longer identifies them as misspelled words
Customizing spell-checking and grammar checking features	Many word processors automatically flag (e.g. underline in color) potential spelling and grammar errors as you write, allowing you to right-click on any questionable term or phrase and replace it with a suggested word. Some will also "guess" at errors and replace these as you type (for instance ensuring there is a capital letter at the beginning of a sentence). The Options or Preferences section of your program allows you to enable or disable these features
Using Macros	See Chapter 2

A word of caution about...

Word Processing

Working with any document over a long period of time can often produce unanticipated problems. For instance, many researchers (including us!) have experienced file corruption issues when working on their long documents. Forewarned is forearmed. Talking to experienced users or joining online support groups will provide you with valuable insights into the potential pitfalls. No program can guarantee 100% fail-safe performance. Your best defense is to be absolutely disciplined in your security, backup and versioning practices.

Typographical considerations

Academic writing has traditions in typography[1] that are historically rather than practically, optically or aesthetically justified. In fact, many formatting traditions in academia have remained unchallenged since the days of typewriters and carbon paper. With developments in technology and the ability to edit work onscreen, many of these traditions have become outdated. For example, you may be all too familiar with the double spacing, wide margins and highly regulated presentation requirements of the traditional undergraduate essay. These traditions have, in many institutions, carried through to thesis presentation and, while there are some arguments for continued use of these features (such as allowing examiners to make editorial annotations on hard copies), thesis presentation standards are far from approximating the professional and reader-friendly format of a published book.

The thesis is not the only document you will produce as a researcher – others include books, reports, journal papers, surveys, posters, flyers, promotional material and presentations. Typographical decisions influence the mood and tone of a document and can greatly influence the impact on your readers. There is much that academic writers can learn from the art and science of typographical design. Unfortunately, all too often researchers overlook or do not understand the need to produce and present documents that are professionally formatted, aesthetically appealing and appropriate for their target audience. We have seen survey forms designed for print distribution spaced out over 4½ pages, with unnecessary gaps, wide margins and little to grab the eye, motivate or enthuse respondents. We have also seen promotional flyers produced to recruit research participants using large blocks of text with the font all the same size, with wide margins. While you may not be in a position to challenge thesis presentation requirements, there are many other documents that allow you greater creativity in presentation. Here are some key insights from typography that may be useful for some of your research documentation:

- **Select an appropriate typeface.** *Sans Serif* typefaces do not have finishing strokes at the ends of the letterforms. Examples include Arial, Avante Garde, Century Gothic and Helvetica. *Serif* typefaces have lines or curves projecting from the end of a letterform. Examples include Times Roman, Palatino, Bookman, and New Century Schoolbook. Serif typefaces are more legible for long stretches of printed text, but sans serif is more readable on a monitor. Verdana is a font that was specifically developed for screen display. Script typefaces (which simulate handwriting) and other decorative fonts are usually harder to read and should be used sparingly – only for headings and other features; never for blocks of text. The most readable type sizes are between 9 and 12 point; 11 is a good compromise.
- **Use bold** for headings and *italics* for emphasis within text. Overuse of either on a page loses the effect and can tire the reader.

- **Avoid underlining** for emphasis as in many publishing contexts this signifies a hyperlink.
- **Add spacing between paragraphs** to increase readability, particularly on screen. Some disciplines and publishers set out paragraphs with an indentation instead of a blank line between paragraphs.
- **Choose your line spacing carefully.** Spacing that is too tight decreases readability while spacing which is quite spread out feels tedious and unnecessarily long and hinders skim or speed reading. While single and double spacing is common, most word processors will provide options for 1½ line spacing and also allow you to stipulate specific spacing.
- **Adjust line length** for readability. If a line is too long, our eyes have trouble finding the beginning of the next sentence.

  If a line is too
  short, it
  breaks up the
  continuity of the
  phrase.

- **Use white space strategically** as it can aid readability even more than font size or writing style.
- **Indent bullets** and indent sub-bullets even further. This greatly aids readability and supports the structuring of your arguments.
- **Avoid using BLOCK CAPITAL LETTERS** as they are difficult to read and are considered by many as "shouting" (bad manners or just plain lazy, indicating lack of effort to use appropriate capitalization).
- **Consider how you align text.** Text alignment refers to the shape of the text block in relation to the margins. Most software programs allow left alignment (sometimes called flush left), right alignment (sometimes called flush right), centre alignment, justified alignment, and force justify alignment. Justified alignment, while it looks "neat" can lead to spacing issues between words which need to be overcome with use of hyphenation.

Improving writing efficiency

How do you usually approach your writing? Does it come easily or do you struggle over every sentence? Do you work from a structure or allow it to emerge as you write? How efficient are you in getting your ideas down?

Writing is as individual as personal style. You may prefer to write in a logical and structured manner from beginning to end (the "perfect draft" strategy) or you may write thoughts as they occur to you, dropping random ideas into sections and then coming back and tightening up arguments as you go (the "successive refinement" strategy).[2] Whatever your preferred approach, some of the tips we offer here may prove useful to improve your writing efficiency. You may find that some strategies work best in contexts where you are not as familiar with the concepts you are writing about, while other strategies work best when you are more confident about your content. Different sections of your write-up (e.g. literature review versus methods section) may also call for different writing approaches.

Managing writing and overcoming writers' block

- **Start writing from the very beginning** of your research process. Don't wait for some magical time when you think you will feel "ready." Write, write, write. Options are to write in a journal (see Chapter 3); keep notes in electronic format in separate word documents or in your bibliographic software (Chapter 9); or write directly into your thesis or report.
- **Use your word processor for all jottings and notes**, including summarizing the literature you are reading (see Chapter 9). You will find this can significantly decrease the amount of work to do later in thesis writing.
- **Improve your typing skills**. If you aren't a fluent typist then it may be worth familiarizing yourself with good typing techniques. While you may not want to spend time doing a typing course, you will certainly get lots of practice throughout your research career.
- **Build an outline, using styles, and keep adding into that structure.** Of course your outline structure will change, shuffle and grow as your writing develops.
- **Brainstorm or mind map ideas** (see Chapter 3) to get you started on a particular section of writing or to free yourself from writers' block.
- **Be strategic about when to write**. Identify which sections you think will be hard going and which will be easier to write. Tackle the most difficult sections at the time of day when you know you do your best thinking.
- **Set yourself specific writing goals** such as "today I will write the section on resilience" or "today I will write 4 paragraphs on my methodological decisions" or "I will write 3 paragraphs before lunch."
- **Give yourself time and space to think through ideas**. It is common practice to move from writing new ideas to editing then returning to composing.
- **Try "blind writing"**[3] whereby you turn off or turn down your monitor while typing so you are not tempted to self-edit and distract your train of thought.
- **Try hand writing without stopping** or taking your pen off the page for 10–15 minutes. Don't censor your writing. This is helpful to start ideas flowing and to overcome resistance to writing.

Editing your drafts

- **Make a one-page list of your editorial decisions** to aid consistency. For instance, include decisions about:

  - **capitalization** of certain words and phrases, such as names of theories, "chapter" or "Chapter," "section" or "Section" and so on;
  - **number formats**, for example "Chapter One" versus "Chapter 1";
  - **hyphenation**, for example "Web page" versus "Web-page" versus "Webpage" versus "webpage."

- **Decide what type of editing to do electronically and what to do on hard copy.** Reorganizing whole sections, for instance, may be better done on the computer while paper-based editing can often allow you to gain insights and see editorial problems that somehow remain invisible on the screen.

- **Don't print drafts of your chapters too frequently.** Not only is this expensive and environmentally wasteful, it also adds to the amount of paper you are shuffling and impacts on your capacity to keep organized. Don't print until you are *really* ready to work on a printed version as the drafts quickly become redundant if you continue editing on screen.

- **Keep considering the logic of the structure of your writing** (i.e. the headings and subheadings). Outline view or the document map (see above) can assist with this. As your writing develops, old structures can become redundant and may actually impede your ability to construct your emerging arguments. Get feedback on your structure from your supervisor and peers.

- **Be consistent with the symbols you use to mark-up your document** when editing on paper.

- **Use different colored text or highlighting for different types of editing decisions** (on screen or on paper), as we suggested in Table 12.5 for collaborative writing. For instance, you might use green for references that need to be checked; red for questions for your supervisor; blue for structural changes and so on. This makes it easier to scan through your document when you are focused on one task, such as reference checking.

- **Use distinguishing marks or symbols,** such as A, B, C to note sections (on paper) that need to be moved to different locations. Make sure you then use the same symbols to indicate where those sections should go.

- **Create a "darlings" file.** As you tighten your writing and get feedback, there will be sections, often quite large, that you need to delete as they no longer fit with your overall structure or argument. You may have invested considerable time, intellectual effort and passion into writing these sections and be reluctant to see them go (hence the term "darlings" – they're like our children who are really ready to leave home, even if we're not ready for them to!). Creating a special document allows you to return to these deleted sections for later consideration. You may find a new place for them somewhere in your thesis (or even in a journal publication) or their relevance may wane.

Writing with others

- **Use a data projector to project your work on to a screen** and write collaboratively into the one document, if you are able to meet face-to-face.
- **Use synchronous communication systems** if you can't meet face-to-face, particularly document-sharing features (see Chapter 6).
- **Make use of comments**, highlighting and tracked changes (see above) to record notes to each other. Different colors might be used to distinguish notes to, or contributions from, different collaborators.
- **Monitor who is working on each section at any one time**. A spreadsheet can help with this, or use careful versioning (see Chapter 4).
- **Use software that enables documents to be saved to a central server** and facilitates checking in and checking out (see Chapter 5).

Using a combination of these writing and editing strategies made our writing of the manuscript for this book both enjoyable and efficient. In the latter stages, which involved fine-grained editing, group meetings with a data projector proved to be particularly productive.

Writing for screen

In Chapter 4 we discussed the advantages and disadvantages of reading on screen. While many people choose not to read long documents at their computer, much of the readability of on-screen documents has to do with how they have been written. Writing for screen is thus an art form in its own right. You may find yourself creating a website (see Chapter 6); publishing your thesis or other papers online; creating online surveys; or using e-mail as a primary form of communication. If so, the following guidelines will make your documents more readable on screen:

- use shorter paragraphs;
- use sans serif typefaces;
- make more use of headings;
- include key points in the first sentence of each paragraph;
- make good use of point form and bulleted lists; and
- use color judiciously.

Nonlinear writing

The concept of hyperlinking has made possible new forms of writing that provide readers with the opportunity to find multiple pathways through a document.[4] This textual nonlinearity means the reader doesn't have to read from beginning to end in a preestablished order, and different readers can navigate their way through the document in very different ways (a little like a "choose your own adventure" novel). In fact, hypertext writing has developed into a literature form in its own right and has rapidly gained legitimacy as an acceptable publishing format.[5]

It is not only webpages (.html documents) that support hyperlinked text. Word processed documents, spreadsheets, presentation software, PDF documents, in fact most publishing forms, now support hyperlinking. In Chapter 13 we consider the benefits of nonlinear presentations. Nonlinear writing formats can be particularly useful for qualitative research because they[6]:

- **preserve the original streams of consciousness** that qualitative data so often reveal but are so difficult to carry through to representation;
- **can help to reduce de-contextualization problems** (i.e. the isolation of concepts from their original context);
- **assist qualitative researchers to represent the diversity of their interpretations of data**, thereby disrupting the "fixed" interpretation that linear text can imply (even if it intellectually challenges this).

On a cautionary note, it is important to remember that:

- the links and pathways you devise are still imposed on the reader, who can only go where you let them, even though there may be many other possibilities;
- if you put in too many links and allow too many pathways through the text, it can quickly become bewildering and unnavigable.

Over to you...

1. What features of your word processor would be useful for you to improve your particular research writing task?
2. How could you customize your word processor to speed up your frequently performed tasks?
3. What strategies could you start using to make the writing process more effective and enjoyable?
4. How do you prefer to edit your work? How could you improve your editing strategies to create greater efficiencies?
5. Under what circumstances could you see yourself using nonlinear writing formats?

Notes

1 Typography is the selection and arrangement of typefaces, sizes and spacing on a printed publication or webpage. Typography has a major impact on the overall look and image of your page and its overall quality.
2 Palmquist and Zimmerman 1999.
3 Blind writing is a strategy suggested by Palmquist and Zimmerman 1999.
4 Coffey et al. 1996.
5 Brown 2002.
6 Points are derived from Brown 2002.

Chapter 13

Presenting and Publishing Your Research

You might be tempted to see your written thesis or dissertation as the primary output and culmination of your research process. If this is the case, it is likely that the only people who get to know and understand what you have done in your research are your supervisors and your thesis examiners. Producing your thesis is really only one step in your research career. Publishing and disseminating your work, both during and after candidature, is not only demanded by competitive academic and industry environments, but is also a great way to be recognized and acknowledged for your hard work and contribution to knowledge. In this chapter we focus on skills and strategies that can assist you to make the most of communicating your research to a wider audience. In particular, we cover:

- tips on giving oral presentations;
- how to make the most of presentation software (such as Power Point), including production of self-running and nonlinear presentations;
- tips on producing posters for conferences;
- strategies for presenting to the media;
- how to plan a publication strategy, including targeting journals and converting your thesis to a book;
- peer review and manuscript management systems.

Oral presentations

Postgraduate research students are frequently required to present their work to others in an oral form, either as part of their course requirements (e.g. some universities require an oral defense of the thesis); through departmental seminars; or at conferences, seminars or other functions. For maximum impact, such oral presentations require effective public speaking skills, good preparation and plenty of practice. At times your may also be in a position to talk to or write for the popular media.

Visual supports (including the integration of graphs, diagrams, photographs, sounds and video) can assist greatly in engaging your audience and conveying your ideas clearly, succinctly and effectively. Poster presentations and self-running displays are examples of alternate presentation formats where a few extra skills can enhance your impact considerably. While presentation technologies offer many possibilities to increase the effectiveness of your presentations, it is important to be aware of their traps and ways they can be misused.

Strategies to improve public speaking

During our research for this book, many of the professors we talked with emphasized the importance of public speaking as an essential skill that most new researchers need to develop and/or improve. One professor regarded public speaking skills as so important to the researcher's role of contributing to public life that he personally paid for each of his graduate students to join Toastmasters International, a global network of clubs that provide a supportive learning environment for people of all levels and walks of life to learn public speaking and leadership skills.

There is no doubt that an ability to speak clearly and to communicate effectively with an audience is one of the key characteristics of a successful researcher, no matter what stage of their research career they are in:

- **postgraduate research students** may need to apply these skills to presentations at conferences, faculty seminars and *viva voca* examinations;
- **early career researchers** will need good public speaking skills for conference presentations and job interviews;
- **established researchers** will inevitably be called upon to give keynote addresses, media interviews and perhaps pitches for large research grants or commercial partnerships.

Few people are naturally good presenters and speakers and almost everyone finds it a daunting and nerve-racking task. It is particularly so for new researchers (as well as many who are more experienced) who have to stand up in front of peers or experts in their field. We offer here some suggestions that may assist in making a strong impact and overcoming presentation nerves.

Preparing your speech

- **Take as many opportunities as possible to speak in public.** The best way to overcome nervousness is to put yourself in situations where you stand up in front of people. This might mean asking questions in conference sessions, making an announcement at a public gathering or giving a speech at a wedding. There is probably no way to get rid of nerves before a presentation, but they *can* work for you. The adrenaline that comes with nerves helps you stay alert and focused and the nerves will usually disappear as you get into your presentation.
- **Know your audience**. Work from the basis of "what does the audience want to know" rather than "what do I want to tell them." What is it that will be *new* in your talk for them, and what will they already know? Find out as much as you can about their background knowledge and interests and shape your presentation accordingly.
- **Plan the structure** of your talk and make sure it flows logically. Let your audience know up front how your talk will proceed and what you will cover.
- **Practice your speech as many times as possible,** particularly making sure you are well within the required time frame. Take the opportunity to practice with your peers and get some feedback on how you're coming across. You can also rehearse it in front of a mirror, like a performance. That way you may pick up any awkward hand gestures and you can practice standing tall and delivering confidently, smiling, etc.
- **Have everything you need for your presentation ready well beforehand.** Distributing handouts before the presentation means people won't take notes unnecessarily and you won't have to disrupt the flow of your presentation by distributing paper. Avoid transferring your presentation files to the appropriate computer at the last minute as time will be at a premium. Others may all want to do the same and this just becomes an invitation for things to go wrong.
- **Get to know the room you will be in for your presentation.** Make sure there are no cords that can trip you. Notice where you can stand so that each person in the audience can see you; familiarize yourself with the equipment set-up; and alert conference organizers to any problems that need rectifying.
- **Greet a few people as they arrive.** A smile, a handshake and a friendly chat before your talk can help take away any fear of the audience.

Delivering your speech

- **Control nerves before you start** by taking a few deep slow breaths (rather than a few stiff drinks).

- **Have a glass of water at hand.** Adrenaline gives you a dry mouth and it's much better to pause and calmly take a sip of water than to try to struggle on speaking with a dry mouth.
- **Know the *exact* words you are going to start with.** It makes for a confident start which can calm the nerves.
- **Make an initial impact.** Consider starting the presentation in a novel way – a funny or engaging story, an image or a question to the audience can be effective.
- **Acknowledge your audience.** Thank them for coming; acknowledge any people who have supported your work; and recognize the expertise that is present.
- **Be confident.** Your audience is there because people are interested in what you have to say. Focus on them, not yourself. Know your strong points and work to those. If you make an error, correct it and continue. There is no need to make excuses or apologize profusely.
- **Keep your talk very simple with a few main points**. Don't try to present too much information. Plan which parts you might leave out if time is short.
- **Do not read your paper or your slides.** If you are presenting at a conference, your presentation should advertise your paper, which people can read later. Reading the content of your slides, when the audience is more than capable of doing this themselves, can seem condescending (we give more tips on using presentation software effectively below). Elaborate on points rather than reading them. Reading also means your voice loses modulation and can be boring for your audience. It is far better to stumble over a few words through being conversational than to read in a flat voice. Pretend you are talking to a group of friends or pick a person in the audience and speak to them as though you were having a private conversation.
- **Speak slowly and clearly**. Use varied vocal tone and move around a little.
- **Use pauses to good effect**. They can be very effective in giving you a chance to catch your breath and giving the audience time to think about what you have said. You can even use pauses to ask the audience to reflect a moment, or in a longer speech, give them the opportunity to take a minute or so to talk to their neighbor about an issue you may have raised or a controversial point they may want to discuss.
- **Avoid padding out your content.** Repetition is useful in some instances, but use it strategically. For instance, recap your main points at the end of your presentation, but avoid restating points you have just made.
- **Avoid filler words such as um, ah, okay, sort of, you know etc**. A pause is much easier to listen to than an um or ah. Listening to a tape recording of yourself speaking or getting feedback in a practice session can help you identify any bad speaking habits.

- **Establish eye contact and rapport with your audience**. Try to include everyone by looking around the room.
- **Incorporate some humor or narrative.** Stories and light jokes are great for engaging your audience.
- **Manage your time well.** Plan to use *less* than your allocated time. Your presentation will almost always take longer than you think. Overrunning can be disrespectful to your audience and the next presenter. If you have only been given a very short amount of time (5–10 minutes), all is not lost. It is better to make one or two points strongly and clearly than try to pack too much into the available time.
- **Be prepared to be flexible**. If what you prepared is not getting across to your audience, or if the mood of the conference or seminar is different from what you expected, have a little confidence (mixed with instinct and common sense) to vary from your original plan, but only if you have the opportunity (for instance 30 minutes between sessions) to rethink your strategy.

Concluding your speech

- **Acknowledge people who helped you along the way,** not your mother and aunt (unless they *were* really helpful), but your supervisors or peers. This doesn't need to take time out of the presentation; perhaps just put this on the final slide and only speak to it if necessary.
- **Remember to conclude**. Knowing when and how to stop is an art in itself. Have an interesting ending prepared, summarize your points and avoid saying something like "that's it!" A simple "thank you" is most effective, followed by an invitation to ask questions, if time allows.
- **Use question and discussion time well.** It can be more valuable for getting your message across than the presentation time. Engage with your audience and make your responses concise and informative. Don't get thrown by a tricky question; if you aren't sure how to respond, say so and indicate you'd be keen to discuss this with the audience member after the session.
- **Above all, enjoy yourself.** If you do, so will your audience.

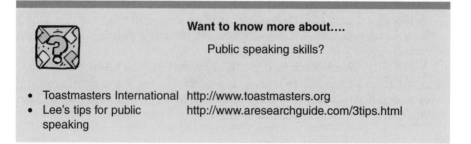

Want to know more about....

Public speaking skills?

- Toastmasters International http://www.toastmasters.org
- Lee's tips for public   http://www.aresearchguide.com/3tips.html
  speaking

(Continued)

- Orman's How to Conquer Public Speaking Fear
  http://www.stresscure.com/jobstress/speak.html
- Strategies to Succeed in Public Speaking
  http://www.school-for-champions.com/speaking.htm
- A free guide to speech writing and delivery
  http://www.speechtips.com
- Presentation Helper
  http://www.presentationhelper.co.uk
- Presenters University
  http://www.presentersuniversity.com

Using presentation software

A visual accompaniment to a presentation can considerably enhance the impact of your message and technology has come a long way since the days when the slide carousel or overhead projector was the favored method employed by the confident conference presenter. Presentation software is designed specifically to help you create visual presentations to support your public speaking. While we offer in this section a number of strategies for using such software, it is important to remember the tips above about developing good presentation skills. The visual technology should not dominate or drive your talk, but instead be a useful adjunct or enhancement. Audiences want to watch you, not the screen.

Generally presentation programs produce a series of slides which combine into a "show," providing a computer-based alternative to overhead transparencies. The most well-known presentation software is Microsoft PowerPoint (although it is only one such program). However, if you learn how to produce a website (see Chapter 6), you can use these same skills to develop a series of linked pages that will function as a presentation. Given that in our experience most beginning researchers use PowerPoint, it is the example we use for the discussion to follow; however the main ideas should be transferable to other programs.

Presentation software features

- **Templates**. Most people develop their presentations from pre-designed backgrounds, layouts and color schemes (known as templates) which are supplied with the program. Additional templates can usually be downloaded from the software producer's site. Be aware that you don't *have* to use these schemes. Formatting the slide design yourself may be preferable when you are using lots of images (diagrams or charts) or when you want the look and feel to be more relevant to your research.

While there are good reasons for consistency across your presentation, variation on an occasional slide can lend an impact. A design can be applied either to the whole presentation or just one slide at a time.

- **The Slide Master allows you to alter the templates** which lie behind the slides, for instance to add a header and footer or other logo or copyright information that will appear on every slide.
- **All objects on your slides (e.g. blocks of words in "text boxes" or images) can be moved or resized** by clicking and dragging on the corners or edges. You can also add additional text boxes to supplement those provided by the template. It is a good idea to break from the standard layout to add variety, or to shape the layout specifically to your content.
- **A transition is a special effect used to introduce a slide** during a slide show. For example, you can fade in from black or dissolve from one slide to another. In PowerPoint you can alter the transitions between different slides and can vary the speed of each. Again, *only* use these for good reason as they can be distracting. Your audience is more interested in what you have to say than in your special effects.
- **An animation is a visual or sound effect added to the text or an object** within your slides. For example, you can have your bulleted text points fly in from the left, one at a time. Customizing animations allows you to select particular parts of your slide (graphics or text) and animate them separately, for example to have components of a flowchart appear as you describe them. Many people overuse transitions and animations or use them inappropriately. Sound effects can be particularly off-putting to an audience. Making every dot point appear separately is unnecessarily time consuming. Again, use animations only to good effect, not because they are there to play with.
- **PowerPoint provides a Notes page** (look under the View menu) which is an area at the bottom of the page to type in notes relevant to your presentation, usually the longer version of what you want to say in your presentation. This is a great place to record speakers' notes, keeping them organized with the slides themselves. One option is to print this notes page (with the slide image) prior to your presentation (see tips on printing below). Technically it is possible to project the slide only and to display the notes on your own local screen. To do this you need to turn on multiple-monitor support (on a PC do this within the Display options in your Control Panel) as well as set the presentation options within the program. In our experience this doesn't always work for all computers and all projectors, and it is important to test this out well ahead of your presentation. Have a printout as a backup.
- **The slide show (or presentation) view is what your audience sees**. It takes away all the menus and icons and just leaves your presentation. To move through your presentation simply click your mouse or use the forward arrow. To end your presentation, press the escape key. Other useful keyboard shortcuts that you can use include pressing "B" to display a

black screen (which is great to get the audience's attention back to you or before you start); or Control-P which turns your pointer to a pen, which you can use to make annotations on the slides. To find out more of these, look up "Slide Show" in the Help section.

- **Your printing options** include:

  - one slide to a page (to produce overhead projector transparencies);
  - handouts (2, 3 or 6 slides to a page perhaps with room for listeners to write their own notes);
  - speakers' notes (as above);
  - an outline (contains the summarized content of the slides); or
  - one slide at a time (the current slide), all the slides, or a selection of slides in a range.

To select the format of the printout you need, first select "Print" from the File menu and then change the "Print What" options at the bottom of the screen.

- **Saving a presentation as a PowerPoint Show** (file type .pps) means that it will open up directly in viewing mode. This can make for a more professional start to your presentation.
- **The "Pack and Go Wizard"** puts all the required components into one file which you can then copy to another computer. You can also include a small "viewer" program, which means that the presentation will display even if the other computer doesn't have PowerPoint installed.

Self-running presentations

Later in this chapter we discuss poster sessions. If you are traveling great distances and anticipate having trouble transporting your poster, or you are looking to provide a different type of display, a self-running presentation is an option. This means that you can create and set-up a PowerPoint (or other) presentation to run through the series of transitions and animations itself, according to a timing scheme you have established. You can loop the presentation to go back to the beginning after reaching the end. In this way, displaying the presentation on a laptop, monitor or other projection device can serve as an alternative or supplement to a poster or display. Here are some pointers:

- After creating your presentation you can record timings (from the Slide Show menu) by simply clicking through at the desired pace.
- You can record a narration for your presentation (from the Slide Show menu) which will provide your voice over each slide, as you might do if you were presenting a paper.
- If you want to create a more interactive display, consider a nonlinear format (described below) and allow your viewers to click through themselves.
- Invest in a security cable so you can leave your laptop or desktop unattended (briefly).

Nonlinear presentations

One of the issues with using software as the basis for your presentation is that it can lock you into a very linear and inflexible format. However, by conceptualizing your presentation a little differently, and using some simple skills such as hyperlinking, you can move between different sections of your presentation as your need or audience interest dictates. We have even seen a presenter use a dice (with audience participation) to determine how her presentation would unfold. Here are some tips for creating nonlinear presentations:

- **Start as usual with a welcome or introduction slide (or two).**
- **Create a "table of contents" slide** which you can use for navigation. It need not just be text; you could use images, a flowchart or a mind map (see Chapter 3).
- **Produce all your slides, using one or more for each of the concepts that you listed** or refer to on your table of contents. While the order isn't strictly important, it might be preferable to use a logical order just in case you decide to change from a nonlinear delivery to a linear one.
- **Create hyperlinks from the table of contents slide to the other slides.** Highlight the words you want to create into a link, select Insert – Hyperlink, then choose the slide you wish to link to. Note that you can also link to another document (such as a Word or Excel document) (see Figure 13.1).
- **Create links from each of your slides back to the table of contents.** Action buttons (look under Slide Show) can be used to create a hyperlinked "button" on your page, such as a "home" or "information" icon.

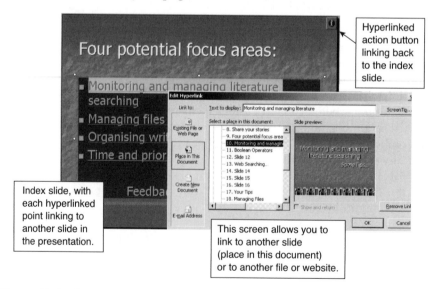

Figure 13.1   Producing a nonlinear slide presentation

Example is from Microsoft PowerPoint

Design and delivery of your presentation

While the last section discussed the technical skills in producing a PowerPoint presentation, just as much thought needs to go into designing the content of the slides and how you will deliver or speak to them. When using presentation software (or even when using overhead projectors or OHPs) there are a number of "golden rules" which can enhance the effectiveness of your presentation:

- **Don't underestimate the amount of time** that it will take to prepare your slides.
- **Keep slides simple.** Slides with fewer words are far preferable to lengthy text (see notes above about reading your presentation). Slides should *only* contain your key points, intermingled with short simple quotes or multimedia inclusions (images or a movie). Reserve explanations for the oral presentation.
- **Keep headings short, relevant and informative**.
- **Make conscious and reasoned typographical decisions.** For instance, use a large, easy-to-read font (preferably sans serif, no less than 28 point). Avoid using more than three colors, and make sure they are highly contrasting (see also Chapter 12).
- **Never photocopy from a book without enlarging (for OHPs)** and don't try to get the whole printed page on one OHP.
- **Provide your name and institution** on the footer of each slide or OHP in case people ask for copies.
- **Never start explaining a slide by saying "I know you can't read this but..."** Better still, avoid putting yourself in that position in the first place!
- **Check all equipment is set up** and in good working order prior to the presentation. Check that people in the back and sides of the room can see. Avoid having to ask by wandering around the room yourself beforehand.
- **Have a Plan B in place if the technology doesn't work.** It won't be the end of the world if you know your content. Reverting to overheads for just key diagrams or images (rather than all of your dot points) generally goes down just fine, so have key slides printed as overheads, just in case.
- **If things go wrong, don't get flustered.** Others in the audience or conference organizers are bound to be able to assist. Move temporarily to a

Want to know more about...

Presentation software?

Tufte 2003   http://www.dwardtufte.com/tufte
Norvig 2000   http://www.norvig.com/Gettysburg

different approach (such as talking less formally to the audience) while someone else looks at the issue.

- **Do not over-dazzle your audience** with excessive animation, sound, or gaudy colors. Many people will be annoyed by this and it only distracts from your main message.
- **A picture really does tell a thousand words** but only use one if it is relevant or has a story to convey.
- **Present data as graphs rather than complex tables.** Keep them super-simple.
- **Practice using a laser pointer** if you intend to use one. If you do, be slow and deliberate with your movements.
- **Include an "end" slide** which contains either a summary of your key points *or* your contact details. Have this slide display during question time, rather than your last content slide.

Producing posters

A poster is a (generally) static display mounted on a board that presents one or more concepts from your research in a visual form. Many conferences run poster sessions, where they allocate a physical area for display of posters and provide a designated time (usually several hours, perhaps broken up over 2–3 days) when conference delegates can move around the posters and talk to the researcher or the person responsible for creating them. Posters are useful for disseminating information about work in progress, particularly when you may not have sufficient data to warrant a full paper or have not had a paper accepted for oral presentation at the conference (quite common with large international conferences). They are a great way of getting initial feedback on your research, making contacts and building your research network.

Posters need to be eye-catching, informative and portable, particularly if you are traveling a distance to your conference (although see also the section on self-running presentations above). In this section we offer advice on how to design, create and present a poster.

Design considerations

- **Posters must attract the audience.** You will be in competition with others to entice delegates towards your display. See it as an advertisement for your work, and use techniques which the advertisement industry find so beneficial. A catchy title is critical. See Figure 13.2.
- **Use your layout and imagery to present information and convey your message.** Use photographs, charts, samples of children's work and/or graphs (see Chapter 2 for more on creating images). Make sure that all images are labeled.

- **Decide what your focus will be**. There are two approaches you can take to poster content. One is to represent a general overview of your project. In this case the poster should tell us what, when, where, how, why, and now what? It could be built around your research proposal structure, i.e. your title, author(s), aim, rationale, related literature, method, findings, implications, acknowledgments, and your contact details. Another approach is to just focus on one or two interesting ideas, concepts or findings from your research, and explore them in more detail. Do include a brief reference list of articles that are important to your research. It can help your audience position your work within a theoretical framework.
- **Don't try to cover too much.** It is a good idea to limit your poster to about 1000 words (do a word count) and make sure it can be read in about 10 minutes.
- **Consider typographical issues** (see Chapter 12). The title should be at least 72 point with 36 point for subheadings and 14–18 point for the text. Break large blocks of text down into shorter paragraphs. Lines of text should contain no more than 10–12 words. Use lots of white space. Your poster should be able to be read from about 1.5 meters (6 feet) away.
- **Choose colors carefully.** Use bright and eye-catching backgrounds *or* headings (but not both) and make sure text contrasts sufficiently. Be aware of colors that are difficult for people with color blindness (such as red and green). Be consistent in your color scheme (it works well to use four colors, including black and white; with a single color dominating 70% of the poster).
- **Guide the reader through content in your preferred sequence.** Generally speaking, the poster should flow from the top left to the bottom right; down columns or along the rows. You could use flow charts or diagrams with arrows or numbers to clarify the sequence of elements on the poster.
- **Obtain and adhere to poster guidelines.** You will need to know how big your poster should be (its dimensions) and how posters will be fixed onto walls so that you will have the right forms of adhesive (tacks, Velcro or double-sided tape).
- **Mention any assistance and financial support.** A poster is an important opportunity to acknowledge sponsorship.
- **Consider a format that can be used multiple times.** If you invest the time and money creating the poster, you should get maximum benefit from it.
- **Get feedback before final production.** Producing a poster can be a relatively expensive endeavor, particularly if you get it professionally printed. Have people look over your drafts and provide you with feedback on style, flow, clarity, design and editing.
- **Leave enough time for printing.** If you are getting it professionally printed and laminated (see below) you may need to allow several days.

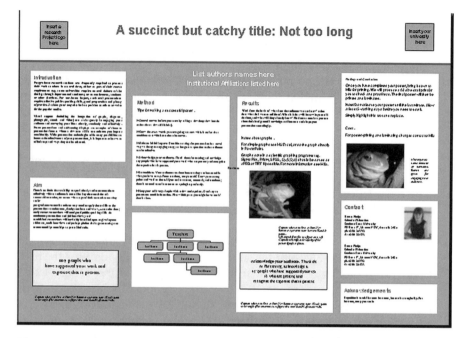

Figure 13.2   A poster developed as a single slide using presentation software

Example is from Microsoft PowerPoint.

Technical considerations

Having explored what your poster might contain and the design issues you should consider, we will now provide some guidance on how you actually create your poster. Historically this involved typing up blocks of text, printing them out, shuffling them around to get the best layout and then pasting them on large cardboard sheets. You may prefer to follow this approach, particularly if your finances are limited.

However, a range of graphic and presentation software can be used to lay out all information and graphical elements on screen before the final product is printed professionally at poster size (you'll need to check with local printing shops to see if this is possible, and to get quotes). If you create your poster digitally:

- **Choose what software you would prefer to use.** Again, you may use a graphics program (see Chapter 2) or a word processing or desktop publishing program. A common strategy is to use Microsoft PowerPoint and to lay out your information on a single slide which then is printed at poster size. Given that PowerPoint is widely accessible, we will focus on tips for its use.

- **Look at available templates.** A range of these can be found on the Web. Try a Web search for "poster template +Powerpoint." You can then use these by replacing the example text and graphics with your own content.
- **Alternatively, create a layout from scratch.** Simply select Page Setup, and designate the width and height for your desired poster. This is important as it ensures you do not run the risk of graphics losing resolution when they are enlarged. It is probably wise to check with your local printing shop and ask them about their preferences or recommendations.
- **Ask to have your poster laminated** as well as printed. It will look far more professional and last longer. If possible, use a matte finish to minimize glare.
- **See also the section above on creating a digital poster** as a self-running presentation.

Presentation considerations

Poster sessions are as much about talking to your audience as just pinning a piece of cardboard on the wall. Make sure to consider the following:

- **Be available to talk to people.** Try to organize to have your cup of tea at other times so that you can make the most of break times when delegates are likely to be visiting.
- **Dress professionally and wear a name tag** so that delegates know that the poster belongs to you.
- **Provide business cards and/or handouts.** Providing something that people can walk away with will help them remember you and your work. It will also ensure they know how to get in contact with you afterwards. A small variety of handouts (such as a one-page flyer and a full paper) provide choice as to the level of information available to interested people.
- **Display a picture of yourself** near, or as part of the poster, so that interested viewers who look at your poster when you aren't there may be able to track you down.

Want to know more about ...

Designing posters?

- Swarthmore College – Designing scientific posters
- Arts and science libraries

- George Hess (NC State University) & Leon Liegel (Oregon State University)
- US Department of energy

- Poster templates

http://www.swarthmore.edu/NatSci/ scpurrin1/posteradvice.htm
http://ublib.buffalo.edu/libraries/ asl/guides/bio/posters.html#Intro
http://www.ncsu.edu/project/posters

http://www.osti.gov/em52/workshop/ tips-exhibits.html
http://miu.med.unsw.edu.au/downloads.htm

Presenting to the media

Presenting information to your peers and experienced researchers through conferences and seminars is only one way of getting your message out. You may find yourself with the opportunity to communicate about your research to a much broader audience. Your research may be of general interest to the public or address issues that are topical at a particular time. If this is the case, you may need to develop skills in communicating with the popular media, whether that be through television, radio or newspapers. We offer here are a few tips and strategies that may be helpful.

- **Use the media officer** of your university or relevant organization wherever possible. It's their job to turn academic ideas into something the media can understand.
- **Make contact with a reliable journalist from a reputable organization** and make sure they have plenty of time to read all the background material and talk to you in depth.
- **Have a clear strategy**, which includes identifying your issue/event, key messages, target audience, target media, timeline and associated risks.
- **Be aware of what it is the media wants to know.** The media are looking for news that is relevant to their audience. They are particularly interested in information that is popular, quirky, new, controversial, or events and activities that the audience can follow up.
- **Make media releases.** These are brief releases in text format of background information that can be used to entice journalists to your story, or to assist them to formulate text or interview questions. When producing a media release include a date, headline, details (who, what, where and when), background information, quotes, and contact details and write it on letterhead. Follow up to see if the media institution has received your release and have a copy with you for your interview. It also pays to ask if your interviewer has seen the media release, in case they have been lost in the organization.
- **Know your target audience** and what they will be interested in. There is a significant difference between presenting to local, national and international media.
- **Know how the medium works**, whether TV, print, radio, or specialist media, and understand the interview format (whether it will be a question and answer session, spoken or in print; how many people will you be talking to; will you be on a panel; will it be live; and so on).
- **Identify your key message** using clear simple language and refer to it throughout the interview. It is better not to make more than three main points. Come back to your main ideas if the journalist seems to be getting sidetracked. Know exactly the points you want to get across and stick to them.
- **Have all the information you need** with you for the interview and stick with the information that you have planned.

- **Prepare for difficult questions** by thinking through responses. Find out what the interviewer's angle is likely to be, or ask what questions they intend to pose ahead of time. If you suspect that the interviewer might be driving a particular agenda, be prepared! That said, memorizing your responses can produce an answer which can appear contrived or inauthentic.
- **Be ready if the journalist wants to take a photo** to go with the story. Make suggestions about using interesting visual props to avoid "head and shoulder" shots.
- **Dress appropriately for TV interviews**. Avoid distracting stripes or busy patterns. Have good posture and vary your focus between the camera and interviewer.
- **Speak slowly and in concise sentences in interviews.** The media generally like to use short quotes, clips or sound bites (8–10 seconds) from what you say. Reporters are especially looking for colorful, lively quotes. It helps to restate the question in giving your response to give the interviewer a complete quotable sentence.
- **Treat all interviews as "on the record."** Don't say anything to an interviewer on or off air that you don't want to be publicly known.
- **If you don't know an answer, say so.** Find it out soon after the interview and get back to them quickly (within the same day), providing follow-up material if necessary.
- **Ask the reporter when the story will run**. Try to gain a commitment from them.
- **Be available after the interview.** You are bound to get follow-up phone calls.
- **Correct errors in newspaper reports** by calling the reporter (not the editor) immediately to ask for a correction. There are often mistakes in media reports, so it's important that the main point you're getting across is clear. Invite the journalist to ring back to check any details. It is better that they double check instead of reporting inaccurately. Live radio is the best medium for ensuring accuracy as you can correct any mistakes on the spot.

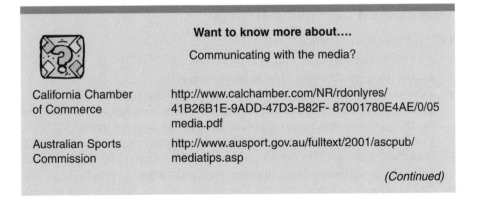

Want to know more about....

Communicating with the media?

| California Chamber of Commerce | http://www.calchamber.com/NR/rdonlyres/ 41B26B1E-9ADD-47D3-B82F- 87001780E4AE/0/05 media.pdf |
| Australian Sports Commission | http://www.ausport.gov.au/fulltext/2001/ascpub/ mediatips.asp |

(Continued)

(Continued)	
Goshen College USA (includes press release template/ example)	http://www.goshen.edu/news/For_GC_faculty/Tips_for_talking_with_media
University of Essex (UK)	http://www.essex.ac.uk/pr/what/mediatips.htm
Queens University (Canada)	http://qnc.queensu.ca/dhtml/mediatips.php

Other presentation approaches

There are, of course, many other forms of research presentation which we have not acknowledged here. Examples include an art exhibition, dramatic presentation, story telling, readers' theatre, musical performance or poetic recital which might convey or depict elements of your research. These presentations might be used on their own or in conjunction with a more conventional presentation or publishing approach.

Publishing your research

While presenting your research is very important for networking and raising your profile, what ultimately counts in the academic world is publishing in respected peer-reviewed journals. In this section we provide guidance on developing a publication strategy, rather than detailed advice on how to write a paper or book, which is usually content and discipline specific. Your supervisor or an experienced researcher in your field can advise you on the best strategies.

Developing a publishing strategy

Why publish your research?

- **Publication lends credibility to your research**.
- **Publishing your work can assist you in preparing for your dissertation**. Writing a paper requires discipline and focus which can be very helpful in clarifying the arguments you want to present in your thesis.
- **Publishing increases your profile as a researcher** and is essential for your future career. The exhortation to "publish or perish" is just as true today in all academic disciplines as it has ever been.
- **Publishing your work can lead to funding** in some cases and is particularly important if you are applying for grants.

Strategies for getting published

- **Be strategic about which journals to target.** Look for opportunities to publish in niche journals from your field. Targeting established journals or those that cover a broad disciplinary area may mean that you are competing with too many other writers. See also Chapter 7 for tools used to identify and monitor journals, and specifically citation indexes which can help you assess a journal's "impact factor." Consider targeting online journals. They have the advantage of an extended and accessible readership; quicker publishing times; and the ability to add supplementary materials (such as multimedia) and hyperlinks.
- **Include publications in your thesis.** If your dissertation includes material that has been published and peer reviewed, this demonstrates to your examiners that your work is of acceptable standard. Publishing during candidature provides a discipline that forces you to make your arguments succinct and has the advantage of ensuring you work to a deadline. Theses by publication are a very specific form of thesis writing and are becoming more frequently used and recommended, particularly in science.
- **Write papers for conferences.** Note whether papers are peer reviewed and published as part of the conference proceedings or will later be published in a journal.
- **Get on to advisory boards for journals.** Many journals are always looking for people for their editorial boards, and if you have already published in their journal this could be a good strategy for raising your profile and being invited to write papers for the journal yourself.
- **Network widely to get invited to write publications.** The more well known you are, the more likely it is that you will be invited to write on particular topics for special issues or edited books.
- **Be guided by the rule "one idea, one paper."** Don't try to cover too much territory in any one paper. Make your arguments for that idea as strong as possible, by drawing on all the knowledge and expertise you have accumulated through your research. If you find yourself wanting to include more than one idea, think about creating another paper.
- **Write collaboratively.** Writing is often much more enjoyable and productive if you can write with others, particularly with those who have experience in getting papers published (see Chapter 12 for tips on collaborative writing).
- **Learn how to write a good abstract.** Abstracts are often read by far more people than will read your full paper. It is therefore very important to know how to write the type of abstract that will lead people to read your full paper. Your abstract should not just flag what you will cover in the paper. It should actually summarize the contents succinctly. The questions in Table 13.1 can form the basis for writing an abstract for a paper, based on an abstract of about 300 words.[1]

Table 13.1   Guidelines for writing an abstract.

Question	Suggested word length
What did you do?	50 words
Why did you do it?	50 words
What happened?	50 words
What do the results mean in theory?	50 words
What do the results mean in practice?	50 words
What is the key benefit for the readers?	25 words
What remains unresolved?	25 words

Tips on getting a paper published in a particular journal

- Determine whether the journal favors particular methodological or theoretical perspectives and write to those.
- Read papers published in the journal to get a sense of the preferred style and content.
- When writing your paper, refer to papers written in that journal.
- Use a catchy title.
- Become familiar with the selection criteria for papers (guidelines to reviewers).
- Check and adhere to journal "guidelines to authors." For example, keep within the preferred word length; use their referencing and heading styles, etc.
- Use the journal's template document (if provided) as a basis for your paper (see Chapter 12 on word processing using styles).
- Expect it to take time to get reviewer feedback and to get the paper published. Editors and reviewers are busy people.
- Be prepared for rejection and don't take it too hard. Remember that very few papers are immediately accepted. Resubmit your paper if the journal wanted to accept it with changes. Alternatively, if the journal rejects it, send it to another journal. Some experienced writers advise that you should start by submitting your paper to high quality and respected journals, and if they reject it, continue trying for others. The main point is not to give up after your first rejection!
- When resubmitting a paper, write a letter to the editor about how you addressed the reviewers' concerns. If you disagree with any comments, say so and justify your stance.

Publishing your thesis

Having written your thesis you may be interested in having it published in some form for a wider readership. There are a number of options to consider:

- converting your thesis to a book for a popular readership;
- converting it to a book for a scholarly readership;
- converting the thesis to a PDF document and putting the thesis on your website;
- having your library include it as part if its online dissertation repository (see Chapter 7);
- self-publishing either through a local printer or directly online (for example, Lulu http://www.lulu.com);
- submitting to Dissertation.com (http://www.dissertation.com), which publishes theses in both e-Book (available over the Internet) and paperback versions (available via booksellers or direct from Dissertation.com). Authors earn between 20 and 40% royalties. PDF versions are submitted to the site and (if accepted) appear in electronic format shortly afterwards, with an ISBN number. If a paperback is produced, this happens in a matter of weeks.

We include here a story of one PhD graduate who converted her thesis to a book for a general readership.

Feature Researcher: Annie Bolitho

Graduate of the University of Technology Sydney, Australia

The process of turning Annie's PhD thesis into a book for a general lay readership was hard work and a deeply thought-provoking experience. Her thesis, written within a cultural studies framework, was titled "New dimensions in water conversation: an inter-animation of writing and water" and won a university award for the best thesis of the year.

Annie won a fellowship[2] to publish her thesis as a book and worked closely with an editor for 6 months to do this. The first step was a formal proposal defining the focus of the book. Given that the theoretical focus of the thesis was far too scholarly for a nonacademic audience, many aspects needed to be rethought. While the thesis was focused on examining "water relations" through a case study writing project, the publisher wanted the focus essentially to be on water. Annie found she had to do a lot of new research to write a book that the publishers would accept. Only one chapter of her thesis went directly into the book.

(Continued)

Through this process, Annie discovered how important the theoretical arguments were in addressing the big questions of her thesis. She points out that a thesis is "the most perfected text you will write in your life," not only because of the rigor required for examination by eminent scholars, but also because of the need to go as deeply as possible into theory to understand the complexity of the phenomena you are studying. Having to bring a strong editorial hand to this "perfected text," to "rip it and shred it and mess around with it" required a balance in negotiations with her editor between speaking for her thesis (doing it justice) and changing it for her new audience.

Writing a thesis prepared Annie for book writing because she knew that what is required is "to do it, do it, do it, until it is done." She learnt from the editorial process that it is essential to have clear and frank discussions and be willing to let go some things that you are attached to, but not give up on what is really important to you from your doctoral work. She discovered also that the time pressure of a publishing deadline is even more uncompromising than that of a dissertation deadline. Annie reflects. It gave me great respect for my thesis, as well as the excitement of making my ideas more widely known."

Peer review and manuscript management systems

If you find yourself in the role of editing, managing or reviewing for a journal, you may be interested in the range of software used for peer review and manuscript management. Even if you aren't (yet) involved in such activities, you may find yourself submitting an article to a journal that uses such software. The features provided by peer review and manuscript management software include[3]:

- **Automated submission.** The software provides templates and/or instructions to authors regarding submission, file conversion and file uploading which is generally done in .html, .pdf or other standard format. It then manages who has access rights to files at each particular stage of the process.
- **Submission tracking and event logging.** The software maintains lists of appropriate and available reviewers and tracks those who choose or are assigned to particular articles. Further communications are also logged, making it easy to check on the status of reviews (completed or pending).
- **Reviewing/copyediting.** The software provides screens for reviewers to record, save and send finished reviews. Some software preserves an original copy of the submitted article in a separate file but allows reviewers to annotate on their own version which can be returned to authors. The software enables the anonymity of authors and/or reviewers to be maintained.
- **Automated notifications.** The software generates e-mails to editors, reviewers and authors, notifying them or following up the status of

articles throughout the reviewing process. This can include alerts and reminders of overdue reviews. Some software can also be used to notify subscribers when a new issue is released.

- **Reviewer and author information and performance tracking.** The software can maintain data such as contact information and availability or the frequency with which reviewers have been required to review a paper.

Want to know more about ...

Peer review and manuscript management systems?

One example is Open Journal Systems (OJS), a free open source system produced by the University of British Columbia. http://www.pkp.ubc.ca/ojs
Many other such systems are available commercially. Try a Web search.
For further information you might consult:

- SPARC (Scholarly Publishing and Academic Resources Coalition), an alliance of universities, research libraries, and organizations focused on enhancing broad and cost-effective access to peer-reviewed scholarship. http://www.arl.org/sparc
- Shapiro, K. Electronic Peer Review Management. Report prepared for the Scholarly Publishing Office, University of Michigan. http://spo.umdl.umich.edu/monthly/peerreview.html

---

Over to you...

1. What has been your experience with public speaking? What could you do to give yourself more opportunities to practice?
2. What features of presentation software could you use to enhance your next presentation?
3. At the next conference you attend, consider the advantages of presenting your research as a dynamic self-running display. What could you include in such a presentation?
4. Reflect on what opportunities you have to communicate your research to your local media. Consider contacting your local radio station to arrange an interview.
5. Make a list of ideas arising from your research that could form the basis of journal papers. For each, make a list of appropriate journals you could target, including online journals. Discuss a publication strategy with your supervisor or colleagues.

Notes

1   Based on Brown 1994.
2   Sydney University's "Thesis-to-book" project, a linkage project with publishers Pan MacMillan, was funded by the Australian Research Council 2005–2007, offering six scholars fellowships to write creative nonfiction books.
3   An excellent review is provided by Shapiro (http://spo.umdl.umich.edu/monthly/peerreview.html). This list of features is drawn from his work.

A final word...

Having read some or all of this book, and perhaps having picked up some of the tips and strategies we have offered in the process, where do you now stand in terms of your relationship with technology? When you use technology, is it controlling what you do, or are you in charge? And perhaps more fundamentally, how confident do you feel in your capacity to be an organized and well-managed researcher? And how will you respond to a future of continual change?

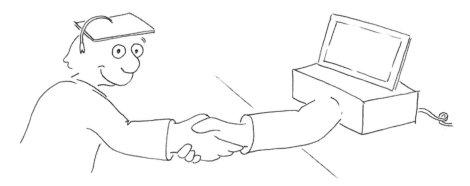

Bibliography

Basit, T. (2003) 'Manual or electronic? The role of coding in qualitative data analysis', *Educational Research*, 45(2), 143–154.

Bazeley, P. and Richards, L. (2000) *The NVivo Qualitative Project Book*. London: Sage.

Berners-Lee, T., Hendler, J. and Lassila, O. (2001) 'The Semantic Web', *Scientific American*, May, 35–43.

Bogdan, R. and Biklen, S. (c.1982) *Qualitative Research for Education: An Introduction to Theory and Methods*. Boston: Allyn and Bacon.

Bong, S. A. (2002) 'Debunking myths in qualitative data analysis'. *FQS: Forum Qualitative Social Research*, 3(2). Available online at: http://www.qualitative-research.net/fqs-texte/2-02/2-02bong-e.htm

Brown, D. (2002) 'Going digital and staying qualitative: Some alternative strategies for digitizing the qualitative research process'. *FQS: Forum Qualitative Social Research*, 3(2). Available online at: http://www.qualitative-research.net/fqs-texte/2-02/2-02brown-e.htm

Brown, R. (1994) 'The "Big Picture" About Managing Writing', in O. Zuber-Skerritt and Y. Ryan (eds.), *Quality in Postgraduate Education*. London: Kogan Page, pp. 90–109.

Bryant, M. (2004) *The Portable Dissertation Advisor*. Thousand Oaks, California: Sage.

Centre of Staff Development (2001) *Student Perceptions of Research Supervision (SPORS)*. Perth: University of Western Australia.

Chen, P. and Hinton, S. (1999) 'Realtime interviewing using the World Wide Web'. *Sociological Research Online*, 4(3). Available online at: http://www.socresonline.org.uk/4/3/chen.html

Coffey, A., Holbrook, B. and Atkinson, P. (1996) 'Qualitative data analysis: Technologies and representations'. *Sociological Research Online*, 1(1). Available online at: http://www.socresonline.org.uk/socresonine/1/1/4.html

Coombes, H. (2001) *Research Using IT*. Hampshire: Palgrave.

Covey, S. (1989) *The Seven Habits of Highly Effective People: Restoring the Character Ethic*. New York: Simon and Schuster.

Denzin, N. K. and Lincoln, Y. S. (1994) Major paradigms and perspectives, in N. K. Denzin and Y. S. Lincoln (eds.), *Handbook of Qualitative Research*. Thousand Oaks, California: Sage, pp. 99–104.

Edyburn, D. (1999) *The Electronic Scholar: Enhancing Research Productivity with Technology*. New Jersey: Merrill.

Ellis, D. (1989) 'Database design and the generation, communication and utilization of information by academic social scientists'. Proceedings of the Information Technology and the Research Process Conference, Cranfield Institute of Technology, UK, 18–21 July.

Fielding, N. G. and Lee, R. M. (eds.) (1991) *Using Computers in Qualitative Research*. London: Sage.

Fielding, N. G. and Lee, R. M. (eds.) (1998) *Computer Analysis and Qualitative Research*. London: Sage.

Fisher, K. (2006) 'Peer support groups', in T. Evans and C. Denholm (eds.), *Doctorates Down Under: Keys to Successful Doctoral Study in Australia and New Zealand*. Melbourne: ACER, pp. 41–49.

Gahan, C. and Hannibal, M. (1998) *Doing Qualitative Research using QSR NUD.IST*. London: Sage.

Gilbert, N. and Troitzsch, K. (1999) *Simulation for the Social Scientist*. Buckingham: Open University.

Giles, J. (2005) 'Special Report: Internet encyclopaedias go head to head'. *Nature, 438*, 900–901. Available online at: http://www.nature.com/nature/journal/v438/n7070/full/438900a.html

Glaser, B. G. and Strauss, A. L. (1967) *The Discovery of Grounded Theory: Strategies for Qualitative Research*. New York: Aldine De Gruyter.

Green, R. (2004) 'Augmented reality user interfaces for biomechanical data overlays'. Paper presented at the Mathematics and Computers in Sport Conference, Palmerston, New Zealand, August 30–September 1, pp. 159–163.

Hall, R. (2000) 'Videorecording as theory', in A. Kelly and R. Lesh (eds.), *Handbook of Research Design in Mathematics and Science Education*. Mahwah, New Jersey: Lawrence Erlbaum, pp. 647–664.

Hammond, J. (2004) 'Using performance analysis technology to evaluate the instructional process in sport'. Paper presented at the Mathematics and Computers in Sport Conference, Palmerston, New Zealand, August 30–September 1, pp. 172–181.

Hart, C. (2000) *Doing a Literature Review*. London: Sage.

Henninger, M. (1999) *Don't Just Surf: Effective Research Strategies for the Net* (2nd edn). Sydney: University of New South Wales.

Hewson, C., Yule, P., Laurent, D. and Vogel, C. (2003) *Internet Research Methods: A Practical Guide for the Social and Behavioural Sciences*. London: Sage.

Johnson, R. B. and Onwuegbuzie, A. (2004) 'Mixed methods research: A research paradigm whose time has come'. *Educational Researcher, 33*(7), 14–26.

Kelly, G. (1955) *The Psychology of Personal Constructs*. 2 vols. New York: Norton.

Keppell, M., Au, E., Ma, A. and Chan, C. (2005) 'Curriculum development in technology-enhanced environments', in C. Howard, P. Rogers, J. V. Boettcher, G. A. Berg, L. Justice and K. Schenk (eds.), *Encyclopedia of Distance Learning*. Vol. I–IV. Hershey: IDEA Reference Group, pp. 492–504.

Kosnik, C. (2001) 'The effects of an inquiry-oriented teacher education program on a faculty member: Some critical incidents and my journey'. *Reflective Practice, 2*(1), 65–80.

Leedy, P. (2005) *Practical Research: Planning and Design* (8th edn). Upper Saddle River, N.J.: Pearson/Merrill Prentice Hall.

Lesh, R. and Lehrer, R. (2000) 'Iterative refinement cycles for videotape analysis of conceptual change', in A. Kelly and R. Lesh (eds.), *Handbook of Research Design in*

Mathematics and Science Education. Mahwah, New Jersey: Lawrence Erlbaum, pp. 665–708.

Lewins, A. and Silver, C. (2005) *Choosing a CAQDAS Package: A working paper by CAQDAS Networking Project*. Available online at: http://caqdas.soc.surrey.ac.uk/

Marshall, H. (2003) 'How long to spend on coding'. *QSR Insight*. Available online at: http://www.qsrinternational.com

May, D. (1997) 'Planning time', in N. Graves and V. Varma (eds.), *Working for a Doctorate: A Guide for the Humanities and Social Sciences*. London: Routledge.

Miles, M. B. and Huberman, A. M. (1994) *Qualitative Data Analysis: An Expanded Sourcebook* (2nd edn). Thousand Oaks, California: Sage.

Mousley, J. A. (1998) 'Ethnographic research in mathematics education: Using different types of visual data refined from videotapes', in C. Kanes, M. Goos and E. Warren (eds.), *Teaching Mathematics in New Times*. Gold Coast, Australia: MERGA, pp. 397–403.

Mousley, J. A. (2000) 'Video transparency: Window on mathematical understanding', in S. Groves and R. Tytler (eds.), *Contemporary Approaches to Research in Mathematics and Science Education*. Melbourne: Deakin University, pp. 13–17.

O'Leary, Z. (2004) *The Essential Guide to Doing Research*. London: Sage.

Oliver, P. (2004) *Writing your Thesis*. London: Sage.

Ormiston, M. (2004) *Conquering Infoclutter: Timesaving Technology Solutions for Teachers*. Thousand Oaks, California: Corwin Press.

Palmquist, M. and Zimmerman, D. (1999) *Writing with a Computer*. Boston: Allyn and Bacon.

Patton, M. (2002) *Qualitative Research and Evaluation Methods*. Thousand Oaks, California: Sage.

Phelps, R., Fisher, K. and Ellis, A. (2006) 'Organisational and technological skills: The overlooked dimension of research training', *Australian Journal of Educational Technology*, 22(2), 145–165. Available online at: http://www.ascilite.org.au/ajet/ajet22/res/phelps.html

Popping, R. (2000) *Computer-assisted Text Analysis*. London: Sage.

Roberts, C. M. (2004) *The Dissertation Journey: A Practical and Comprehensive Guide to Planning, Writing and Defending your Dissertation*. Thousand Oaks, California: Sage.

Roschelle, J. (2000) 'Choosing and using video equipment for data collection', in A. Kelly and R. Lesh (eds.), *Handbook of Research Design in Mathematics and Science Education*. Mahwah, New Jersey: Lawrence Erlbaum, pp. 709–729.

Rudestam, K. and Newton, R. (2001) *Surviving your Dissertation: A Comprehensive Guide to Content and Process*. Thousand Oaks, California: Sage.

Schonlau, M., Fricker, R. and Elliott, M. (2001) *Conducting research surveys via e-mail and the Web*. Available online at: http://www.rand.org/publications/MR/MR1480/

Seidel, J. (1991) 'Method and madness in the application of computer technology to qualitative data analysis', in N. G. Fielding and R. M. Lee (eds.), *Using Computers in Qualitative Research*. London: Sage, pp. 107–118.

Sheskin, D. (2000) *Handbook of Parametric and Nonparametric Statistical Procedures* (2nd edn). Boca Raton, FL: Chapman & Hall/CRC.

Sternberg, D. (1981) *How to Complete and Survive a Doctoral Dissertation*. New York: St. Martin's Press.

Stevens, K. and Asmar, C. (1999) *Doing Postgraduate Research in Australia*. Melbourne: Melbourne University Press.

Stockdale, A. (2002) 'Tools for digital audio recording in qualitative research'. *Social Research Update, 38*. Available online at: http://www.soc.surrey.ac.uk/sru/SRU38.html

Stroh, M. (2000) 'Computers and qualitative data analysis: to use or not to use … ?' in D. Burton (ed.), *Research Training for Social Scientists*. London: Sage, pp. 226–243.

Tashakkori, A. and Teddlie, C. (eds.) (2003) *Handbook of Mixed Methods in Social and Behavioral Research*. Thousand Oaks, California: Sage.

Tesch, R. (1990) *Qualitative Research: Analysis Types and Software Tools*. New York: The Falmer Press.

Tesch, R. (1991) 'Software for qualitative researchers: analysis needs and program capabilities', in N. G. Fielding and R. M. Lee (eds.), *Using Computers in Qualitative Research*. London: Sage, pp. 16–37.

Turney, L. and Pocknee, C. (2005) 'Virtual focus groups: New frontiers in research', *International Journal of Qualitative Methods, 4*(2). Available online at: http://www.ualberta.ca/~ijqm/english/engframeset.html

Weitzman, E. (2000) 'Software and qualitative research', in N. K. Denzin and Y. S. Lincoln (eds.), *Handbook of Qualitative Research*. Thousand Oaks, California: Sage, pp. 803–820.

Weitzman, E. A. and Miles, M. B. (1995) *Computer Programs for Qualitative Data Analysis: A Software Sourcebook*. Thousand Oaks, California: Sage.

Index

accountability 50
address book 22, 110
Adobe Acrobat *see* PDF
ADSL 27
annotating 64, 65
antivirus software 75
Apple computers *see* Macintosh
applications *see* software
appointments 48
archiving 69, 71
asset management *see* data management
asynchronous communication 92, 106–17
atlases 163
attachments 109
audio 155, 180, 181–85
    podcasting 116
autocorrect 250

backing up 73, 76
bandwidth 27
behavioural observation software 191–93
bibliographic software 167–73
    examples 177
    for data management 78
    selecting 170
    use when filing 174
    use when literature searching 138
    use when note taking 175,
        176, 253
    use with master documents 246
BiblioWeb 173
blogs 106, 115–16, 161
    for data collection 198
    for journaling 42
    for professional networking 105
Bluetooth 14

bookmarks 160
    filing 63
books 142
    e-books 65, 143–44
boolean logic 132, 157
broadband 27
browsers 28
    security settings 75
budgets 17, 91–98
bullets 242

CAQDAS 210–17, 227–33
catalogues, library 140–42
CD-ROMS 73
chairs 59
charts *see* graphs
chat 26, 104, 117–20
    focus groups 198
    interviewing 197, 198
citation indexes 130, 135, 139–40
code and categorize 212, 215
comments 248
communication 104–25
compression 71
computer terminology 12
computer-based data input systems 205
concept mapping *see* mind mapping
conferences 105, 106
Critical Path Method 88
cross referencing 240
customizing programs 31–32, 249–50

data
    audio 181–85
    collection 81, 179–201, 207–37
    multimedia 181–90

data *cont.*
    organizing 22
    video 186–88
data analysis 207–25
data management utilities 77
databases 21–23, 136, 210
    literature 22, 136, 137
    searching 136
demonstration software 17
desk space 57
desktop computers 13
diagrams 23
diaries 39, 40, 41–42, 61, 188
dictionaries 12, 83, 162, 163, 250
digital sound recorders 182–83
Digital Subscriber Lines *see* DSL
discussion boards 106, 114–15
    for data collection 197, 198, 199
    for professional networking 105
    for project management 89
document delivery services 138, 144
downloading 75
drag and drop 12
drawing programs 23
DSL 27
DVDS 73

e-books *see* books
editing 254
Elluminate Live! 119
e-mail 26, 106–13
    addresses, locating 106
    features 109
    filing 63
    for professional networking 105
    hoaxes 75
    managing 112
    virus transfer 75
encryption 72
encyclopaedias 16, 163
endnotes 247
EndNote *see* bibliographic software
ergonomics *see* health and safety
    ergonomic software 59
ethics 64
evaluating information 162
expectations 46
expert system software 80–83
exploratory learning 11
Extensible Markup Language *see* XML

Favorites *see* bookmarks
fields *see* databases
figures 245
files
    backing up 73, 76
    cataloguing 77

files *cont.*
    file extensions 16, 25
    file formats 16, 24
    file size 25, 67, 71, 109
    linking 33, 240, 246
    managing 69–78, 71
    naming 16
    opening 75
    physical 57
    saving 17, 32, 44, 74, 76, 77, 160, 174
    version control 74
filing 62, 67
    electronic documents 70
    e-mails 110, 112
    filing cabinets 67–68
    filing schema 61, 62–64, 68, 70, 71, 110, 160,
        172, 174
    literature 173–74
filters 111
finance management software 98
finances *see* budgets
find and replace 247
firewalls 75, 76
firewire 188
flowcharts 23
focus groups, online 198
folders 60, 68
footers 240
footnotes 247
freeware 17
FTP server 14
funding *see* grants

Gantt charts 23, 85, 87, 88, 90
Global Positioning Systems
        (GPS) 14
glossaries 240
goal setting 11, 60
Google Scholar 152
grants 80, 91–95
graphics 24, 146, 186
    as data 189
    locating 155
    resizing 264
    software 23–25
graphs 21, 23, 82, 268

hardware 13–14
    requirements 18
headers 240
headings 241, 242
    numbering 243
health and safety 57–59, 64
help function 12
highlighting 64, 65, 248
hoaxes 75
homepage 161

HTML 29, 123
  HTML editing software 125, 126
human movement recognition systems 193
hyperlinks 28, 42, 255
  creating 247, 266
Hypertext Markup Language *see* HTML

icons 18, 32, 264
  adding to toolbars 250
images *see* graphics
indexes 240
infoclutter 56
information literacy 129
inter-library loan 138, 144
Internet 26
  connecting 27
Internet Service Provider *see* ISP
Internet telephony 117, 120
interviewing 184–85, 189
  online 197–98
interviews, with media 272–74
isolation 49
ISP 28, 108

journals *see* periodicals; diaries

keyboards 58

LAN 27
laptops 13, 57, 60
layers 24
letters 249
librarians 146
library catalogues 140, 141
licensing 17–18, 91
lighting 59
Linux 15
literature
  databases 22, 137
  filing 173
  handling 173
  labeling 174–75
  managing and organizing 134, 166–76
  monitoring 130, 146, 147
  reviewing xii, 43, 44, 80, 128, 146, 253
  searching 128–46
Local Area Networks *see* LAN
logbooks 41–42

Macintosh 7, 13, 14, 15, 71
macros 33
mailboxes 110
mailing lists 26, 106, 107, 114–15
  for data collection 198
  locating 152, 157
malware 74, 76
manuscript management systems 278
margins 240

master documents 240, 246
media, presenting to 272–74
menus 11, 32
merging documents 248
meta-search engines 151
Methodologist's Toolchest 80, 95
Microsoft Excel *see* spreadsheets
Microsoft Excel add ins 223
Microsoft Office 16
Microsoft Word *see* word processors
milestones *see* time management
mind mapping xii, 41, 42–45, 53
  as data collection 189
  software 23, 44, 53, 189
MiniDiscs 182
modem 27
monitors 58, 65
multimedia
  data 181–90
  searches 155–56
  software 203

newspapers 146
nonlinear presentations 266
nonlinear writing 255
note taking 175–76
notebooks *see* laptops
notes 40, 41
  utilities 41
numbering 243

OCR 66–67
offices 60, 61
  shared 61
online interviews 197–98
open source software 17
operating system software 15, 18
Optical Character Recognition *see* OCR
options 12
oral presentations *see* presentations
outline view 243

paint programs 23
palmtops 14, 18, 40, 90, 182, 190
PDAs *see* palmtops
PDF 25–26
peer support groups 49–52
periodical directories 144–45
periodicals
  monitoring 147
peripherals 13
Personal Digital Assistants *see* palmtops
phone calls 40
photocopying 59, 64, 65, 66, 92
photographs 23, 142
  as data 188
  file formats 16
  in presentations 259, 268

physical environment 56–64
planning 80–87
    data collection 180
    literature searches 129–35
    quantitative research 221
plug-in 29
podcasts 105, 106, 116
popups 75
Portable Document Format *see* PDF
posters 268–71
    designing 268
    presentation 271
    technical considerations 270
powerbooks *see* laptops
Powerpoint *see* presentations, software
preferences 12, 250
presentations 259–74
    concluding 262
    delivering 260
    designing 267
    media presentations 272–74
    non-linear 266
    preparing 260
    public speaking 259–63
    self-running 265
    software 263–65
printing 65, 66, 70, 254
    presentations 265
    printing the screen 24
    saving paper 65
prioritizing 37–38, 44, 60
project management 79–98
    software 5, 87–90, 100
proposal 80, 84, 94, 98
proprietary software 17
proxy settings 28
public speaking *see* presentations
publishing 274–79
    your thesis 277

qualitative data analysis 208–11
    computer-based 210
    manual 209
    software *see* CAQDAS
quantitative data analysis 217–25
    software *see* statistical analysis
quotation sites 163
quotes 242

radio 272
Random Access Memory (RAM) 13
reading 173, 175–76
Really Simple Syndication *see* RSS
records *see* databases
references 242
relationships, managing 48
repertory grid 193–94
Repetitive Stress Injury *see* RSI

reporting 87
repositories 152, 200
research jobs 163
research plan 80–87
research-in-progress 148
resolution 67
Rich Text Format *see* RTF
right clicking 12
risk management 11, 72, 76
RSI 57, 58
RSS feeds 161
RTF 16

sampling 81, 180, 222
saving *see* files
scanning 66–67, 92
screen grabs 24
search directories 152
search engines 151
search visualization 153, 155
searching strategies 129
section breaks 240
security 60
server 14
SFX 140
shareware 17
shortcuts 31–32, 70
signatures 110
simulation software 194
Skyview 156
software 15–26
    antivirus software 75
    applications 16
    bibliographic 78, 138, 167–73, 174, 175,
        176, 177, 246, 253
    browsers 28
    CAQDAS 210, 227–33
    data input software 205
    data management 77
    databases 21–23
    downloading 18
    drawing 23
    e-mail 106–13
    expert systems 80–83
    finance management 98
    graphics 23–25
    HTML editors 125, 126
    installing 70
    licensing 17
    mind mapping 23, 44, 53, 189
    multimedia 203
    operating system 15
    painting 23
    presentation 263–65
    project management 5,
        87–90, 100
    selecting 7, 18
    simulation 194

software *cont.*
   spreadsheets 19–21, 90, 95, 148, 210, 223, 224, 225, 256
   statistical 222–25, 234
   survey 205
   text to speech 31
   utilities 16, 40
   voice recognition 30, 59
   word processing 23, 74, 238–50
sound annotations 248
spam 113
spell-checking 250
spreadsheets 19–21, 90, 223, 224, 225
   calculating expenses 95
   hyperlinking 256
   monitoring journals 148
   organizing data 210
spyware 74, 76
statistical analysis software 222–25, 234
statistics 81, 192, 200, 218–21
sticky notes 40
stress *see* health and safety
styles 240, 241
Styles Organizer 245
supervisors 3, 9, 45–49
support 18, 49
survey software 205
surveys 118, 180, 247, 249, 251, 255
surveys, online 195–97
symbols 247
synchronous communication 117–21

table of contents services 147
tables 242, 247
   list of 245
tables of contents 244
telephone interviewing 184
templates 8, 112, 245, 263
terminology 12
text boxes 24
text retrievers 211
text to speech 31
textbase managers 212
thesis publishing 277
time management 37, 38–41, 84, 85
timelines *see* time management
to-do lists 39
toolbars 32
tools 12
track changes 248
transcribing 183–84
translation 122
truncators 133
TV 272
typeface 251
typing 30, 58, 59
typography 251–52

Ulrich's Periodicals Directory 144
Universal Resource Indicator *see* URIs
UNIX 15
URIs 157
URLs 157
USB memory sticks 73
utility software 16, 40

version control 74, 248
video 186–88
   analysis 191
   data analysis 217
   data management 77
   in communication 197
   in data collection 198
   journaling 42
   podcasting 116
video conferencing 121
Virtual Private Network *see* VPN
viruses 74, 76
visualization software *see* mind mapping
voice recognition software 30, 59
VoIP *see* Internet telephony
VPN 108

Web 26, 150–64
   evaluating 162
   saving search results 160
   search tools 151–57, 152, 153
   searching 150–59
   searching, improving results 157
   Web browser *see* browser
Web pages, creating 123–25
Wikipedia 16, 115
wikis 106, 115–16
wildcards 133
windows 15, 240
Windows Explorer 70
wireless 27
word processing 23, 74, 238–50
   long documents 239
   styles 241
workspaces 36
workstations 13
World Wide Web *see* Web
worms 74
writers' block 253
writing 238–56
   collaboratively 248, 255
   for screen 255
   improving efficiency 252
   nonlinear 255
   structure 254

XML 29

zipping files *see* compression